Mustn'
Grumb

Mustn't Grumble

The Autobiography

TERRY WOGAN

First published in hardback in Great Britain in 2006 by
Orion Books
an imprint of the Orion Publishing Group Ltd
Orion House, 5 Upper St Martin's Lane,
London WC2H 9EA

5 7 9 10 8 6 4

A CIP catalogue record for this book is available
from the British Library.

ISBN-13: 978 0 75287 438 8 (Hardback)
ISBN-10: 0 75287 438 1 (Hardback)
ISBN-13: 978 0 75287 615 3 (Export Trade Paperback)
ISBN-10: 0 75287 615 5 (Export Trade Paperback)

Typeset by Input Data Services Ltd, Frome

Printed in Great Britain by Clays Ltd, St Ives plc

The Orion Publishing Group's policy is to use papers that are
natural, renewable and recyclable and made from wood grown in sustainable
forests. The logging and manufacturing processes are expected to conform
to the environmental regulations of the country of origin.

Every effort has been made to fulfil requirements with regard to
reproducing copyright material. The author and publisher will
be glad to rectify any omissions at the earliest opportunity.

www.orionbooks.co.uk

For my son, Mark, and Luigi Bonomi, without whose drive and enthusiasm I might have spent most of the year just lying about enjoying myself ... For my ever expanding family: Alan, Katherine, Henry, Susan, Kate, Freddie and the Queen of my heart, Helen, without whom none of it would be worth a tinker's curse ...

Acknowledgements

Thanks will never be enough for the irreplaceable Jo Gurnett, the wonderful Amanda Harris and all at Orion, my dear friend Paul Walters, the 'team', Deadly, Boggy and Fran, Alan Boyd, Lesley Douglas and all the great people with whom it's been such a pleasure to work on the Coffin-Dodgers network, BBC Radio 2. Would that I could mention my loyal TOGs by name, but all I know is their pseudonyms; they're my joy, my constant friends and inspiration. I know that they won't mind if I single out the brilliant Mick Sturbs, whose inspired 'Janet and John' tales regularly reduce million to tears and mild hysteria, and have been instrumental in raising almost a million pounds for *Children in Need*.

Contents

Mustn't
Grumble

Prologue

This finely honed little tome, through which you are thumbing before returning it, unbought, to the bookstore shelf, is by way of what they call in Dublin a 'follier-uppier' to my last oeuvre, *Is It Me?* That went surprisingly well, except with a little old man in Belfast. I'd gone there, in the grand tradition of bookselling, as part of a tour of the UK, hawking my little book shamelessly from Reading to Cambridge, from Norwich to Bristol, from Bath to Belfast. Jolly crowds greeted me everywhere, some even bought the book. A man in Reading rushed to my side in the bookstore there, and asked me fervently to sign his prayerbook. I did so, with an even-handed flourish. He looked a little puzzled, smiling wanly as he left. The sales assistant was most sympathetic: 'He thought you were Terry Waite,' she explained.

For reasons that now escape me, unless it was the usual one of a boys' night out, two of my underlings from *Wake Up to Wogan*, an obscure radio show that need not detain us here, accompanied me to Northern Ireland for the book tour. Paul Walters, my producer, otherwise known as Dr Wallington P. de Wynter Courtney Claibourne Magillicuddy Walters, or, for short, 'Doctor Wally', was one, and hanging on, like grim death, to our coat tails, Alan Dedicoat, otherwise known as Deadly

Alancoat, the Wealdstone Weather-Boy, the Voice of the Balls, or, to keep it short, 'Deadly', was the other.

Naturally, Deadly was not allowed to travel with us across the Irish Sea, but magically materialised at our hotel outside Belfast. Walters and I had made the mistake of travelling with him once before, on British Midland. Appropriately enough, the Voice of the Balls was seated on the other side of the blue curtain which, in all aeroplanes, separates the well-to-do from the riff-raff. As Paul and I toasted each other in lukewarm champagne, on the other side of the curtain the unfortunates were being doled out dishwater and rolls wrapped in clingfilm. Deadly made the mistake of thinking the customer might choose the filling in his stale roll. 'Ham?' he mildly inquired. 'Have you got ham?' The impertinence of the request struck the ancient stewardess dumb, but when she found her voice, the whole plane heard it: ''Am?!' she shrieked. ''Am? There's no 'am 'ere! That's on the other side of the curtain! There's cheese or tuna, which d'ya want? 'Am! Honestly, some people . . .'

The great Michael Devine had come up from Dublin to drive us around Belfast. Michael Devine is one of those rare beings, who, quietly and without fuss, can do anything, make all your dreams come true. This is a quiet-spoken, gentle Dublin man, who looks after all the celebrities and stars who come to Ireland. Julia Roberts stays in his little house in the Dublin suburbs when she craves anonymity. A few years ago when Julia wanted to be alone, Michael borrowed The Edge's (of U2) house on the banks of Lough Corrib in Galway, and looked after the superstar there. Julia gave him her apartment in New York when Ireland were playing in the World Cup in the Big Apple. When Julia got married a year or so ago, she flew Michael and his family to the

West Coast to attend the joyous nuptials. And guess who, *in loco parentis*, gave away the biggest female film star in the world? A Dublin taxi driver named Michael Devine. Whenever Ireland won the Eurovision, which it seemed to do every second year in the nineties, I'd get in touch with the great Michael. He catered for our every whim in Dublin, but his tour de force was the Big Night. Up to our hotel would roar a full police escort. Into Michael's limos we'd get and off we'd go, at breakneck speed, to the Point, where the Contest was being staged. Through the narrow streets and backroads of Dublin we'd scream, ignoring red lights and roundabouts, pedestrians, cyclists and other road-users, as first one and then another police motorcyclist roared ahead of us to hold back the traffic. You can keep your roller coaster and your Wall of Death – these were white-knuckle rides I will never forget. At the end of it, we were deposited at the front door of the Point, and Michael slipped the sergeant-in-charge a handful of crisp oncers. 'Right, lads,' said Michael, 'off you go to the Park.' And off the bikes would roar to the residence of the President of Ireland. I often wonder if she knew that we had first use of her escort. . .

As we travelled from one book-signing to another, Michael tried to explain the intricacies of Northern Ireland to the eejits from England.

'This is green,' he would say, 'a Republican, Nationalist area.'

'How do you know?' asked Deadly.

'You just do,' explained Michael, 'and this is an Orange street.'

'How do you know?'

Michael gave a sigh: 'You just do. A couple of streets over there, it's all Black.'

'Ah,' said Doctor Wally, 'like Brixton, in London.'

'No,' said Michael Devine, struggling to keep a pitying look off his face, 'Black Protestants.'

The Doctor and Deadly fell silent.

'That's a Catholic dog,' I said.

'How do you know?'

'I know from the look of it . . .'

It's very difficult to explain the religious differences that separate Northern Ireland to a secular Englishman, but trying to explain that you can tell a Nationalist from a Unionist, a Catholic from a Protestant just by looking at them is impossible. An Irish person, whether of Northerly or Southerly persuasion, knows immediately what you're talking about. My wife thought *I* was a Protestant when we first met. I had the look of one, she said. To think that that foolishness still prevails in certain parts of these islands makes you want to weep . . . And if you can't tell them apart by their looks, you can tell by their names, or how they spell them. Don't ask . . .

After two years without any contact with her family or friends, a young Irish girl returns home.

'B'jesus yer safe!' says her father. 'Thank the Lord – we were worried sick! Why didn't you contact us?! Why didn't you let us know you were OK? The last two years have been a nightmare.'

'Sit down, Da. There's something I have to tell you.'

He sits down and she continues, 'Da, I've become a prostitute.'

'You WHAT?! How could you?! How dare you . . .'

'Da, don't . . .'

'Whaddaymean, DON'T? I'll give you DON'T! What reaction did you expect?! And what are you doing here anyway?'

'I came here today to make amends. I have the deeds for me Ma to sign for a £450,000 detached property in County Cork; I've booked you both on a "round the world" cruise for six weeks whilst the removal men take all yer stuff from here and move it to the new place – I've even arranged for a private designer to come and talk to me Ma about how she wants it fitted out; I've bought a horse each for the two bairns and have paid for their tuition fees at the fancy girls' school in Dublin – only the best for me little sisters! And I've got me brother his very own pub in Templegate – he can run it as his own and get out of that rough Tinker-owned Clover place down the road – he can make his fortune. And for you, Da, just for you; here are the keys for the E-type Jaguar you always wanted . . .'

'What is it you said you'd become?'

'A prostitute, Da!'

'Oh that's fine – I thought you said a Protestant. Come and give your auld Da a hug!'

The funniest Eurovision incidents always happened in Ireland: hardly surprising in view of the ever-cheery nature of the inhabitants of my native place. Ronan Keating was one of the presenters about five years ago. He was, even then, a huge international star, as the lead singer of Boyzone, and certainly Ireland's most famous export and probably the best-known face in the country. After the show, we all repaired to a huge barn of a place in the University College Dublin grounds, for the usual, terrible, overcrowded, anti-climactic post-Eurovision party. Loyally enough, Ronan himself turned up. He didn't get in though. The woman on the door turned him away because he didn't have an invitation with him . . . It was the Irish, not the Australians who invented the 'tall poppy' syndrome. 'Sure, I knew his oul' fella.' Actually, I didn't, but my dear brother Brian knew Ronan Keating as a lad; his family lived nearby. In view of Brian's two stunning daughters, it's no surprise that Ronan and the local Lotharios hung around my brother's household quite a bit. Ronan always wanted to sing, to be a pop star, and one evening Brian offered him a word of good advice: 'Now listen, Ronan. Give up all this old pop-singing nonsense; it'll get you nowhere. Concentrate on your studies. Do your exams, and make something of yourself.' We fast-forwarded some years, and my brother and his old jalopy are held up in traffic near his home. A limousine with blacked-out windows slows down opposite Brian's car. The window slips noiselessly down, and Ronan Keating looks out: 'Ah, there you are, Mr Wogan! How're ya?' The brother winds down his creaky window: 'Ronan!' says Brian. 'Well – was I not right?' . . .

Michael decanted us at a bookshop where I was to sign a couple of hundred of my books, but it wasn't to be a public appearance, as I had already flung myself at the unfortunate denizens of Belfast at a public meeting the night before, and another bookstore that morning. Publishers get their money's worth. As I sat in a corner of the store, signing away good-oh, with the beginnings of repetitive strain injury nagging at my shoulder, a little man materialised at my side. He was about seventy, neatly dressed in quiet sports coat, slacks and suede shoes, and appropriately hatted. He had an umbrella over his arm, always a wise move in Ireland. He leaned over me. I smiled encouragingly.

'You're a lickspittle,' he said. No, he snarled it.

I watched him as he walked to the door, his every fibre quivering with rage. He turned.

'*A lickspittle!*' he shouted.

He exited, and walked off down the street, a nicely dressed, respectable, harmless old man. And one with 'hatred' in his heart. For me.

OK, I'm not Saint Anthony, and I understand that as soon as you stick your head above the parapet, somebody's going to want to knock your block off. Dislike I understand. The more some like what you do, on television or radio, the more will find you a pain in the proverbial. But *hatred*? Splenetic, fierce loathing? And 'lickspittle'? Old-fashioned, Edwardian, a preacher's curse. Only in Norn Iron. No. My mother was born there, in a British Army barracks. I love the place, as I love my Dublin, my Limerick. Some of my funniest correspondents to the Radio 2 morning extravaganza write to me from Ulster. 'The Crooked Man of Old Bangor Town', or as we know him 'Crooky'.

> *Spring has sprung, the week's begun*
> *Ready to be filled with Godfrey fun.*
> *Your other listener can fear no harm*
> *When surrounded by her bouncy charm.*
> *Since May's well out without a doubt*
> *She'll be casting many a fleecy clout.*
> *And make us privy to home-life facts*
> *Delighting chaps in dirty macs.*
> *With charming anecdotal quips*
> *About her bathroom and its drips.*
> *Tilers, plumbers, painters too*
> *She'll eagerly discuss with me and you.*
> *But since she acts so prim and proper*
> *Nobody's got the heart to stop her.*

Mustn't Grumble

For ever since the Beeb began
No totty's been toppier than our dear Fran.

Whether they love me, I would not presume to conjecture. As long as I keep to myself in Britain, I'm OK. The Irish, like the Scots, have always preferred 'the King across the water' . . .

1

I knew him when he was a young fella

⌒

'Let the tap run.' Nellie Nolan's watchword. My mother always had to leave the kitchen, in case one of the two Nellies would catch her smiling. The other Nellie was her eldest sister, whose misanthropic view of life my mother always found ridiculous and, usually, hilarious. As soon as we were out of earshot, my mother would explode into laughter.

"'Let the tap run, Nell." She says it every time she's offered a glass of water! Does she think everybody's an eejit except herself?'

In Ireland, in those days, everybody let the tap run before they had a glass of water. The popular notion was that it got the lead out. These days, it's a slang term for getting a move on, but in the hungry forties in Ireland, there wasn't a lot of trust in public utilities. There was the Gas Board, the Electricity Board, the Water Board, the Turf Board. Nothing to do with racing – for 'turf', read 'peat'. All of them had Gaelic names, and you couldn't get a job in any of them unless you were educated by the Christian Brothers and had had the native tongue beaten into you until you were senseless. For countless years, life in Ireland was hoisted on the ridiculous petard of an archaic language that nobody loved, and nobody, apart from a few native-speakers and those my mother called 'blood to the beak', craw-thumping politicians, ever spoke. Only those who love it speak it now; it's not a political football any more. Every so often, a Northern Irish Republican will drag the old language out to show that he's more Irish than the other side, but otherwise, certainly as far as the urban Southern Irish are concerned, Gaelic is with O'Donovan Rossa, in the grave.

I slipped into a calumny there, as far as the Irish are concerned: 'Southern' Ireland. Try saying that in Davy Byrnes or Nearys in Dublin, and you'll soon get your head bitten off. 'Eire' is another word that might get you into trouble, particularly if, like most English people, you pronounce it 'Ire', as in 'anger'. It'll certainly provoke that. For the 'Southern' Irish, their country is called 'Ireland', or, at a push, 'the Republic'. The vexatious bit on the top right-hand corner is termed 'Northern Ireland'. Recently, at a rather snobby do in London, an elegant woman with a slight Northern Irish twang asked where I came from, in 'Southern' Ireland. 'Limerick,' I said, 'in Ireland.' I'd been away too long and forgotten the old sensitivities, the real prejudice, and, yes, hatred, that bubbles just below the surface of the sad old problem. The lady bristled: 'Ireland? It's got at least four names!' I could have riposted that Northern Ireland has got at least four as well – Six Counties, Ulster, Northern and Great Britain – but, like most good comebacks, I didn't think of it in time, and anyway, the conversation had frozen over.

Nellie Nolan, a formidable battleship of a woman, never without a hat, was the bosom friend of my Auntie Nellie, who was in charge of curtains in Clerys: at the time, the only department store worthy of the name in Dublin. Clery, they used to say, was the original family name of Desirée Clary, who gave Napoleon all that trouble. That's the kind of thing they say in Ireland, and if you're a big enough eejit to believe it, then fair enoughski. The two Nellies, invariably clad in black, went everywhere together. These days, people would look knowingly at the two of them and speculate about the true nature of their friendship. Sorry and all that, but homosexuality did not exist in Ireland in the forties. Nor the fifties or sixties. There was no such thing. I never came across it once, in the classroom, in the showers, in the rugby scrum. I certainly never met it while clerking in the bank. I have a vague recollection of a priest grabbing me by the arm and telling me that I was his favourite, but the clearer memory is of the same priest trying to knock my hand off with a leather strap. One of my classmates once said to me: 'I love you in the manner of Gide,' but he laughed as he said it, and his nose was running at the time . . .

My dear Auntie May had a special friend as well, Enda Fitzgerald. Enda is one of those Irish names that can work for a man as well as a woman. I think Saint Enda was a man; perhaps there was a doubt about his sexual orientation, but probably not, for the reasons stated earlier. It was Bertie Wooster who said to his man, upon hearing the name of a newly christened child: 'There's some raw work done at the baptismal font, Jeeves.' Nowhere more so than in Ireland. Obscure saints come into their own: I know somebody saddled with the handle 'Berchmanns'. How do you fancy Fursey? Setanta? Oisin? Cornelius? There are families who zealously name their infants after foreign saints – Majella, Attracta – and at least one I know who named their four babies after the Portuguese children who claimed to witness the miracle at Fatima. The least dangerous of those was Carmencita. The baby in question went on to become the mayor of Dublin. Perhaps it's not a bad idea to give your child an extra hurdle to overcome. Now that I think of it, Terry swings both ways as well. Let's not even go there . . .

Auntie May and Enda, or Auntie Enda as I called her, were the antithesis of the two Nellies. They loved a laugh, and they smoked like chimneys. Together or apart they were two of a kind: loving, warm, and, like my mother, deeply committed to having a good jeer at anybody and everybody. Instead of coming to the church and the reception on the day Helen and I got married, Auntie Enda stayed in the little house in Drumcondra to look after my frail granny, Muds. We stopped, on our way from the church, to see them both. It was one of the last times I saw my Granny alive. And one of the last times I saw Auntie Enda. Auntie Enda's marriage came as a bolt from the blue. I thought she and Auntie May would soldier on together for ever. I've got a picture of Enda's wedding, sent to me by her niece. Have a look at it. The gang's all there. The two Nellies are on the left.

When he was on holidays, Michael Wogan wore a beret. When he was cycling back and forward, up and down the Ennis Road, back and forward over Sarsfield Bridge and round the back of O'Connell Street by the Franciscan church, to and from Leverette & Frye, victualler to the gentry, the horse-people, the remittance men and the middle-class wives of solicitors and dentists ('A half a pound of ham, Mr Wogan, that'll do us for the weekend'), the Da wore a cap. A beret, in the streets of Limerick, was an invitation to the abuse of corner-boys and the sniggering of bank clerks, cattle jobbers and other lousers.

Just to stop some well-meaning editor from sticking his or her quill in here, the word is 'louser' not 'loser', 'losser', 'tosser' or any other word with which the Anglo-Saxon ear may be more familiar. A 'louser' is essentially a Dublin form of expression, beloved of my father, to describe a ne'er-do-well, a sneak, a rotter. Politicians were lousers to a man, as were most policemen, a fair few priests, and anyone else who did not come up to my father's exacting moral standards. The kindest man who ever walked, he could forgive cheating, stealing, lying and, probably, manslaughter, but not if it became a habit. The curse of the Irish – legendary small-mindedness, craw-thumping, back-biting and downright treachery, were all the mark of the 'rotten louser' in my Da's book. He wasn't a great judge of character, and got let down more than once by people he had liked, and promoted; like the rest of us, he liked people who appeared to like him. I rarely give advice to my children, mainly because they are adults now and have more sense than me, but if there is a sage word left in my locker, it would be: 'Those who flatter you are not necessarily your friends, and those who give it to you straight, like it or not, are not necessarily your enemies.'

Anyway, Michael Wogan's beret. It was a brave and strange choice for such a conventional man in the strait-laced Ireland of the forties and fifties, where any deviation from the norm was looked upon as a sin, against either the faith, de Valera, or Holy Mother Ireland herself. The beret, like the cigar, the bow tie or any drink other than a pint of Guinness, was foreign, pretentious, an attempt to rise above your appointed station in life. Bettering yourself was not regarded as a virtue in the Ireland of my youth. Knowing your place was. And staying in it, that was the main thing. A beret would be regarded as a shout for notice, the last thing any self-respecting person would want. The greatest sin was vanity, in the absence of sex, which was, indeed, itself conspicuous by its absence, at least as far as Irish newspapers and the radio were concerned. Occasionally, an English Sunday newspaper would sneak in under the razor wire of censorship, and the scandalised talk in the snugs and parlours of Limerick would be of vicars and scout masters and London's naughty Square Mile. 'Never happen here, in Holy Catholic Ireland . . .'

Sex only reared its ugly head once a year in my home town, when Redemptorist preachers took over certain churches for a week to breathe fire and brimstone, promising eternal damnation in the fires of hell for even the most trivial of offences. You were toast for thousands of years for a venial sin such as lying or bad language; anything more serious – for instance, one of the seven 'deadly' sins: pride, covetousness, lust, anger, gluttony, envy or sloth – and you were a goner for all eternity: 'Think of it: when you burn your finger on the stove – that would not be a millionth part of the eternal agony you would suffer, every single second of every single day of eternity in the fires of hell!' This for eating too much, or fancying one of the girls from Laurel Hill convent. And people believed it. Some people still do. I wonder if the preacher from hell believed it himself? My father certainly didn't, and my mother's sense of humour wouldn't allow her to, either. There was always an element of schism and doubt in the Wogan household. Blind faith, and an unquestioning belief in the rantings of an apparently deranged priest, were just not a factor of everyday life in 18 Elm Park, Limerick.

So was my father's beret a cry for attention, a still, small shout of 'me, me, me'? No, the beret simply meant 'holiday'. He went to work in a cap, to Mass in a hat, and to the various seaside resorts we went to on family holidays in a beret. It was probably the only beret in Ireland. I never saw anyone else sporting one. Berets don't suit the Irish, and my father was no exception. He never looked right in it; it needed to be pulled forward and tilted at a rakish angle. His was pushed too far back on his head and gave him a boiled-egg look, particularly when he'd caught the sun. The beret is the least attractive head-covering known to man. Even the French have trouble with it. You never saw Maurice Chevalier or Charles Boyer in a beret, did you? And Gerard Depardieu? Don't make me laugh. Even in France nobody under eighty wears a beret, and even then I'm sure it's only worn by one of those little old actors employed by the French government to walk up and down the streets of deserted French towns with a baguette under their arm to give the illusion that there are actually people living there. They don't fool me – there's nobody at home in rural France. Those shutters never open, it's all a film set, and all those agricultural subsidies are being trousered by the boys in the sharp suits in the Elysée Palace. Isn't it extraordinary how we of the Outer Islands jeer Johnny Foreigner, and the French in particular? And at the same time live there in our hundreds of thousands, and flee there in our millions every summer?

My father, who had never been further afield than the Isle of Man, once visited France on a wine-tasting trip. This was after his brains and hard work had promoted him to the heady heights of general manager of Leverette & Frye, which subsequently became the Peter Dominic chain of wine shops, and a director of the distinguished wine and spirits merchants, Gilbeys. Loudenne was their Chateau on the Gironde, near Bordeaux, and the visit one of the highlights of the Da's life. On his return he talked about it incessantly, until the penny finally dropped that all this talk of fine food and delicious sauces was getting on my mother's nerves, a woman with no patience for cooking, whose idea of a sauce was either something you poured from a bottle, or a cube of something or other that you crumbled into hot water. What really got up my mother's nose, however, was 'the woman'. A paragon, apparently; a woman of surpassing beauty and charm, as skilled at the skillet as she was at the decanter, and whose sparkling repartee kept the entire company in fits. A passing reference to this combination of Joan of Arc and Catherine Deneuve might just have passed muster, but my dad was an innocent in the ways of women, and went on and on as the frost that was setting over our house threatened to become a glacier.

Mr Michael Thomas was not wise in the ways of women, but then, who is? Recently, when introducing the topic of 'Womanly Wiles: How to Combat Them Before Finally Giving In', on my admittedly too self-consciously intellectual radio programme, someone asked how best to counter the perennial feminine query: 'Does My Bum Look Big in This?'. Forty years of marriage had prepared me for just such a question. There is only one answer: 'No', delivered à la de Gaulle – resoundingly, positively, without a scintilla of doubt. Anything else – an aversion of the eyes, a flicker of the lids, a moistening of the lips, or, worst of all, a nanosecond's hesitation before replying – can only end in an inquisition to rival Torquemada at his best, inevitably ending with an exasperated 'I don't know why I bother!', a brisk turn of the heel, and the slamming of several doors. I received enough material from my listeners on this vital question to fill a slim volume. Indeed, I toyed with the idea of a thesis. Imagine me, with a doctorate!

Actually, you can. A couple of years ago, Professor Kevin Ryan astounded me with a letter, inviting me to accept an Honorary Doctorate of Letters at the University of Limerick. Would I? I'd have swum the Shannon for it. Those who followed my last adventure into autobiography will know that I had already swum in the Shannon at Corbally, where my great hero, Gordon Wood, had taught me to swim. In all truth, he wasn't much of a teacher, thinking that everyone was, like himself, built like Johnny Weissmuller and a natural athlete, so all a poor, half-grown, measly muscled young limb like myself would have to do would be to fling myself into the freezing river and thrash about like a young Mark Spitz. Gordon saved me from drowning several times; it was the least he could do, since he'd thrown me in in the first place.

When I think of how my two boys, Alan and Mark, learned to swim: underwater, in the Hilton hotel pool in Nicosia, Cyprus. The water warm, the teacher gentle and encouraging. And now I suppose you expect me to tell you that they grew up soft and unable to do more than paddle about in the shallow end, along the timeworn lines of, 'They don't know they're born,' and, 'It never did me any harm.' Well, they may not, and it didn't, but they're both better swimmers than me. Mark was the Maidenhead and District Champion. It must be said that neither could match my leg-thrash, but I could only keep that up for fifty metres. I'm much the same on a tennis court – you ask Dr Bev Daily, who used to play with me before our legs and backs gave out. Mind you, he'll claim the same electric pace over ten metres as I have myself, being also Celtic-bodied, with short legs and long trunk – a mesomorph from the Principality. The original Wogans came from there as well, which probably accounts for my thirty-inch inner leg and short arms. Incidentally, I find it reprehensible that jacket- and shirtmakers make their stuff with arms long enough for simians. How many gentlemen do we see these days with their knuckles brushing the ground? French rugby players excepted, of course . . .

Ah, rugby. I played the great game from the time I was eight when I moved to the gentle ministrations of the holy Jesuit Fathers at Crescent College. Crescent was a famous rugby school in Limerick, the very heartland, the soul, of Irish rugby. Everybody in Limerick who could raise a fist played rugby. Dockers, solicitors, doctors, cement factory and mill-workers, cornerboys, shopkeepers and small sons of grocery-store managers. Limerick was more like a Welsh town, where the only class that mattered was what you showed on the rugby field. Thomond Park, Limerick, was where I saw the Springboks play, the 'Afrikaanse' men as I heard them call themselves. I always loved language, and that one word has stayed with me, like 'appelkose', which the Da used to sell in his extraordinary Fortnum & Mason-type emporium on O'Connell Street, Limerick. He pronounced it 'appelkosay', but why wouldn't he? Lychees were always 'Lichees' to him. Later, when he retired, he would cross the road to the pub on Ballymun Avenue, Dublin, and order a 'Kronenburge'. Nobody corrects your pronunciation in Dublin; it's considered bad manners, and it is. Someone once corrected me on my pronunciation of 'salade niçoise', and I've never forgiven them. Here's another word to the wise: don't be a smart-ass if you know something; keep it to yourself. Wait until people ask you for your opinion.

A national newspaper once complimented me on my cleverness in not allowing people to know how clever I really was. Cracked it! I've fooled 'em by giving the impression of being more clever than I really am. I'm a product of an Irish education, a butterfly brain. I can trot out small bursts of Greek, Latin, Gaelic, German, Spanish and French without being fluent in any of them. I know the first couple of lines of any classic poem you care to name, and can throw in the telling Shakespearean quote whether called for or not. I know a lot of words, I find it easy to speak and write (although as you plough through this, you could easily point out that it's not that easy to read . . .). Maybe that *is* a definition of cleverness, but I don't think any of my teachers at the Salesian Convent or the Jesuits of Belvedere and Crescent Colleges would agree. A little above average, I think they'd say, and, mercifully, there's none of them alive to say more.

Cleverness comes in many forms, and is often confused with intelligence, but it's not the same thing. The former US President, Bill Clinton, an Oxford Scholar, is undoubtedly clever, but his social intelligence is that of a caveman. And for all his cleverness, history will show Ronald Reagan, forever lampooned here as a moronic B-movie actor, to have been the better president. I never met Ron, although I interviewed the elfin Nancy, but I saw Bill Clinton once, in a West End theatre. He was in a box beside the stalls, and the Americans in the audience spotted him early. At the interval, they swarmed around his box, mostly women, it must be said, simpering and squealing like teenagers. How is it that men who treat women badly seem to attract them like flies to a honey-pot? Anyway, the normally sedate interval became a maelstrom of female excitement, an American woman beside me returning to her seat, flushed: 'I got it! Bill Clinton's autograph! Imagine! Wow!' and other expressions of high transatlantic delight. All around me, the British remained motionless, scarcely deigning to look in the direction of Bill's box. I thought I caught the censorious clicking of a tongue . . . Maybe I'm being a bit hard on Clinton; I'm sure he could interact socially with the best of them. Charm, you could call it – I'm sure he has that in spades. So had dear old Ron. What Bill really lacked was sexual intelligence. His brains had a habit of drifting southwards in the presence of anything in a skirt.

I came to women late myself. Everybody did in my gang in Limerick, but I think I was particularly backward. The table football crowd that I mixed with in my early teens just didn't see girls. They weren't there. They didn't play our games, go to school with us, or talk about the same things. What did we talk about? I'm racking my brains here, and it's not all due to my admittedly declining powers, but I can't remember anything. I know we talked about football, about school, about our friends and foes, about films – but never about books, politics, the radio (I was an avid listener to the BBC Light Programme; they listened to Irish Radio, because their parents did). There was no television. What would today's teens talk about if there was no television? The one topic that I'm quite certain never came up was sex. We weren't shy or afraid of it, we just knew nothing about it. You'd be a long time waiting for the Jesuits to instruct us in it, and our parents had yet to come up with the goods.

As it turned out, mine never did, apart from a passing reference by my father to a 'secret sin' that flew in the face of God and His Holy Mother, and could leave a person mentally impaired. He probably felt he should say something in view of the fact that my bed sheets were standing up of their own accord every morning. We boys, lads, growing young men, never talked about it. There were the precocious ones, who talked in innuendos, and made sniggering references that I pretended to understand. I got the general gist, of course, but it never occurred to me that I would meet, talk and generally socialise with a girl on a one-to-one basis. My friend Billy came to his senses early, probably because he had a sister. I've always felt that fellows with sisters were that important step ahead. Sisters have friends, you see. Now that I think of it, I hadn't enough friends who had sisters – it obviously stunted my growth.

Billy was one of the few. His sister Mary was very pretty, and I think her mother thought that Mary and I might be friends, but Mary wasn't really interested in boys, and the whole business was over my head. Billy started to slip away from our little coterie. I saw him cycling into town early one evening. 'I'm going to the pictures,' he said with a knowing grin as he whizzed by. We remained fast friends, and still never talked about sex, nor bandied women's names about, but I knew who he was going to the pictures with. Not that I could understand why . . . Then Billy began to smoke. James didn't, and John didn't, and I didn't, but Billy had a wild streak. Cigarettes and women – the rocky road to hell. Billy began to affect an American twang, and then, one day, he took me aside to tell me he'd changed his name. 'Ned,' he said. 'That's what they call me now.' He'd never liked 'Billy' very much, and he had my sympathy; I'd never liked 'Terry'. He felt he had a right to call himself Ned – it was his name, Edmond, but it was also his father's, and his mother had called him by his second name, William, 'Billy', to avoid confusion.

Precisely the same thing as had happened as soon as Rose Wogan had got her firstborn home to 18 Elm Park. Michael's my name, but it was also my father's, so my second, Terence, became my real name, 'Terry'. I don't mind it now, but I'm still not crazy about it. It's always seemed on the effeminate side to me, and as soon as I got over here, it became 'Tel', which is even worse. I suppose if I'd stuck with Michael, it would be Mickey or 'Mick' by now, so I must be grateful for small mercies. Tom Lynch, the uncrowned king of Ireland's storytellers (which is saying something in a country where nobody shuts up), hates being called 'Tommy', but, like all of us, he has been called worse. As a young man with an uncontrollable mop of hair, he took to pulling on one of his sister's hairnets before he retired to his trundle bed of an evening, in an effort to look less like a hedgehog the following morning. His friends called round, his mother showed them up to his bedroom, and from then on he was known as 'Rosebud'. Tom Lynch's marvellous stories of his family life are something that he can tell much better than I can, but I've always been affected by his recounting of the evening he opened his front door to drink in the last of the setting sun over Dublin docks, and let rip with the ripe, resounding fart that he had been building nicely to all night. Even as he did, he heard the muffled groan of his sister, who had been kissing her boyfriend a fond goodnight on the other side of the door . . .

Many a casual liaison was cemented in the doorways of

Ireland. Where else were you going to get a 'coort'? That's the Irish version of 'court' – when couples started going out together on a regular basis, they were said to be 'coorting'. This could take the form of long walks together down dusty boreens, just holding hands, meeting every weekend at the 'ballrooms of romance', and cycling the ten miles home abreast or being asked round to the girlfriend's house for tea on a Sunday. This happened to me when I started coorting Helen, and it came as a particularly nasty shock when, after a tasty dish of rashers and egg and homemade cake to follow, we all went down on our knees for the family rosary, something that never happened in our house. Luckily, Helen's father, Tim, was a quick man with the responses, so we didn't dwell over the sorrowful mysteries, but I got to my feet shaken.

Then came an even more severe jar: the dreaded sing-song. Why the Irish feel that they have to burst into song and ruin a decent meal, or a reflective pint of stout, has always been a mystery to me. Nobody ever burst into song in my house, or they'd be looked on as a complete eejit. You can't walk into a pub in Ireland without some gobdaws launching into 'The Fields of Athenry' at the slightest gap in the conversation. The next thing, someone produces a banjo from their vest pocket, out comes a tin whistle, then a bodhran, and the whole evening's banjaxed. I think it's something the Irish feel they have to do, that somehow they're letting down those who fought and died for the Ould Country if they don't intone a dirge. It's called the 'craic', a word that fills me with horror. I'm an effete, urban Irishman. If anybody starts playing a banjo or an accordion around me or my family, we throw a couple of coppers in his hat. Unfortunately, good Dublin bourgeois common sense has long since gone out the window. They're all at it, even the 'new' Irish, the multimillionaire big players who seem to be coming out of the country on a production line. A wealthy young Englishwoman told me of how she abhors that frightening moment after dinner in an Irish house in Barbados, when the host says, 'Now then, Cosima, you'll give us a song.' And it's not as if anyone enjoys it. Take a look around the next time you're caught in the pub and they strike up 'The Irish Rover'. Unless he's past caring and inoculated by the demon drink, the soloist is performing self-consciously, as if his mother has forced him to do it. Everybody else is looking at everybody else and smiling rictus-like, desperately pretending to be having a good time, and wishing the row would stop and they could go back to their pint and a good old chinwag. It never does, of course, and in the end, with the drink dulling their wits and their inhibitions stunned, everybody joins in, and they stagger off home in the wee small hours thinking that they've had a good time. It's happened to me, and every time it does, I can't believe it . . .

I couldn't believe it when it happened in Helen's house, that first time. 'Helen will give us a song,' commanded her mother Ellie. I've always put Ellie together with my beloved granny, Muds, as the gentlest, sweetest-natured people I've ever met. Along with the present Mrs Wogan, of course. (That was a close one.) Beneath the almost angelic face and soft voice, though, Ellie had steel. She had to – Tim Joyce, at his worst, was a bully and a tyrant. (At his best, which he was during the long years of Ellie's illness, he was a saint, considerate, caring and loving. A man who had for years required his soup to be cooled on the window sill at one o'clock on the dot, back rashers only, and the skin to be taken from his chicken, became a cook, house-

24

keeper and nurse without a murmur ...) So, Helen obliged with a song, 'My Love is Like a Red, Red Rose'. Everybody seemed to enjoy it, but they weren't fooling me. I knew what was going on in their heads: exactly what was panicking me: 'Whose turn is it next? What the hell am I going to sing? I don't know the words to anything.' The fear that stalks the family sing-song: nobody knows the words. You think you know them as you sing along with the radio, but on your own, you're dead after the first couple of lines. My good friend and radio producer Paul Walters has twelve guitars, and a long nail on one of his thumbs for playing them, which he does in public only under threat of death, or at a Christmas carol concert. I've been there, when he's played for people who want a good old singalong knees-up.

'Play "The House of the Rising Sun"!'

'*There is a house in New Orleans, they call the Rising Sun – and it's been the ruin of many a poor boy, and Lord, I think I'm one ... The ... I ... My ...* I don't know any more ... What about "Cathy's Clown"? Oh, no, I don't know that, either ...'

And so the long night wears on. At least the Irish can finish a song, if they're still standing. Or maybe they only think they can. My reaction to the threat of being called upon to sing of a Sunday evening in Helen Joyce's front room in Rathmines, Dublin, was the coward's way out: I hid. Behind the sofa. I made myself invisible. I can do that. You have to, if you're shy, or have a low threshold of embarrassment. I can 'slip away' – ask Helen or any of my friends.

My mother always said, in later years, that I was a 'strange' child. Having dutifully played with my little friends in Elm Park, I would come through our front gate, closing it firmly behind me in case any of them would follow. The child is father to the man. I've been like that all my life. They say that to travel is more important than to arrive, but for me, knowing when to leave is more important than either. And sooner, rather than later. I'll sneak away from anything – receptions, cocktail parties, weddings, dinners, even grand dos at Buck House. I've been privileged to attend there more than once at Her Majesty's request, but I feel that once I've bowed and exchanged a word or two of airy badinage with Their Majesties, they wouldn't be too distraught if they didn't see me again that evening; or possibly ever . . . So I sidle away through the madding crowd, and I'm tucked up in my bed while the marble halls are still echoing to their chatter.

A year or so ago, the Queen and Prince Philip hosted a grand levee at the Palace to celebrate the music industry's contribution to the public purse, and British life in general. I got there early and was given a special badge, then ushered through one great room after another, hung with magnificent paintings and imposs-ible chandeliers. Gilt was everywhere, on the walls, the ceilings, the chairs. It was overwhelming, and there I was, the boy from Limerick, alone in this grand room, awaiting the arrival of the Queen of England. What would Michael and Rose Wogan have said? Or Auntie May, Muds or Great-Aunt Maggie? Or all those teachers who thought I was OK, but would never amount to much? All those years in short trousers, on the crossbar of my father's bike, playing table football with myself on the floor of the front room in Elm Park – were they all leading up to this?

Then the other rooms started to fill up, but only one or two joined me in what I was beginning to think was my own personal salon. Shirley Bassey, Vera Lynn, Tim Rice, Tessa Jowell, Phil

Collins. In another room, Brian May from Queen and Eric Clapton were just a couple of the great names of British music who hadn't made the final cut. We lined up, Shirley Bassey knocking over an occasional table in her nervousness, and Her Majesty and Prince Philip entered, all welcoming smiles. They moved slowly down the line, exchanging pleasantries. When the Queen came to me, she told me what a wonderful musical afternoon she'd enjoyed, listening to the music of, among others, Katie Melua. She complimented me on my discovery of such a bright talent. I blushed modestly, but didn't have time to tell Her Majesty that the discovery was my producer Paul Walters', not mine, because with that charming smile of hers she had moved on to exchange airy badinage with the next in line, Phil Collins. Prince Philip asked me how I kept up my incessant babble every morning on the radio, and I said I was just babbling to myself, which seemed to satisfy him, and he followed the Queen, who by now was making her way to the door and the next bunch of hobbledehoys and ne'er-do-wells.

As she did so, Phil Collins whistled the five notes from *Close Encounters of the Third Kind*.

The Queen turned, still smiling, but puzzled.

'What was that?' she inquired.

Collins was speechless.

'He was calling ET, Ma'am,' I said, even as I said it wishing I'd kept my mouth shut.

'Ah,' said the Queen, nodding understandingly. They'd obviously warned her about the kinds of idiots she'd be meeting that evening.

As the door closed, Phil Collins turned to me, whining piteously. 'Why did I do that? What came over me?'

'The Royal Effect,' I answered sagely. 'You say the first thing that comes into your head, and you carry the memory of your foolishness with you to the grave.'

Then I slipped away into the night, as swiftly as I had come.

Speaking of Her Majesty, many years ago, when the world was young, a doddering old geezer would wheel his mobile commode into my radio studio and, unbidden, rattle off, in a wheezy baritone, the supposed highlights of his programme, which used to follow mine, like a wounded snake. Every week, I would cling to the forlorn hope that his wheels would come off, or the monkey-gland injections fail, but then came the dreadful news: in a moment of weakness, the Queen had given the old bloke a gong! I knew then that there'd be no getting rid of him, and in fact I was the first to crack, running off in desperation to television for nine years. And you'll never believe it, but he was still there when I came back . . .

On the day after Jimbo got his gong, he walked in virtually unaided, wheezing away, and pointed to the medal swinging against his chicken chest.

'It's the OBE!' he chortled, going into another paroxysm.

'Congratulations, Jimbo,' I snarled through gritted teeth.

'Yes, and do you know what she told me?'

'If you mean our beloved Queen . . .'

'Yes, she said she listens to our little chinwag, what about that?'

'Well,' I replied, with a hint of petulance, 'why didn't I get a gong as well?'

'Har-har,' he chuckled, bringing on another fit of coughing. 'Har! She says it's the part of *my* programme she enjoys best, har-har . . .'

How I didn't spit live on the air, I'll never know. The listeners, of course, who never knew any better, were impressed, and one old soldier who claimed to be a contemporary of Jimbo wrote in praise, 'Jimmy Young did sterling work in the war, and us chaps home from the Veldt on leave liked nothing better than to take a popsy to the old Alhambra in Leicester Square to see the old boy perform. His rendition of "The Boers Have Got My Daddy" will live long in the memory . . .'

It's but a hazy recollection, but I think it was dear Jim who gave me a piece of advice, shortly after he realised that I was not there solely as his warm-up man:

'Always remember, lad, don't bleed in front of the men.'

They don't make 'em like that any more.

2

I must be talking to myself . . .

⁓

Jimmy Young went on to get a knighthood, and then left us all in the lurch in what can only be described as a marked manner. It was sad that a great broadcaster, held in affection and respect by millions of his daily listeners, and widely respected, too, as a first-class political interviewer, particularly by Margaret Thatcher, should leave the BBC, to whom he had given such service, under a cloud. Jimmy was never an easy man. He had fought his way up the bill in variety in the forties and fifties, became one of the biggest names in British popular music with huge hits such as 'The Man from Laramie', and then, when pop music changed the Hit Parade, carved another career for himself as a disc jockey, presenter and, finally, an interviewer that every politician wanted to talk to. He'd come up the hard way, and was ever fierce in his defence of himself and his radio show. That show was everything to Jim. He lived it; his whole life revolved around it. Although his programme didn't start until midday, he would be in at half-eight in the morning, checking the papers, reading the research, formulating the questions for the interviews. With my incapacity for any kind of preparation or rehearsal, it made me tired just to look at him. Even his relationship with, and subsequent marriage to, his delightful and supportive Alisha didn't soften his commitment to his beloved show. But, as everybody in radio and television knows, what we do is not permanent and pensionable. We know it, but we don't believe it, and Jimmy Young was no exception.

I've always said that I hope I'll have enough sense to get off the beach before the tide comes in, but mark well that word 'hope'. Will I be able to walk away when my time has come? How will I know when my time has come? As I've said elsewhere, one of my defining virtues, or perhaps vices, is to leave; and sooner, rather than later. I walked away from *Come Dancing* in the early seventies (hard to believe that Bruce Forsyth would revitalise his career by walking back into the ballroom in his early seventies). I gave *Blankety Blank* the elbow when I felt the public had had enough (Les Dawson proved me wrong). *Auntie's Bloomers* had run its course when I took a powder (Lily Savage and Anne Robinson continued to flog the dead horse for several more years), but I didn't listen to my instinct for escape with *Wogan*, and was persuaded to continue with it for at least two years longer than I should have. You remember they were building that village, Eldorado, in Spain and needed to drag me out until it was finished.

Nobody was brave or honest enough to tell me, of course, which is exactly what happened to Jimmy Young. Them upstairs had made their decision to say goodbye to him long before they told him. He was in his eighties, he didn't fit with the new image of Radio 2, which was aiming for a younger market to take up the slack left by the continuing failure of Radio 1. Nobody explained it to Jim, nobody took him out to lunch to break it to him gently. Not, in fairness, that you could break that kind of thing gently to Jim, who was spiky, defensive, resistant to any change. Still, he did deserve better than the unholy mess that marked his departure. I think the suits were hoping that he'd just disappear without them saying anything. It remains one of the greatest faults of BBC management: nobody ever says anything to your face. Confrontation is a dirty word, much better to send a memo. The one for the chop is expected to read the signs, interpret the body language, read between the lines, then do the decent thing and fall on his sword.

Michael Aspel tells a poignant story about being wined and dined, flattered and cajoled, and then, after an excellent meal, convinced that all was well and that his contract was being renewed for another two years. Actually, he was being fired. Exceptions prove the rule, naturally, and the BBC exception was Alistair Milne, who'd come up through the ranks as an outstanding producer, full of brains and ability, to the heady heights of Director-General. This was a man who fired from the hip, exemplified by his dismissal of a Managing Director of Television. They'd spent the day together delightfully, at a shooting party. Several brace of game bird were in the boot, and, suffused in the warm glow induced by good claret and game pie, they sat together companionably in the back of their BBC car.

'A good day,' remarked Alistair.

'Wonderful,' agreed his managing director.

There was a pause, then Milne spoke again.

'Oh, by the way, boy. You're fired. Clear your desk by midday tomorrow.'

It may not be coincidental that Alistair Milne is the only Director-General of the BBC in living memory not to be ennobled . . .

Jimmy Young's and my morning exchanges became part of the warp and weft of our listeners' daily lives; as a lady from Benfleet, Joan Wells, put it, 'Whoever it was, was right, in saying the JY interlude is the best part of your show, but then it's also the best part of Jim's.' Dammit, Jimbo and I made the cover of the *Radio Times* on the strength of it, the ultimate accolade. Actually, the more important accolades are those that come unbidden from the likes of the aforementioned St Joan:

> *In the rarefied air of the BBC*
> *Two minds magnificent meet and mingle*
> *And the brilliant flashes of repartee*
> *Are sufficient to make one's toenails tingle.*
> *The shafts of conversational wit*
> *The serendipitous well-turned phrase*
> *Illumine the world of the listening TWIT,*
> *And set his questioning mind ablaze.*

There's more in that vein, but I've never encouraged flattery nor sycophancy, believing that when friends communicate, it's usually on a level of gentle persiflage. Which is why I'm the subject of dog's abuse from my listeners, particularly when I appear on television: 'My old granddad recognised that suit you wore last night, it was his demob one, which Oxfam took away in pity in 1950. He says he left half-a-crown in the pocket. Hand it over.' And that's a particularly gentle example of what I've put up with over the long, weary years.

I don't know why it struck me that the Radio 1 jocks were doing it wrong when I arrived to relieve Jimmy Young in late 1969. All I could hear was people reading cards and letters in praise of themselves: 'Dear Tony, Dave, Pete, Rosko, we think your programme is fab!' Nearly forty years on, I still hear far too much of it: 'Keep up the good work.' 'We love your programme.' Sorry, but it's sickening. If they're heaping praise on your unworthy head, blush modestly by all means, but keep it to yourself.

Radio presenters get the mail they encourage; they get what they deserve. For all those years, the people who write to me know what I want to hear, and it's not gratitude nor platitude. I'm looking for wit, originality, a keen eye for the ridiculous, lateral thinking, a laugh at life. Ever since I took over the afternoon Radio 1 and 2 joint show in 1972, my listeners have obliged. As I've often said, without them and their marvellous letters I'd have sat there, mumchance, in front of the microphone for years on end. Nowadays, we rejoice in the flights of fancy of Mick Sturbs, Willie Gofar, Edina Cloud and the thousands of others who write under an assumed name, some of them blatant in their attempts to trip up an honest broadcaster about his daily toil: a Miss Tickles, first name Tess; the Bushes, Tudor and Anita; a Mr Hucker, first name Rudolph; Mr Peacock, first name Drew; and a charmer who claimed to live in 2 Effin Close, Far Corfe, Dorset. In olden times, in the seventies and early eighties, people were decent and unsuspecting enough to sign their real name, but the tone was always, as it has remained, the same – foolish but fun.

Lately, that fine upstanding young limb of a broadcaster, Richard Allinson, reminded me of how his mother had rejoiced in the late seventies to the daily reports of the man who took his budgie for a walk in Birmingham. Luckily his doings are recounted in an earlier tome of mine, *The Day Job*. Apparently, our man would stroll along every day as far as the Robin Hood roundabout, and stand there letting his feathered friend breathe in the health-giving fumes, causing many a dented bumper to the unsuspecting passing motorist. Denizens of Solihull and Hale Green wrote in their hundreds to tell me that they'd met the man who took his budgie for a walk, and not to make fun of him because he was a nice little man and they didn't want him upset. 'Anyway,' said one, 'we need something around here to make us famous. We do not have a park, a swimming bath, a nursery school, a place where you can get a cup of tea, or a Sainsbury's' . . . Many claimed to know who he was: a man from Wolverhampton thought that he might be his Uncle Andy, whom he had carelessly mislaid at the Spaghetti Junction Lupin Festival. Another identified him as Jim Smith, then manager of Birmingham City, claiming that the supporters had given Jim the bird, and that it was an albatross, not a budgie, and that he was doomed to stop one in three to tell his sad tale . . .

Then, from Wales, the Celtic fringe lifted, and another one made his escape, this time from Swansea. 'Taking a budgie for a walk is nothing, look you. I knew a man once who took his goldfish for a walk. It took years of training, starting by taking the fish out of the water for a few seconds, and gradually increasing the time. While this was going on, the water in the tank was gradually reduced, until the fish became totally "oxygenised". After all this effort, tragedy. One day, while they were crossing a bridge, the fish slipped its lead, fell into the river below, and was drowned.' You could see that coming, but there was no avoiding it. That's often the case, but half the fun is in the terrible inevitability of the punchline.

We've often whiled away the idle hour with punchlines alone: 'Don't push me past me mother's'; 'No, not a twelve-inch pianist', 'How much?' (the dreaded Preston joke). A day doesn't go by without recycling, 'Are you a doctor, then?' 'No, I never really bothered.' (Antony Aloysius St John Hancock), or the perennial, politically incorrect, 'Waiter, this chicken is rubbery.' 'Oh, thank you velly much.' Daily radio is about familiarity, repetition and even predictability. For instance, the only possible reaction to a good ol' country song is, 'Ee-hah, dang ma britches,' or, 'Set a spell and let your saddle cool.' A romantic ballad requires a simple postscript, such as, 'I am promised to another, you hussy.' A tear-jerker may be pre-empted by, 'Here's one to wring the withers,' and followed by, 'It's hard to beat a good laugh.' 'Give the woman in the bed more porther' is still acceptable after a burst of hooligan music, and anything vaguely Mexican or Latino must of necessity have 'Arriba, arriba, andale' as a postscript. These traditions have been handed down through the ages of *Wake Up to Wogan*, and it's much too late to change them now. Anyway, I can't think of anything new.

Nothing dates like humour, but although the names of my listeners have changed, the quality of their contributions seems permanent. Or maybe that's because we share the same sense of humour. Back in the seventies a man called Pat Carr of Norwich used to write to me, and his flights of fancy could only be compared to the magnificent Milligan. A report had come through of a Channel swimmer (why do so few people do that any more?) who, on landing at Dover, claimed to have slept part of the way from Cap Gris Nez. I cast some doubt on this, feeling that sleeping while swimming was a sovereign way to sink to the bottom like a stone. Carr wrote:

> Following the news of this fellow swimming the Channel while asleep, I decided to be the first person to swim the Channel while tied to a lamppost in Birmingham. Sadly, due to the swarms of greenfly sticking to the margarine covering my body, I was arrested on the M6 as a sexual pervert. This was a fatal blow to my chances, and I've had to postpone my attempt. Please send best wishes to my wife who is waiting for me in Calais with the key to the chains, and say 'Hurry home.'

Plus ça change. A couple of years ago, inflamed by the efforts of Richard Branson, my friend Willie Gofar attempted a solo balloon flight around the world from Peterborough. He was hampered by wishing to go home every night for his tea, requiring the balloon to be tethered to a convenient lamppost every evening at dusk, and further held back by having to keep one foot on the ground, in the interests of safety.

Anybody listening to *Wake Up to Wogan* in 1993, when I began my second incarnation as a daily radio presenter, would have been listening to an entirely different type of show than what passes for entertainment between 7.30 and 9.30 a.m. on Radio 2 these days. The content now is entirely different. The music has changed, to cater for a newer, younger, bigger audience. And it's not just me chunter any more; I can hardly get a word in edgeways for Doctor Wally's petulant mumbling, the Voice of the Balls' vibrant intonation, John Marsh's curmudgeonly moaning, and Fran Godfrey's incessant chirruping, 'Me, me, me.' What's really interesting is that nobody's noticed. The show is constantly changing, while remaining the same.

I've never believed in standing still; my whole professional career has been one of change, and, if you like, risk-taking. I left Ireland in 1969, having established myself there on radio and television, for a thirteen-week contract with BBC Radio. On the strength of that, I moved my little family of wife and son from the comfort of a charming bungalow overlooking Dublin Bay to a nondescript rented house miles from London. That Helen never complained is something I will never forget. The new BBC job didn't pay as much as I was making in Ireland, so I reversed what I had been doing between 1967 and 1969, and in 1970 started commuting the other way, from London to Dublin, to record the commercial radio shows I was still doing in Ireland. It never occurred to me that the BBC might not renew my contract, and I might have to crawl back to Ireland under cover of darkness. I'm not all that sure I'd take the same risk now . . .

The essence of any daily show, but particularly one in the sensitive early-morning hours, is, as I've said, familiarity. One of the reasons for my show's popularity is the fact that the public have been listening to me, man and boy, granny and grandchild, since Mafeking was relieved. I receive letters on a daily basis from fathers and mothers who tell me that they are now forcing their children to listen to me, just as their parents did. I know I should find that heartening, but somehow . . .

I've always maintained that you can't contrive at change. I'm still there, clinging to the wreckage, but I've learned from experience that the very idea that you think a cracker, the one that will run and run, is the one that dies without a murmur, while Paul Walters remarking that he had a special affection for rhubarb, and tinned, at that, produced an enormous listener reaction (punchline: 'We put custard on ours') that is revived every year by the Wakefield Rhubarb Festival. You can force rhubarb, but you can't force change on the listeners, you can only respond to their whims, their changing moods. You can suggest, even point, but you must let them lead the way. Nobody knows better than Paul and me the ever changing face of Britain, the new directions taken by public opinion. We'd have to be pretty thick not to know the way things are going, and what the public wants, with up to six hundred emails on our computer overnight, and another couple of hundred in the course of the programme.

The biggest factor in the show's changing face has been the email. In my previous incarnation on the Radio 2 morning show, 7.30 to 10, with added Jimmy Young from 1972 to 1984, all my incoming mail was by card or letter. I would initiate a topic, and it would take at least three or four days before I got a response. Or a listener would come up with a blinding notion, but again it would be several days before the rest of the gang caught the ball and ran with it. It was fine while the show was trundling on, but as you can imagine, there was something of a hiatus when I took a holiday. When I reinstated the whole rotten business in 1993, I asked for faxes, to get a more instant response, but within a year or so the email had taken over. Many of my listeners actually bought computers so that they could communicate with the programme on an instant basis. It is marvellous to have a reaction to the previous day awaiting you in the morning, and even better to have yourself shouted down within minutes of opening your mouth.

Dear Sir,

On the 50th anniversary of the famous *Waiting for Godot*, I, literary impresario Winston Flange, have managed to unearth this early 1st draft of the famous play by Samuel Buckett:

WAITING FOR WOGAN

VLADIMIR: Is he going to say something significant soon?

ESTRAGON: Who?

VLADIMIR: Wogan – I've been listening for weeks but nothing ever happens.

ESTRAGON: Yes, it's ridiculous – the whole show is completely meaningless.

VLADIMIR: Shall we switch off then?

(*They do not move. Silence.*)

ESTRAGON: There's nothing else to do. We'd better carry on listening.

And there the manuscript breaks off.

> *I remember way back around '78*
> *We tuned in to Radio 2*
> *To find Terry Wogan was 'Fighting the Flab'*
> *Though his waistline mysteriously grew.*

Our Terry went on to host Children in Need
And a chat show that ran on the telly,
It was usually all right but one terrible night
Anne Bancroft reduced him to jelly.

They made him a knight in 2005
For his services and his quips,
With his thick Irish brogue, this old Limerick rogue
Is now more English than fish and chips.

So here's to our Terry, the Master of TOGs,
Here's to him wherever he roams,
He's the king of the wits (with a silent T)
And the thinking man's Eamonn Holmes!

W.B. Yeast

Things were slower in days of yore, but my listener was just as sharp. The topics that exercised them are lost in the mists of time, but I can easily recall taking a deal of unfair comment on my interpretation of the Cornish Floral Dance. To refresh your jaded memory, an instrumental version of that grand old tune became a surprise hit in the mid-seventies by the Brighouse and Rastrick Brass Band, or as they were known to my crowd, the Faggots and Gastric. I started to intone along with the crowd-pleaser, remembering my father's relentless outpouring of the same thing every evening as he shaved.

Eventually, a chap called Mike Redway, who should have known better, produced my vocal version, and it, in turn, became a hit. The glow of pardonable pride that I feel when remembering this grand achievement is vitiated by the hurtful remarks I endure with strong resolve to this very day. While joining a long queue to enter Turkey for the Eurovision Song Contest the other year, out of the blue a voice with a distinct Cornish burr said, 'We'll never forgive you for what you did to the Floral Dance.' 'And the rest of the world will never forgive you for your damned pasties,' I retorted, and as Wodehouse put it, I meant it to wound. For heaven's sake, Cornwall, get over it! I suppose that I should be inured to it, for God knows I had my share of contumely at the time:

> *I thought I heard the curious tone*
> *Of Terry Wogan on the gramophone,*
> *Grunting here and groaning there,*
> *Devoid of timing, tone and flair,*
> *Trying to make the most of his chance*
> *With his hideous attempt at the Floral Dance*

As I've said before, I'm supposed to have no feelings.

Back then we spent some time on Knickers of World War Two, with particular reference to Messerschmitts, which came down without a fight; *Dallas*, and the endless machinations of J.R. and the Ewing family, whose fabulous wealth only afforded them one phone, wire coathangers and a small space in front of the garage where they held weddings and parties. 'Who killed J.R.?' took years off my life. Those who nowadays think that Dirty Den returning from the dead is a big deal should have been around when Bobby Ewing got out of the shower and it turned out that everything we'd been watching for the past six months had been a figment of his imagination . . .

Listeners liked word-play in those olden times. Paul McCartney's 'Mull of Kintyre' became 'Muck in the Byre', 'Mulligan's Tyres'. Kenny Rogers's 'Lucille' – '*You picked a fine time to leave me Lucille, with four hungry children and a crop in the field*' – provoked the unusual reaction that it was no wonder the woman left, with four hundred children and a croc in the field. Nana Mouskouri became Nana Moussaka, Shirley Bassey, Burly Chassis. And at Wimbledon, there was an American tennis player of pleasing and reputed playboy tendencies (it's all become a bit serious and intense these days) who rejoiced in the name of Vitas Gerulaitis. Now, what could you do with a name like that? Plenty, if you're one of mine:

Oh Vitas Gerulaitis
All in shining whites
With your shorts all nice and tightus
I could really fancy you
Oh Vitas Gerulaitis
I won't put up a fightus
Come round and have a bitus
And a mug of Aqua Vitus
And I'll get nicely Titus
Andronicus with you . . .

As I've said before, if you were paying attention, times change but some things remain the same: the weather and its ways has been a constant source of inspiration and vexation to the thinking listener. Sometime in the very early eighties, a misguided fan of our feathered friends remarked that, apart from a man's best

I must be talking to myself . . .

friend being his duck, these gifted birds repaid observation in the matter of weather forecasting. Naturally, there was a come-back:

> *If your duck goes ballroom dancing*
> *Swallows you will soon be glancing*
> *But if your duck throws off his sequins*
> *A freak frost will do your beans in.*

And,

> *If your duck do bite you twice*
> *'Tis certain that there will be ice.*
> *If your duck stamp on your toe*
> *You can expect a fall of snow.*
> *If your duck do kick your nethers*
> *You probably won't care what the weathers.*

That was from someone who claimed to be named Bill Waddell, probably the first example of the use of the pseudonym on my show. I'll get *Time Team* on to it. Come on, Carenza . . .

All these talented contributors thought of themselves as TWITS, the forerunners of my beloved TOGs. Incidentally, it's indicative of Radio 2's ever growing new audience that I'm continually being asked, 'What's a TOG?' You young limb, a TOG is a Terry's Old Geezer or Gal. Don't ask me again, or I'll set your granny on you. A simple example of Togdom will suffice for now:

The clock radio came to life at 7.30 after a long weekend. Ah well! Back to work.

Leaping out of bed, I decided not to wake her majesty: let her have a lie in, she deserves it.

I hurriedly dressed, had a quick bowl of cornflakes, made the tea and toast, and just as the 8 o'clock (Dance with me) pips were sounding, I took a cup of tea in for her.

'Here you are my dear, a nice cup of tea to wake you up. I'm just off before the traffic gets too bad.'

She yawned and sleepily sat up. 'Thank you. It's a long time since you brought me tea in the morning.'

'Yes, well, can't stop, see you at dinner time.'

I was outside heading for the car when she opened the bedroom window. 'Where are you going?' she called.

'To work of course.' I could see what she was thinking – it was a Bank Holiday weekend, and she was still half asleep. She thought it was Monday but in fact the Bank Holiday was yesterday. 'Wake up, it's Tuesday today. Just listen to the radio and you'll see. Wogan's back,' I yelled.

I turned away with a wave, and as I opened the car door she shouted, 'But you don't go to work any more, you retired two years ago.'

Francis Frogbound

The TWITS were the Terry Wogan Is Tops Society, and, like TOGs, they seemed to evolve spontaneously, a Big Bang of Broadcasting. One minute they weren't there, the next they were all over the shop when I'd open a supermarket, wearing

46

their TWITS T-shirts with my fizzog all over them. Unlike TOGs, who have a national convention every year and regional get-togethers whenever their trained senses tell them, the TWITS claimed to hold their AGM in a phone box somewhere in Wigan. Like TOGs, they had their own secret handshake and sign, and may well have carried something for taking the stones out of horses' hooves. But where the TOGs have been content to increase and multiply 'neath one proud banner with a single device, the TWITS lost control from an early stage. I regret that I didn't impose some sort of structure, a coven, even a committee, for it all got out of hand. Breakaway groups proliferated, TWIRL (Terry Wogan Is Really Lovely), TWADDLE (Terry Wogan And Daffy Duck Look Effeminate), TWINKLETOES (Terry Wogan Is Not Kinky Like Everyone Thinks Or Everyone Says). Then it got really personal: WIDOW (Wogan Is a Dreadful Old Woman) and WOGANS (Workshy, Overpaid, Grouser And Naggers Society). In the end, they all passed as the idle wind when I folded my tent and made my weary way to television. I like to think that somewhere, a small group of the intelligentsia still meet under the forbidden sign of IDIOTS (I Drool Incessantly Over Terry Society).

Of all the topics I've introduced to my demented pack, none have produced, before or since, such a reaction as my light-hearted comment on motorway cones. I lightly touched on the fact that although mile after mile of motorway lane was 'coned off', nary a soul was to be seen working on the other side of the little red and white blighters. The British public fell on the cones like ravening wolves. They sent me photographs of ones about their evil work – encircling holes in the road and telegraph poles, hijacking lorries, intimidating police cars. Everyone had a tale of cone horror, but of course, being TWITS, sanity broke through, and a young lady from Penarth produced a fragrant nosegay of children's rhymes:

> *Terry, Terry, quite contrary,*
> *How do the motorways grow?*
> *With tarmac grey*
> *And men who play*
> *With pretty cones all in a row.*
>
> *Oh where oh where have the workmen gone?*
> *Oh where oh where can they be?*
> *With a cone put here and a cone put there*
> *They must have gone to their tea.*
>
> *Pat-a-cone, pat-a-cone motorwayman,*
> *Close me a lane as fast as you can.*
> *Stop it and block it, and mark it with glee,*
> *Put out your cones, and go home to your tea.*

I still have people reminding me of the Days of the Cone – it seemed to leave an indelible mark on the unfortunate motorist's psyche. Of course, worse things have happened since, such as congestion charging and bus lanes, but the cones are still with us, miles and miles of them, without even a man leaning on a shovel on the other side.

A couple of years ago, in a rush of blood to the head, the Highways Agency put up signs here and there on motorways and A-roads. 'Cones Hotline' was the bold message, with a phone number the exasperated traveller might ring if it all got too much for him. It was too good an opportunity to miss, even for the beleaguered British motorist, bowed down by fuel prices, road taxes that didn't pay for roads, speed cameras and traffic jams. At last, an opportunity to let fly and tell them, whoever they were, where to get off . . . After a year, the Highways Agency withdrew the 'Cones Hotline'. It wasn't the success they had been hoping for, they said. Ninety-five per cent of the complaints they got were wrong. And did you know that the man who was responsible for the bus lane on the M4 (you know the one, it's on the outside lane, and has never seen a bus. Motorbikes and taxis, yes) was awarded an OBE for his fine work?

I suppose that I could go on jumping up and down in the same old rut about motorways, cones and the sad lot of the nation's abused majority, the motorists, but I suppose I've become infected by the classic phlegmatism of the British, and can't be bothered banging on, when I know that neither the Highways Authority nor the Government give a rattling damn, because they know that the 'silent majority' are not called that for nothing. It's minorities that change the world; if you belong to a minority, you're on the pig's back, as the Granny used to say. Look at the money that's spent on Radio 3 . . .

3

On the other hand, talk is cheap

~⌒~

In 1982 Michael Parkinson left his comfy chair as chat show host to the nation with the BBC, and joined David Frost, Robert Kee, Anna Ford and Angela Rippon, the Famous Five, in their ill-starred adventure into breakfast television. The BBC countered with their old reliable, Frank Bough, and Selina Scott, whom they had pinched from ITN. The Famous Five foundered, not because of Bough's cardigans, nor brisk professional style, but because of the sensational Scott, who always looked as if she had just fallen off the chaise longue after a night to remember. Nobody, before or since, has brought such languid sex appeal to early morning television. Thank goodness, otherwise I wouldn't have given you odds on the well-being of early-morning radio in Britain. Mercifully, Selina seemed to disappear into the mist. The thinking viewer still misses her of a morn, I'll be bound . . .

It is extraordinary how breakfast television has failed to make any real impact. Whenever I go to the States, and wake up of an early morn to my sunny-side-up with crispy Canadian bacon and coffee that tastes of nothing, I turn on the television, not the radio. Maybe that's because I'm in a hotel bedroom, but it's due, at least in part, to the way they do it in America. The mood is light, the presenters attractive, the pace smart, and it's all done with professional ease. There's none of the self-consciousness, the uncomfortable lack of rapport, of the British breakfast sofa. I suppose this criticism could be levelled more at GMTV than the BBC, but the Corporation's idea of breakfast news is flawed, in its turn, by not being quite sure whether it's supposed to be light-hearted or serious. So the attractive presenters are caught between two stools, and the interaction between them in the lighter moments seems forced, rather like John Humphrys' desperate attempts at badinage on Radio 4's *Today*.

Everything today is about image, not substance, and it was Tony Blair and new Labour's realisation, and masterly exploitation, of this fact that brought them to power and has kept them there. If any endeavour should realise this, it's television and radio. Yet how often do we see, on television news, reporters who look like unmade beds? Unattractive, badly dressed, unkempt reporters are a distraction, just as bad as the stumbling verbal incompetence we hear far too often from contributors to radio news. Ums and aahs, monotonous untutored tones, and even lisps. It reminds me of the little fellow I met, years ago, in Henry Street, Dublin.

'Hello, Sean,' says I.

'Hello yourthelf,' he said.

'Where are you off to?' I inquired.

'I'm off to the radio thathion,' he said, 'to do an audithion to be a newthreader.'

'Good man,' I said, 'good luck.'

'Ah thure, luck won't come intho it. I should geth ith, eathy.'

Some weeks later, I met him again.

'Ah there, Sean,' I asked, 'did you get the job?'

He looked a little downcast. 'Didn't geth ith,' he answered, 'too thmall' . . .

When I joined Radio Eireann, we had a month of training, every day of the week, in how to speak on the radio: intonation, pronunciation, inflection, emphasis and expression. And after all that, I was the only one who got a job at £17 3s 4d a week, rising by annual increments of pitiable amounts. I was poor, but I was a trained broadcaster. I'm sure that they used to do it that way in the BBC, but I'm equally sure they don't do it that way now. Journalism has become more important than presentation, and that's the wrong way round, lads – ask Tony Blair . . . On *Sky News*, I watched a reporter from the Fox Network in America deliver from a hurricane-lashed location a perfect interpretation of what was going on around her – no hesitation, no stumbling, no verbal crutches, no looking down at the script. It was straight-forward, succinct, without acting or affectation. Oh, and she was young and beautiful. That was the reason the Fox Network picked her, then they checked out her brains and journalistic ability, and found that they excelled even her beauty. Please don't tell me that British universities are not churning out just such young women and men in their thousands from media studies courses every year. So who's picking television news-hounds who look like bag ladies and tramps? Don't tell me that it can't be easy to look your best if you're 'embedded'. Or on a rain-lashed promontory in Caithness. What's the cameraman there for, if not to tell you that your hair is sticking up at the back, your nose is running, your anorak is cheap and nasty, and you look like the wrath of God?

So Parky left the chat show (or 'prat show', as it's called in Holland) leaving the unfortunate viewing public to darkness, and to me. The Saturday night talk spot was mine, the producer Marcus Plantin, whom I'd worked with first when he was assisting the great (in every sense of the word) Stewart Morris, and with whom I soldiered through the muck and bullets of *Blankety Blank*. Though the memories are hazy, I think I enjoyed it, and the critics and reviewers were kind. Robin Day came on as a guest, and was his usual blustering self, but told me how much better I was than Michael Parkinson. I put the blessed Parky's name in full there, just to show that we're pals, and I know his first name. One of the more hurtful, yet perceptive, letters I received lately was one that pointed out the oddity that those whom the British public revere and love are known universally by their first names: Cilla, Elton, Ant and Dec, John, George, Paul and Ringo. Those in the public eye that they hold in little regard, not to mention disgust, they know by their surnames: Hitler, Crippen, Chirac, every prime minister and football manager since Churchill and Ramsey, Mussolini, de Gaulle and, dammit, Wogan. And – sorry, Mike – Parkinson!

Robin Day's compliment wasn't worth tuppence, as I found out a couple of years later when, in a fit of pique over his wages from the BBC for politically pontificating, he fulminated like a gas boiler when some minion wound him up by telling him how much *I* was earning with my far less important, and even trivial, chattering. Robin, who rightly saw himself as the British political inquisitor par excellence, had earlier become as a coiled spring when he heard what his equivalent on US television, Dan Rather, was trousering. Robin could not contain himself, bursting into print and dragging my name all over the papers with him. At the time I was on holiday with the family, and when I returned, Michael Grade (the head honcho for one brief shining hour, before he left in a marked manner when he found that John Birt had the power to second-guess him), insisted that Day should come on *Wogan* so that we could have a proper dust-up for the public's delectation.

I didn't like the idea, and I was right. The late lamented Sir Robin had spent most of his life bullying, blustering and shouting opponents down, and I was no match for him. When the show was over, he was sweetness and light itself, introducing me to his son. Light entertainment always pays more than news-based shows; bigger audiences will always bring higher rewards. They should have paid the old curmudgeon more – he was an actor, an entertainer to his fingertips. He would be pleased, and probably jealous, that his tradition of dogged, aggressive hectoring of the great and the good is being carried on today by John Humphrys and Jeremy Paxman, two right Dobermanns, their bite as bad as their bark, and socially two of the most civilised, urbane gentlemen you could meet.

Elsewhere, I've said that chat show hosts are never remembered by their triumphs, but by their disasters. After eight to nine years of relentless chatter, live, three nights a week at peak time, all *Wogan* will ever be remembered for will be George Best, drunk as a skunk. Possibly Anne Bancroft, for her dumb act.

The producer of *Wogan*, my friend the late, and sadly missed,

Peter Estall, kept a record of my infamous interview with Anne Bancroft. A model of its kind, it should be preserved in a vault in the deepest recesses of the Haunted Doughnut, to be brought out only when some presenter who has enjoyed success on a gardening programme or a 'reality' show thinks that the time is ripe for a chat show. I began the Nightmare of Shepherds Bush by asking the lady about her meeting with royalty at her film premiere the night before:

WOGAN: Did you get to exchange words with any members of royalty?

BANCROFT: I did.

WOGAN: Didn't speak until you were spoken to, I hope?

BANCROFT: I don't remember.

WOGAN: I had the pleasure of interviewing your husband, Mel Brooks, about four years ago. He told me that I had to talk to you.

BANCROFT: Why?

WOGAN: Because he said that you're his inspiration.

BANCROFT: That's not true.

WOGAN: Is he a help to you?

BANCROFT: No. We barely see each other, to tell you the truth.

WOGAN: That's not good, is it?

BANCROFT: Well, yes it is.

WOGAN: In your new film *84 Charing Cross Road* you swap letters with Anthony Hopkins, but you don't meet him. He's in London and you're in New York. You acted separately – how did you do that?

BANCROFT: What do you mean, how?

WOGAN: It must be difficult.

BANCROFT: It's a lot easier than this.

WOGAN: Didn't Mel Brooks give you *84 Charing Cross Road* as a birthday present?

BANCROFT: That's a pack of lies.

WOGAN: Why do you hate this kind of interview so much? Is it me?

BANCROFT: Probably.

WOGAN: Do you do this kind of thing in the States?

BANCROFT: No.

WOGAN: Are you glad you did this?

BANCROFT: No.

WOGAN: Thank you, Anne Bancroft . . .

And Michael Parkinson thinks he had a hard time with Meg Ryan . . .

Over the years I've tried to excuse her extraordinary, unprofessional behaviour, but I'm not going to bother any more, having read what her husband, Mel Brooks, had to say about it. He said that she was furious that we had used a sexy still from *The Graduate* to spice up the programme. Since the movie was about the seduction of a young man by an older woman, and Bancroft spent much of it in bra and pants in the bedroom, I think I'll pass on that excuse, and put it down charitably to a bad day at the office for a fine actress.

Paradoxically, I've always felt that the best, most spontaneous interview I ever conducted was with the brilliant Mel Brooks on my old Saturday night show. It was verbal ping-pong, and I loved it, although it's probably true that the public's enjoyment of something is in inverse proportion to the presenter's. So what I'll be remembered for will be Georgie and Annie. Parkinson will never escape the memory of that blasted Emu, the late Russell Harty for Grace Jones's slap in the face, Richard White-ley (I miss him yet) for the ferret attached to his finger. My own personal favourite is not a disaster at all, but a *Tomorrow's World* piece in black and white, by Raymond Baxter. A new and exciting invention that would revolutionise the music world, he pro-claimed – the compact disc! And its greatest asset was its dur-ability: he threw it on the ground, he smeared jam on it, he had a tractor roll over it, and still it played! Several centuries on, I play compact discs every day on the radio, and know from sad experience that if you as much as graze the surface with a finger-mark, the damned thing won't play . . .

The Saturday evening Wogan show had its frissons too: I mind well Raquel Welch getting into a right two-and-eight about some-thing. I've a vague recollection that she wanted to be taken ser-iously, not all that easy in view of her previous form in a fur bikini in some prehistoric romp. I do recall her telling me that she was married to a renaissance man. She and Leonardo da Vinci parted soon afterwards . . . And I will always remember the pleased expression on the face of Chevy Chase, then a big American com-edian turned movie star. Whenever I asked him a question, he would smile benevolently and wink roguishly at the studio audi-ence, but not a word came from his lips. Obviously that was enough to reduce American audiences to helpless hilarity, but our lot were bemused. I think he may well have thought he had delivered himself of a blinder, it just didn't get past his teeth. Another of that ilk was the great rock and roll pianist hell-raiser, Jerry Lee Lewis. He, too, gave me the silent treatment, while leaving me with the indelible impression, by his merry smile, that he thought that he had delivered a lightning riposte.

The mildest question would set certain people off in a strop. Neil Kinnock threw a wobbly for no particular reason that I could discover on the Saturday night show, Michael Heseltine stormed off after a *Wogan*, letting the producer have a mouthful as he went his patrician way. Heseltine always bore himself like a patrician, although didn't some Tory grandee dismiss him because 'he had to buy his own furniture'? Vanessa Redgrave, unsurprisingly, just got up in the middle of a show and left. Bored, I suppose. Some I would have preferred to leave or not turn up, if it was their intention to sit there like stuffed dummies. I'm bound to say this only happened occasionally, and usually with American film stars whose eyes had already glazed over in make-up. I never decided whether this was preferable to American film stars on whom whatever they were taking had the opposite effect. There are few things more disconcerting than an interviewee doing handsprings in the middle of a conversation.

Then, in 1988 began my great American adventure. A charming Californian named David Simon, who was minding Mickey's interests for Walt Disney in Britain, rang me up and asked me to lunch. He said that he'd been watching *Wogan*, and thought that I'd be the very man to do a similar thing for Walt and his boys in the States. Calming my natural excitement at the prospect of breaking through in the Mother of All Televisions, I agreed to talk about it. And talk about it we certainly did: high-flying executives rushed to my side from Burbank, Hollywood, and we talked the talk, while they indulged themselves in what is known in the States as 'fine dining', followed by port, cognac and cigars. Eventually, the vexed subject of money came up, and there seemed to be plenty on offer, with a five-year contract and ten per cent of the net profit. This latter incentive didn't seem to me all that rosy, not having come up the Shannon on the last lily, and knowing that these endeavours usually show a net loss for the taxman, after the tea ladies, grips and best boys have been paid. A small percentage of the gross would suit me better, I said, and we agreed to talk further when I visited the States later that year.

As luck, and the late Peter Estall, my producer, would have it, we were already scheduled for a whole week of *Wogan in Hollywood*. Off we popped to sunny Sunset Boulevard, bringing Helen, and Jo Gurnett, my friend and manager, in case there was any chance of fisticuffs. It was idyllic. I lounged about the pool of the St James Hotel, high in the Hollywood hills, looking down on the smog-enshrouded city of Los Angeles. Then, of an early evening, to the television studios, where before a studio audience who hadn't the smallest notion who the guy with the funny accent was, I recorded two shows a night. An American audience would applaud a fly crawling up the wall if instructed, but such was the strength of the line-up of guests, they didn't need the likes of some Limey to keep their hands warm. Bob Hope, Cyd Charisse, James Caan, the Golden Girls, Dom de Luise, denizens of *Dallas* and *Dynasty*, Harrison Ford made it worth the trip in terms of star names, although Harrison Ford, charming man that he is, delivered most of his replies from behind his hand, being one of the shyest people that I've ever interviewed. Not a fault that you could ever level at Bob Hope, who insisted on whatever he was selling being mentioned in the first ten seconds, and when we'd finished the recording, took over the studio to record a charity appeal, a deal he'd cut as a condition to doing the show. No flies on Bob.

The television shows went well, the Disney people came to

watch, we went out to dinner to bond. It was pleasant enough, but noticeable that the same executives who had indulged themselves in the port, cognac and cigars in London were remarkable for their abstemiousness on their home turf, in front of their colleagues. Eight of us round the table, sharing the bottle of wine . . . It might have stayed that way if Jo Gurnett hadn't said in a loud voice, 'I suppose a second bottle of wine is out of the question?' Mind you, it's true to say that they don't give it a lash in LA in the same wholehearted manner that we're used to when pulling on the old nosebag. Helen and Jo went out to lunch there, and when the wine captain ('I'm only doing this while waiting to produce my own movie, which is in development') asked them their desire in the way of booze, Helen said, 'We'll have a bottle of Chardonnay'.

The honest fellow nearly passed away. 'A bottle?'

'A bottle,' replied herself, calmly, 'chilled as you like.'

Helen swears that the entire kitchen staff came to gape at the two hussies as the news spread around the restaurant like wildfire. The outrage continued when the two ladies then ordered a hearty meal, instead of a green salad and omelette made only with the white of egg.

It all came to a head over brunch in the Beverly Hills Hotel. Helen and I made our way through the tasteful grounds, over a little bridge that spanned a charming small lake, on which swam a stately swan. An overdressed flunky led us to the table where the Disney folk were sitting. One of them said, 'Did you see the swan?' and Helen and I knew from that moment that the Great American Dream was never to be. We didn't tell them that swans were pretty familiar to us, or that waiters in epaulettes and brocade didn't impress. Instead, we ordered a Kir Royale each, which was our mistake, because the drink on the set brunch was a Mimosa. Our hosts, recovering from the body-blow to their expenses nicely, began to tell me of their plans for me: 'Let me just run this by you . . .' Helen says it's the only time in all the years she's had to sit around a table with me that I appeared to be getting smaller. I felt it myself – a terrible, heavy weight of stultifying boredom dragging me beneath the table. Eventually the painful ordeal looked like coming to an end, when the waiter ('I'm not really a waiter, I'm just doing this while an idea I have in development comes through') asked our preference for coffee or tea. Somebody said, 'I'll have a decaffeinated camomile tea,' and Helen and I were on the next plane out of there.

The previous American outing with the *Wogan* crew had been a couple of years earlier, when *Dynasty* ('Dienasty', or even 'Dysentery', to my discerning listener) was pulling in the viewers. *Dynasty* had followed *Dallas* as a homely, ongoing tale of another family of American folk, as rich as Croesus, and lords of all they surveyed in Denver, Colorado. Their palatial home was much grander than Southfork, with sweeping staircases, marble halls and candlelit dinners. The Carringtons never left their orange juice and scrambled eggs behind at breakfast, they power-breakfasted in the corridors, or dining rooms, of power. Nobody ever held a wedding or a party in the drive in front of the garage, like those honky Ewings. They had a chauffeur as well, who, if I remember, put himself about a bit among the female members of the Carrington clan. Otherwise, the show was a carbon copy of *Dallas*. Same treachery, backstabbing, family feuds. People were shafted in every sense of the word, right, left and centre in every episode. The characters were identical to the Ewings and their acolytes, as well. There was Blake Carrington, a steely-haired mixture of Daddy Ewing and J.R., Lucy the Poison Dwarf had her equivalent, various sons, relatives and lovers circled the action, the only difference being a lack of ten-gallon hats. Sue Ellen and Pammy were the undoubted forerunners of Linda Evans and Joan Collins, who were ever at each other's throats, and who invented 'bling' before Posh Spice could pout. To watch those two ladies at it hammer and tongs, all cleavage, shoulder pads and skintight dresses with no visible panty-line, was a weekly treat, and although it never achieved quite the dizzy heights of *Dallas* at its peak, *Dynasty* was not so dusty.

The main reason for the similarity of the two shows, apart from the obvious television rule of beating a good idea to death, was that they were both the brainchild and creature of the producer Aaron Spelling. Aaron was a crowd-pleaser whom the success of *Dallas* had put right at the top of the Hollywood food chain, and a firm believer in the philosophy of 'If You've Got It Flaunt It'. Every year, he would bring down thousands of tons of snow from the mountains to carpet his lawns in seasonal style for Christmas, and every Christmas morning hide little trinkets in the snow, like Cartier watches and Tiffany bracelets, for his children to find. He even had his entire house lifted and moved around, so that it would catch the sun in the morning. 'What a man!' I hear you cry. Well, yes, unless you were relying on him and his production team to deliver on their promises.

Dinner with the Carringtons was the big idea cooked up by my feisty producer, Frances Whittaker – a Christmas special, with the entire Carrington gang gathered round the festive board, exchanging airy badinage with me over the drumsticks, sprouts and stuffing. Helen and I stayed in the eccentric Chateau Marmont Hotel along with Kevin Lygo (then a humble researcher, now Director of Programmes at Channel 4, and I'm sure, destined for even greater things), Jon Plowman (producer, who went on to trail clouds of glory with *Absolutely Fabulous*) and the redoubtable Frances, who never left her room or put down the phone for the entire stay, desperately trying to piece together the shards of a good idea smashed to smithereens by people who, having promised the earth and dragged us all the way to the West Coast of America, couldn't, or couldn't be bothered to, deliver. We got bits and pieces, chats in various locations with the main players; I walked down the staircase of the Carrington mansion. It was OK when it was all edited together – just a series of interviews interwoven – but it was a far cry from the advertised *Christmas with the Carringtons*, and there wasn't much festive cheer when it transmitted. The press lies in wait for those whom they think have had an easy ride, and this was their chance. They panned the thing, and I hate to say it, but they were right. Old Aaron Spelling didn't exactly set the world alight after that. The curse of the Wogans . . .

The late Peter Estall simply loved the States. Any excuse and my *Wogan* producer, who took over after Frances Whittaker had left for pastures new in 1990, was off to LA and the Big Apple. He decided that we should cover the opening in New York of an exciting new restaurant, Planet Hollywood. A poor enough excuse for a trip across the Pond, but this restaurant had Sylvester Stallone, Arnold Schwarzenegger and Bruce Willis as its investors, and they were turning up to add to the glitter, glamour and publicity of the big night.

It had been a rush to get the restaurant up and running for

the opening gala, but with typical American get-up-and-go, there it was, ablaze with lights, Hollywood memorabilia, stars, wannabes, hamburgers and fries. And, mercy me, unlike the unfortunate *Dynasty* debacle, the three major backers were there, and willing to sit down together and talk with me like regular guys. At the time, these were the three most macho, hottest males on the planet, so it was a scoop. Except that I never liked interviewing anyone away from our little grey home in the West, the Shepherds Bush Empire theatre. I missed the audience and their feedback, but mainly the fact that it wasn't 'live'. A talk show is a little thing, cheap television for the audience that it delivers. Apart from the famous faces, surely its only real attraction is the frisson of fear, the thrill of the unexpected when things go wrong, personalities clash or someone or other throws a hissy fit. Talk shows should be unpolished, unedited, with their shirt tails hanging out. I've been on talk shows where deeply uninteresting guests have been allowed to maunder on for thirty minutes or more, in the desperate hope of getting at least five minutes of interesting chat. 'Live' keeps everyone on their toes, but mainly the host . . .

So, the Three Big Bears of the Silver Screen came in to Planet Hollywood and chatted freely, but the most interesting part was before the interview started, when Sly and Arnie engaged in a spirited discussion on how to maximise their pecs.

The sad fact about talk shows is that some of the people who come on them have nothing to say. They'll talk about their movie, their book, their music, but beyond that, zip. Why should they divulge anything about the things we'd really like to know about: their personal lives, beliefs, convictions, relationships, politics? A Paxman, a Humphrys, a dear old Day might bully and incite them to indiscretion, but it wouldn't be much of a series after the word got out to the other stars, their managers and publicity people. After about six weeks, mine host with the incisive questions would be talking to himself. Mrs Merton had a burst of chat show notoriety in the nineties, but in the end ran out of people willing to be the butt of her tart tongue, particularly as it was impossible to have a go back at an ostensibly kindly, old, grey-haired lady. It was a brilliant concept of Caroline Aherne's, but I'm sure that she knew that it wasn't built to last. Alan Yentob plucked Clive Anderson out of his comfortable niche on Channel 4 and tried to make him a major chat show host on a big boy's channel, BBC 1. But what works for a niche audience doesn't necessarily play for the majority, a lesson the BBC has been slow to learn. The energy and obvious talent of Johnnie Vaughan has yet to find a suitable vehicle on BBC, and, at least at the time of writing, Graham Norton, another lured from his wildly successful minority slot by the promise of mass popularity, appears to be still in search of the Grail.

These are all talented people who've enjoyed great success in a narrow context, and talent's not so thick on the ground that you can blame a Head of Light Entertainment or a Controller of Programmes for trying them on a bigger stage. It just doesn't appear to work too often. Except in the case of the brilliant Jonathan Ross, who seems to have made his brand of bad language, doubtful jokes and generally offensive behaviour acceptable to the public at large. Why? Because they can see beyond the Big Act. The same public that hangs on every episode of *EastEnders*, and loves *I'm a Celebrity, Get Me Out of Here!*, is perceptive enough to recognise the qualities it admires in its presenters in Jonathan: humour, wit, warmth and, behind all the fast talk, a man whose family is more important than anything else.

If you're going to make it big on the box, you need a Mr or Ms Big rooting for you. You can have all the talent in the world, and a diligent agent knocking on every door on your behalf, but if someone up there in the corridors of power doesn't take a smack to you, you could be hawking yourself around for ever. I've always said that anybody in our game who fancies that their success is due to their good looks and talent is due for a big fall. Luck – that's what really counts, and anybody who forgets it is a fool.

I have been inordinately lucky with the people who've found something in me that was worth a shot: my wife, of course, without whom it wouldn't have happened (and even if it had, it wouldn't have been any good without her anyway); Denis Meehan, who took me from behind a bank teller's counter in Dublin and stuck me in front of a microphone; Mark White, who rewound a back-to-front tape from some unknown gobdaw in Ireland, and gave him a show on the BBC Light Programme; Barrie Edgar, who persisted with me on *Come Dancing*, even though I didn't smoke a pipe like Peter West and himself; Jimmy Gilbert, who saw something in *A Song for Europe* that was enough for him to give me *Blankety Blank*; Bill Cotton, who thought I was good enough for Saturday nights, and then three nights a week. Michael Parkinson might never have returned to the glories of his BBC chat if it hadn't been for Peter Salmon, newly appointed Controller and a big fan of Mike's. Peter was keen enough on Gaby Roslin, too, to give her her own show, but, at least as far as Noel Edmonds was concerned, Salmon was his nemesis. Which is the other side of the coin: if somebody up there *doesn't* like you, it doesn't matter what the public think, you're for the outer darkness.

A few years ago, two young producers, Angela Ferreira and Paul Smith, had the bright idea of exploiting the popularity of *Wake Up to Wogan* on the radio by making it into a daily mid-morning television show, *Wogan's Web*. Like the radio show, the idea was to keep it loose and fun, with my producer, Paul Walters, collating the emails live on the air, and generally putting himself about in a friendly, handsome manner. He bought a half-dozen new shirts on the strength of it. We had a team of Old Gals answering the phones, marshalled by a young lady so pretty she had to be known as 'Bag of Spanners'. The Voice of the Balls weighed in fruitily, there were guests, contributors, and it was fun. The cameraman, the sound guys, the crew all loved it. So did the public – it grabbed thirty per cent of the audience almost from the start. Not that it got much past the start. After a couple of weeks of success and public approval, it got reduced to three mornings, and then two, and then – zero. You see, a new Head of Daytime had taken over, and she wanted the slot for her friend and new discovery, Vanessa Feltz. The Feltz show didn't last long either, but they didn't ask *Wogan's Web* back. They tell me that the lady who made the decision has never forgiven me for her mistake . . .

When David Liddiment, trailing clouds of glory from Granada TV, took over as Controller of BBC 1, he immediately commissioned a series called *Wogan's Ireland*, which I think you will have read enough of in my first mighty work of auto-biography, *Is It Me?*. If, like many a discerning reader, you missed that, don't trouble yourself. *Wogan's Ireland* never set the turf ablaze, but it was a pleasant enough meander round the Four

Green Fields. I wonder if that poor man who went around County Cavan in his car every night, painting yellow circles around the potholes that are such a feature of that fine county, is still at it, still being arrested for his pains, and still being ignored by the County Council? Liddiment was quite keen to bring me back on a more regular basis on BBC Television, but somebody was standing in the way. This was hinted to me more than once by various producers, but the somebody was all sweetness and light whenever our paths crossed. David Liddiment arranged dinners and lunches between myself and the somebody, and pleasant social occasions they were, with nobody saying anything of any consequence whatsoever. Nothing came of them, David eventually moved elsewhere in television, and, when last I looked, was the Director of the National Theatre. The somebody was still there in the upper reaches of the BBC when last I looked there, a great survivor cast in Teflon.

Maybe my suspicions had no grounds, but after all these years in the business, I cleave to Thoreau's maxim: 'Some circumstantial evidence can be very strong, particularly when you find a trout in the milk . . .'

4

The moving target

⌒

I'm proud of *Wogan*. We did it live, at peak viewing time, for three nights every week for almost nine years, with viewing audiences that they'd die for, these days.

Never mind that it was the agents, managers and their clients, the stars, who dictated terms, which is why we were forced to fly to Cannes for Madonna, Nashville for Dolly Parton and the other junkets I've described, as well as the dreaded satellite interchanges. Most of the time, it really worked. I'd say three nights a week of star-studded chatter would be impossible to sustain in the new millennium, and a nightly show, such as Jay Leno conducts on US television from Hollywood, well-nigh impossible in Britain. The growth of the *Entertainment Tonight*-type show and promotional interviews which are shown on satellite and cable television around the world would seem to have devalued the whole concept of the 'star' interview. It will go on as long as there are movies, plays and books to be sold, but hardly more than once a week as far as British television is concerned.

The beauty of radio is that you can interview who you like, when you like and where you like, and nobody's going to know the difference. You can be halfway up Croagh Patrick on your annual pilgrimage, or potholing in the Pitcairn Islands, but nobody's expecting a picture. You may sound like you're trapped inside a corrugated iron biscuit box, but the listener makes allowance, even if the engineer in London is biting lumps out of his control desk. I've come through loud and clear myself from many a foreign field: in the seventies, Radio 2 was overly keen on the 'outside broadcast', and I found myself at half-past seven on a Bank Holiday morning, microphone in hand, by a deserted funfair on the promenade at Great Yarmouth. It hadn't occurred to my producer, Derek Mills, that the thing didn't open until 10 a.m., coincidentally just when my programme finished. It's not easy talking to yourself on a deserted promenade with only the screaming of the gulls and the crashing of the waves on the shingles for company.

It happened again when we visited Jersey, probably to cover the Battle of the Flowers (you've got to hand it to Radio 2 – a parade of flowers and floats, in sound only. Lord Reith must have been saluting in his grave). My job was to kick the day off – and so I did, once again to the sound of seagulls and surf, on a deserted beach. For reasons that escape me, Aubrey Singer, then Managing Director of BBC Radio, and David Hatch, Controller of Radio 2, accompanied the good Derek Mills and myself to Jersey, and before I started my monologue to the lonely sea and the sky, we all breakfasted together. Dear Derek Mills is no longer with us, but David Hatch still reminds me of the poignant moment when Aubrey said to Derek, 'Pass the honey, will you?'

Derek did as he was bid, with an ingratiating smile.

Aubrey Singer hardly looked up from his toast. 'This is marmalade,' he barked. 'You're fired.'

For a couple of terrible moments, we all watched the colour drain from my producer's face. The Managing Director buttered his toast, looked up slowly, and, upon seeing Derek's stricken look, burst into laughter. It took me the whole day to persuade Derek that it was just old Aubrey's waggish way, and he didn't mean it . . .

I mind well when the bold Aubrey, having been promoted from MD Radio to MD Television, held a celebratory dinner at Broadcasting House. The table undulated like a snake, so that nobody would feel that they were below the salt. Many were the heads of departments who rose to their feet, extolling Singer's Herculean efforts on behalf of radio, and I particularly remember the Head of Radio Drama, Ronnie Mason's, impassioned plea: 'Don't forget about us, Aubrey! Don't forget us!' Aubrey Singer smiled enigmatically, delivered himself of some encouraging words, and the following day moved his desk across London to the Television Centre and forgot about radio. It's understandable, but BBC Radio and BBC Television have never really got on. The radio thinks of itself as the senior service, the bearer of the flame, the upholder of the principles of public service broadcasting, and television is simply not aware of radio's existence. Radio people are dismissive of their counterparts on BBC Television as overpaid and shallow, and the people in White City couldn't care less because they know that television is for the up-and-coming, and radio's for the been-and-gone . . .

I could never understand why we took off on those radio away-days. It seemed to me that by leaving the studio and wandering off into the wide blue yonder, we were leaving our audience behind, abandoning the warmth and familiarity of our, and their, daily routine, and substituting something alien. No letters or faxes, none of the usual contumely and badinage, just seagulls, the sea and bad-tempered holidaymakers who had been dragged to the beach at all hours of the morning by their children. Derek Mills maintained stoutly that it was good for the network, giving us a presence and a sense of our reality to the listeners we met, and talked to, as we made our way around Britain's holiday resorts. It also enabled him to curry favour with old and young alike by giving away Radio 2 pens. We're not talking bagfuls here: Derek was a BBC man of the old school – good husbandry was the watchword. The pens were eked out, almost grudgingly, one at a time, to local dignitaries, or members of the public who had spoken nicely into the microphone. They were BBC pens, and Derek guarded them like his own. Meanwhile, the beat went on: we saw Bridlington and were suitably braced, Mousehole, and Penzance, where the largest pasty in all Christendom fell to the floor and covered the outside broadcast van and all its inhabitants from head to toe in potatoes, turnips and mince . . . And then we went to Singapore.

What the justification was for Derek and me to hop aboard Concorde for its inaugural flight to Singapore, I'm not sure, but I put aside my reservations about outside broadcasts and off we went into the ionosphere. I reported into various programmes as we made our supersonic flight halfway round the world in about six hours. I reported from Dubai ('It's hot here, Jimmy, I can tell you. No, I can't see any camels. I'm in the airport lounge.

Fancy any duty-free perfume?'), then, next stop Singapore. We had three hours there before Concorde turned around and went home. I reported from Singapore ('It's hot here, John, I can tell you. No, I can't tell you about the market in Bugis Street. I'm lying down in my hotel room'). Fifteen minutes at the Shangri-La Hotel, quick cocktail round the pool, back to the airport. I noticed that the side of the plane bearing the logo 'Singapore Airlines' was gleaming. The other side, which said 'British Airways', was still dusty from its outward journey. Some hours later, back in Blighty, I made my final report. ('Well, no, I didn't see much. You can't with Concorde, it's too quick.')

In the early eighties a fresh-faced young limb of a producer called Paul Walters took my helm, and we've been firm friends ever since. He's been producing *Wake Up to Wogan* for over ten years now, and is proving impossible to dislodge. In those early days he was bearded like the pard, but otherwise he was the same laconic, languid, charming eejit that he is today. He likes to get out and about in God's green air when he gets the chance, as well. He accompanies Ken Bruce and me to all the Eurovision Song Contests, and we've blazed a trail to Nashville, British Columbia, Crewe and an oil platform in the North Sea. That was the first trip we took together, out there in the Forties field. I bedded down for the night in one of the oil-workers' bunks, and even as I rose for my early-morning show he got into the bed after his night shift. It made for a fascinating programme, but it wasn't until last year, when he was the worse for drink, that Walters admitted to me that *he* didn't have a hot-bunk turnover on the oil platform all those years ago. He, being the producer, and me a mere hobbledehoy, the oil company had given him a cabin of his own . . . (And this a good ten years after

I had fought my groundbreaking battle to travel first class on British Rail to *Come Dancing* locations. Hitherto, the producer travelled first class, the talent only travelling second class because the railway had abandoned third class. Now that I think of it, I always got the bedroom at the back on all those trips . . .)

Paul Walters has laboured under many a pseudonym since he started to work (work? what am I saying?) with me. He quickly became known as 'Pauly', and then Poorly, the sickly producer, and nowadays the TOGs call him everything from Phil to Reg to Eric. He answers to all, like one of Pavlov's dogs, and particularly to Doctor Wallington De Wynter Magillicuddy Walters, although, as he readily admits, he's not a *real* doctor ('Never really bothered'). As you may be aware, if you're a keen reader and regular listener, I'm a doctor myself, having been awarded an honorary doctorate by the splendid University that graces my home town of Limerick. Dr Wally and I greet each other civilly in the studio as medical men might in the operating theatre each morning.

'Morning, doctor.'

'Morning, doctor.'

A brief roundelay of well-worn medical badinage ensues.

'Pop up on the couch'

'This may smart.'

'Leave your clothes over there beside mine.'

And, 'Oh, doctor, what are you going to do with that?'

'I'm going to open a window . . .' and we're ready to begin another day of unrestrained, unrehearsed, unprofessional, unbelievable numptyness.

The boy Walters and I and other members of our team have flung our nets far and wide, from Nashville to Crewe, taking in

British Columbia on the way. Twice to Nashville, actually, for the Country Music Association Awards. Nashville – the buckle on the Bible Belt – has got a church on every corner, miraculous guitar-players in every bar, and the best spare ribs you ever did eat in the South Street Rib Shack. And I was cream-crackered from the moment I arrived until the moment we left. The six-hour time difference meant that I started my live show at 1.30 in the morning, so the day's routine went as follows: breakfast at ten, then a gentle stroll down Music Row, with a seemingly endless stream of great musicians and singers in every bar, all of them playing for beer and a sandwich, and waiting for their Big Break. Then lunch, and a recorded interview with stars who beat the huge odds and made the breakthrough: Reba MacIntyre, Chely Wright, Faith Hill. For it's the Nashville women who've really made it big, beyond the narrow confines of what used to be called 'country and western', over the last few years. Rafts of female songwriter singers have broken the cowboy hat 'n' boots tradition of the Grand Ol' Opry, and had hits that 'cross-over' from country to pop. Emmylou Harris, Mary Chapin Carpenter, Nanci Griffith, Shawn Colvin, Gretchen Peters, Beth Nielsen Chapman, the list goes on and on. The men, on the other hand, seem stuck in the cowboy rut, unable to break free from their grass roots. Only Kenny Rogers can get away with appearing on the Grand Ol' Opry without a ten-gallon hat, but then he's one of the few males to have cracked the 'cross-over'.

Anyway, to return to the good ol' Nashville routine, after lunch and whatever, Pauly and I would return to our hotel, the Renaissance. We pronounced it in the European manner, Ren-ay-sance, and could never get a taxi driver to take us there.

'Ren-ay-sance? Never heard of it.'

77

'But it's a big hotel, right in the centre of town.'

'Nah.'

'Here, I'll spell it for you.'

'Oh! You mean the Ren-a-sense!' . . .

A little nap in the boudoir, and then down to the hotel's music lounge, where one evening two women and a piano were making the worst racket I've ever heard in my life. They were so off-key, we thought that they must be doing it for a joke, but nobody was laughing. Apart from Pauly and me, who couldn't stay away. Tuneless and toneless, the pair sang and played their hearts out, pausing only when some tone-deaf drunk pressed money into their hands. It was extraordinary to behold, in a town bursting with musical talent breaking its heart to be heard. Off we would pop, spirits restored, and when not putting ourselves outside most of a large pig, we would have one of those combinations so beloved of Americans, like surf and turf, or steak and spaghetti. Then, bursting at the seams, back to the hotel, and bed, for a couple of hours, before tottering to the feet again to make our way to the radio studio for the 1.30 a.m. start. I loved it, but it was a killer. Still, it was worth it for the fried green tomatoes, the off-key women, the guitar-pickin', and the rising country star who sat down beside me in a Nashville restaurant.

'Hey!' he said, sociably. 'So where are you guys from?'

'Well, we're from BBC London, but I'm from Ireland originally.'

'Ireland, huh? That's kinda like Scotland, isn't it?'

The record company executive next to me consoled me.

'Don't worry. I was at a meeting recently, and my American boss was looking in a puzzled manner at a map of Europe. He eventually turned from the map with a hopeless sigh, and said,

'I don't get it. I can't find Japan anywhere there.'

I'm not sure what took Radio 2 to Crewe, but it wasn't to tour the Rolls-Royce factory. I found myself in the signalman's box of the great railway marshalling yard, straining for two hours of entertaining chat as the trains came and went. Members of the public turned up too, thank goodness, but I particularly remember a very well-dressed, youngish, attractive couple who had also been in the hotel's dining room the night before. We exchanged some airy banter, and they went on their way. A week later, a very charming letter arrived from the husband, who asked if Paul and I might meet him and his wife for breakfast when they were next in London. The letter was so well written, and they seemed such charming people, that we felt that we could meet them. And so we did, in a hotel near Broadcasting House, and they were fine, smartly dressed, causing no embarrassment, apart from the man's excessive enthusiasm for the radio show, and for me. Then, as the weeks and months went by, the letters came with increasing frequency, at first good-humoured, and even witty, then slowly drifting into maudlin obsession. I'm sure the poor young wife knew nothing of it, but in long, tortured letters the man told me of his fixation on me, how he thought of me as not just a friend, but his father. Naturally we were very worried by these sad outpourings, but at a loss to know what to do. Replying to the letters, we knew, would certainly make things worse. Then, out of the blue, the tabloids reported the sad story of a man who had got into trouble for persecuting and stalking Ulrika Jonsson. The papers published his picture. It was our man. He had committed suicide . . .

Like everybody who sticks their nose in front of a television camera or a microphone, I've had my share of overenthusiastic fans. They mean no harm, and must always be treated with good manners. No sensible person can have any truck with 'stars' who are uncivil and downright rude to the very people who have put them where they are. Sometimes, the public themselves can be downright rude: 'Here, sign this piece of paper. I can't stand you myself, it's for my wife . . .' It's hard, but the only answer is a smile. Obsession is something else, and has always made me uneasy. For a long time, a young woman would be waiting for me in all weathers as I left the studio in the morning. We'd exchange a few words; that's all she seemed to need. Then, one weekend, I saw her ride by my house. She had joined a stables nearby to be near me. As suddenly as she had appeared, she was no longer there every morning. Her letters had told me that she was a medical student, but they, too, stopped abruptly. A couple of years ago she wrote to me again, this time a sensible, cheery letter, the sort you'd expect to get from a doctor. You shouldn't believe *Green Wing*.

Every year, wee Pauly and I put ourselves forward as prizes – if you like, booby-prizes – on the *Children in Need* Auction for Things that Money Can't Buy, on Radio 2. I know that you'll find it astonishing, but people are prepared to spend good money to be in our doubtful company. Fifteen thousand pounds to play golf with us at Mid-Herts and Doonbeg, ten quid to have lunch with two sad old geezers at the Ivy, and a lot more to accompany our heroes to Sheeprock Lodge at Penticton in British Columbia, Canada. Four good people paid through the nose to join the two of us, with the bonus of Deadly, the Voice of the Balls, to bring added value and lick everybody's plate. Helen came with me, and we all went up and down the snowy mountains on sno-cats, which were so frightening no one felt the cold, and lifts on which it was cold enough to make your hair stand on end. Somewhere in this mighty tome, as you riffle through it in the bookshop without the slightest intention of buying, you'll find a picture of Pauly shortly after he was lifted, rigid, from the ski-lift . . . Penticton was starkly beautiful, a true winterscape, and a skiers' paradise. Well, a serious skiers' paradise. No crowds, but no social life; great runs, but no smart little restaurants on the slopes. Just a hut that served onion soup so hot that you simply gave up trying to break through its molten cheese crust. There was food, of course, at ground level, and Pauly had the buzzard balls. Even with his cast-iron digestion they did him in, but not before he displayed an aptitude for the ancient Canadian sport of 'naggling'. I know, it sounds like something Kenneth Williams, as Rambling Sid Rumpo, would do in *Round the Horne*, but all it involved was ramming a stick into a hole in the middle of a revolving wheel, or something. A child could do it, and Pauly did. He boasts about it frequently, and only a reference to buzzard balls quietens him . . .

The strange thing about the majestic forest that covered the foothills of the mountain was the lack of wildlife. Few birds, and no animals. The area was full of native Americans, or as the vigilantly politically correct Canadians call them, the First Nation. Canadians tiptoe around the First Nation, whether from guilt over ancient wrongs, or to show how much more enlightened they are than their American neighbours over the border. They filled a lake with fish in order to provide the local First Nation with both a pastime and a source of food. The First Nation hired a boat and some dragnets, and cleared the lake of all fish in a couple of days. I think I know where all the wildlife went . . .

We went on to see Vancouver, surely one of the most beautifully situated cities in the world, all shimmering water and bobbing boats. It reminded me of Limerick with scenery; it rains a lot in Vancouver. On the way home on the plane, I passed Pauly half a sleeping tablet. He went out like a light in the middle of a sentence. And this is the man who claims that he bummed around Europe with a guitar, a beard and an Afghan coat in a permanent fog of wacky-baccy. I don't think so . . .

I'd been to Canada a couple of times before Paul and I made the long haul to British Columbia, once at the behest of Bob Burrowes, then the Head of BBC Radio Sport, to drink in the heady atmosphere of Montreal prior to leading the radio coverage of the Olympics there. You need more than a couple of days to get more than a fleeting impression, and all I really remember were the flights out and back. I flew out in the company of Mary Peters, a great Olympic champion, but like myself, sturdily made. We were like a pair of sardines, well to the back of the plane. It might have been painful if it hadn't been for Mary's company. A great athlete, but an even greater person – ever smiling, ever optimistic, Northern Ireland's greatest ambassador, her life given over to the service of her beloved people. If anybody ever deserved to fly first class through life, she does, but it's your BBC and they husband your resources like misers. Unless, of course, you're a very senior executive, or a star they desperately want to sign up for television. Then, the sky's the limit, even if they don't know what to do with the star after they've paid a fortune for him.

Mary and I travelled steerage, but on the way back, Bob Burrowes pulled a few strings and I left Montreal in the first-class cabin for New York. My first time in first class, and I can remember it clearly, thirty years on. The scrambled-egg breakfast, the beef carved from the trolley, the champagne, the wines. I've been lucky enough to turn left at the top of the steps many times since, but nothing has ever come close to my feeling of luxury and well-being on that first first-class flight. It explains why I have no patience with people who fall asleep the minute they park themselves in the premier cabin. They're showing off; it's inverted snobbery: 'Oh, I travel this way all the time . . .' Let me never get so blasé. Another glass of champagne, please, and, yes, I'll have breakfast, lunch, dinner, two movies and all the fine wines you can throw at me. I've paid plenty for it, and I'm going to enjoy it. I'll sleep when I get there, and don't make it too quick . . . (I just love flying – airports I hate. Who could love them? Crowded, stressful, customer unfriendly, where you never see a smiling face. People worried, late, delayed, drained, every single passenger wondering whether any trip or holiday is worth so much mental and physical strain.)

I also went to Edmonton, on the Alberta plains, with my old pal Derek Mills – once again a fleeting glance – preparatory to presenting the Commonwealth Games for Radio Sport. This time we went first class through the kindness of Air Canada, but I have no recollection of scrambled eggs. Edmonton rears out of the landscape like Dallas from the Texan prairie, and still seemed a little raw and unfinished when I was there; I'm sure it's a polished, sophisticated metropolis now. Then, it seemed as if all the beggars and drunks on the street were native Americans, while the well-to-do queued for discos and clubs at 4.30 in the afternoon with dinner at six, and everybody in bed by ten.

I've no more recollection of the Games themselves than I have of the Montreal Olympics, although I recollect that they bankrupted Montreal. Let's hope London 2012 will be a financial, as well as a sporting, success. The Los Angeles Olympics, in 1984, which I covered from an outside broadcast van in a Hollywood back-lot, was the first Olympic Games of the modern era to show a profit. Some twenty-two years on, I can remember nearly everything about those Games: Carl Lewis, Seb Coe, Steve Ovett. The stadium where all the track and field events were held was smack in the poorest part of the city, yet as we passed through the ghetto, on all sides we were greeted with smiles and friendly greetings. As far as I know, no one got robbed, mugged or otherwise dumped on for the entire two weeks of the Games. Hard to reconcile with the subsequent race riots, burnings and the shootings and murders that we hear about, on an almost daily basis, from the City of Angels.

A wonderful woman, now sadly passed on, Julie Lewis, bid a hatful in the Radio 2 auction for Things that Money Can't Buy to witness the cutting-down of the Trafalgar Square Christmas tree in a Norwegian forest, and, once more, there were our two favourite funsters cheering on the sidelines. We all had a marvellous time: sleigh-rides in the snow, decimating whole herds of reindeer at the dining table, and stumbling about Oslo in the gloom. Or maybe that should be gloaming; it's a weird sensation to exit your hotel at eleven in the morning in a kind of oyster light. As you wander about, you expect it to brighten up at any moment. You go in for lunch, and when you come out at three in the afternoon, darkness has fallen. The Norwegians are a remarkably cheery folk, considering . . .

A week later, we joined Julie Lewis for the raising of 'our' Christmas tree in Trafalgar Square. Julie must have enjoyed it, because the following year she bid even more money, and we all went off to Norway again. To hell and back. Hell was chilly, but a jolly outing, with our friends the reindeer playing their full part again at dinner. Scandinavian meals have a quaint formality: your tongue would be hanging out for a drink, but not a drop is offered until the food is served. Then you can't get at the food, because they're up on their feet, downing the akavit with every speech of welcome. When they ran out of people to make speeches, they went out into the streets and dragged in passers-by to say a few words. Then came the lutefisk, a delicacy peculiar to those born north of the Skaggerak. It's a simple enough recipe: you bury a fish in the ground, and when it is sufficiently rotten, you dig it up. Then you eat it. And Pauly thought he'd gone a bridge too far with the buzzard balls . . . Choirs sang for us, and children danced, and we vowed to return, even if hell froze over.

It was raining when we flew into Aberdeen for the Tall Ships Race, but nothing could detract from the sight of those magnificent craft, assembled from all over the world. The towering masts with their huge sails were impressive enough, but the sight of young sailors clambering all over the dizzy riggings was even more remarkable, particularly for someone who can't climb more than three rungs of a ladder without being paralysed with fear. I'm not prone to vertigo, I've never felt the urge to fling myself off heights; I'm just a chicken when it comes to climbing. All vestiges of self-confidence disappear as soon as my feet are off the ground. As a young man, I've embarrassed myself time out of number, transfixed by terror while climbing rocks no more than six feet off a sandy beach. We visited many of the tall ships – smoked salmon, soda bread and whiskey on the Irish ship contrasted with the more meagre fare of the Russian vessel.

Vodka aplenty, but we'd already heard that food was in short supply, and the other nationalities were donating their 'past use-by-date' foodstuffs to the starving Russians. There was a remarkable spirit of camaraderie among the crews; mostly young volunteers. A well-spoken lady said to me, 'Isn't it marvellous to see these young people all mixing together? Boys from the inner city mixing with chaps from the public schools – those poor boys must be learning so much.' It struck me that the public-school boys might be learning a great deal more from the streetwise kids.

Last year, Pauly Walters and I went to the Granite City of Aberdeen again, as part of a grand week of BBC Radio 2 entertainment. The mighty network staged concerts all over town, featuring major artistes. Ken Bruce, Mark Radcliffe, Bob Harris, Richard Allinson all displayed their wares to the general delight of the eager population. I was the only disappointment.

It all started well enough at a civic reception, where councillors and dignitaries of the town warmly welcomed Radio 2 and myself, the veteran broadcaster, and flagship show presenter of the network. I'll let you into a secret that only eight and a half million regular listeners know: this 'veteran' thing is beginning to get on my nerves. I'm always surprised at the age I am, and I'd appreciate it if people would show a bit of manners; everybody knows 'veteran' is a euphemism for 'ancient', 'decrepit' and 'past it'. Whatever happened to 'distinguished', or even 'mature'? Sir David Frost says that age is only important if you're a cheese, but that hardly carries any weight since he's the same age as me. Yes, I know he looks a lot older, but he doesn't take care of himself like I do, with my racing-snake figure and complementary six-pack. I'll admit that I owe much of that to my highly strung temperament and the constant state of nervous tension that causes me to literally burn off the calories, even when I'm just sitting there. I am constantly being exhorted by my colleagues and friends to 'eat more!' I urge them to calm themselves: 'I eat every bit as much as you, but the weight just won't stay on,' I explain. It's breeding; the Duke of Devonshire hadn't a pick on him . . .

Anyway, back in Aberdeen, all was sweetness and light. I had a decent piece of halibut and a tasty viognier for dinner, and slept like a baby. The following morning, we arrived to present the morning show at BBC Scotland's studios, coinciding with the arrival of a mountain of foodstuffs. Pauly, Deadly, Boggy and I make no pretension to be anything other than rugged, no-nonsense trenchermen. Fran Godfrey's a more delicate flower, so we usually eat her share of the available provender as well. Rare indeed is thc week that the show is not victualled from some food source eager for a mention. We've eaten full Christmas dinners, right down to the stuffing and sprouts, at eight o'clock in the morning. Many's the full English breakfast and Ulster fry that gets put away between music and emails, not to mention snorker and bacon butties, Krispy Kremes, Danish pastries and the good old muffin. Pauly and I have shared a curry at quarter past eight in the morning, and been the better for it. People think that you can't eat and broadcast at the same time. Pshaw! All right, I may sound a little indistinct and muffled from time to time, but my listeners understand that blood-sugar levels must be maintained, and the inner man sustained, if high broadcasting standards are not to drop.

There were hampers-full of good things to welcome us to

the studio at Aberdeen: doughnuts aplenty, bacon baps and a great big box of the local delicacy, the Rowie, or Buttery, if you're from Inverness. Aberdonian listeners had been singing the praises of this 'Rowie' for weeks in advance of my arrival there. I was not to miss it, it was the very food of the gods. In far-flung corners of the globe, expats cried themselves to sleep every night for want of a Rowie. I had a box of forty to choose from, so picking a hearty-looking specimen at random, I took a manly chunk . . .

I'll never understand local fascination and delight in their own peculiar little specialities. You'll hear Londoners raving over pie and mash with liquor. If you haven't tried it – don't, it's disgusting. Ditto jellied eels. Irish stew is not something you should ever risk in Ireland, the Pekinese can't do duck, and no one in Kiev should be let near a chicken.

So it is with the Rowie of old Aberdeen – a sort of lardy-cake, with so much salt that it felt like a mouthful of the North Sea. With all my years as a 'veteran' broadcaster, I should have known better than to say so over the airwaves. The good burghers of Aberdeen were aghast, and those who didn't fall into a dead faint at my heretical words were whipped up into a frenzy by the local newspapers. Even the Scottish nationals got in on the act, their headlines expressing shock and horror at my 'outburst', as they put it. An enterprising baker leapt on the band-Wogan and produced a variation on the theme, calling it a 'Wowie'. Alex Salmond, leader of the Scottish National Party, sprang to the inedible thing's defence, just a tad inaccurately: 'Terry Wogan's a judge at the Eurovision, so he can't be much of a judge of the Rowie'. Back to the old drawing board, Alex. I was lucky to get out of town before it all really hit the fan, but naturally, it brought out the worst in a poetic TOG:

The Man Who Put the 'Row' into 'Rowie'
(It's like a Bateman cartoon – you really couldn't make it up . . .)

Noo – dinny think I'm bein' pushy,
but Jings! Ye've caused an awfy stooshie!
It seems that, while in Aiberdeen
you passed remarks on their cuisine?

'This morning rowie tastes like seaweed!'
was not construed as praise indeed –
the comment caused them much distress,
and outrage in the national press!

Nae wonder then, you fled the place
sae quickly, tryin' tae leave wi' grace
ere champions of the salty buttery
could offer you assault and battery . . .

But dinny panic! Mustn't grumble!
You needny grovel or be humble –
for you, as for the Granite City,
there's nae such thing as bad publicity!

Sally Forth

Doonbeg Golf Club, where Pauly and I played on behalf of
Children in Need, is on the Wild West Atlantic coast of Clare,
and the brainchild of an American, the owner of Kiawah Island

89

Golf Club on the East Coast of the States, facing the Atlantic. He wanted it both ways, you might say. Doonbeg has joined the ranks of the great golf clubs that line Ireland's Atlantic coast: Ballybunion, Tralee, Waterville – and, just up the road from Doonbeg, Lahinch. I'm privileged to be a member of both of the latter. Lahinch is the elder by many years, founded by the British garrison in Limerick in the nineteenth century. It's a mighty course, and I have suffered there, usually in the company of my great friends the Clancy clan. The wind blows in off the huge beach with such force that on one occasion when the late, great Michael Clancy sought to take his car out of the garage, a passing zephyr lifted the garage door from its hinges and carried it fifty yards down the road.

I haven't played Lahinch for years, but I visited there last year while I was staying in Doonbeg. Nothing has really changed; the main street with the church at the top, the bar that my family's dear friend, the late Gordon Wood, once owned, still there. The shops and the restaurants look a little brighter, but it was raining the day I went, and I'd only gone anyway because I couldn't face another round at Doonbeg in a force ten gale.

I'd a hangover as well; that's the trouble with Ireland, you can't just go out for a meal and a quiet drink and be back in your little bed in the arms of Morpheus by ten o'clock. In total contrast to Scandinavians, the Irish insist on getting themselves and everybody else stocious with drink before they even see the menu, and long after any sensible nation would have called a halt and staggered off into the night, they're still at it. Only in Ireland is the pint of stout regarded as a digestif, and on this particular occasion it was followed by a variety of drinks that seemed to be in celebration of the European Community: Irish coffee, followed by sambuca, then Cointreau with ice. I swear I saw Peter Houlihan, my convivial host, with a balloon glass of crème de menthe frappé.

Things have changed in Ireland, and not just the stuff they're drinking. The Irish *Wirtschaftswunder*, the Celtic Tiger, has transformed the countryside. When I first went to golf at Lahinch, the houses were few and far between. Deserted cottages dotted the stony hillsides, and the houses that were there were grey and spoke sadly of the region's, and indeed the country's, poverty. Now, on all sides, the houses proliferate and assault the eye with a mad variety of colour. Just as the Irish have changed the colour of their drinks, they've brightened the landscape with rainbow-coloured houses: peppermint-pink bungalows, scarlet cottages, custard-yellow mansions, developments in every pastel shade from primrose to sky-blue. It's as if the Irish want to trumpet their success from their rooftops, and who could begrudge them after so many barren years of hunger, deprivation and emigration? The houses and the drinks have changed colour – the people remain the same: welcoming, funny, generous and with no idea when it's time to go home . . .

No matter what the colour of the houses, or the innate vivacity of their inhabitants, a wet day in Lahinch is not conducive to gaiety, and I remembered when Helen and I had stayed there with Michael and Kathleen Clancy. Devout Catholics, they brought us to Mass with them on Sunday. It was raining, and I can smell the inside of that church to this day. It was like being smothered with a very old wet sock. I didn't chance the church the last time I was in Lahinch. Not only good memories should be treasured, or at least preserved.

Peter Houlihan, a man whose ebullient, cheery nature

embodies the spirit of the new Ireland, asked me to join the advisory board of the Doonbeg Golf Club, and I did so like a shot before wiser counsels at the club prevailed. It's rare enough that I'm asked for my advice on anything, least of all by those who know me. Luckily, there are other, shrewder heads on the board, and I agree with them.

When I go there, I stay with Tony and Maeve at their bed and breakfast, Links Lodge. The bed and breakfast phenomenon broke out in Ireland about twenty years ago and swept through the countryside like a bush fire. There are thousands of them, and the full Irish breakfast rules OK. Bacon, eggs, sausages, mushrooms, toast. A heart attack on a plate. There's black and white pudding as well, and fried bread if you really want to go down with all guns blazing. The healthy option is always proffered – orange juice, fresh fruit, cereals, skimmed milk. It's just that you'd better follow it with the Full Irish, otherwise your hostess is going to be very offended . . .

You'd need plenty of ballast if you're thinking of playing Doonbeg. When the weather's bad at Lahinch, the goats shelter in the lee of the clubhouse, and even the pluckiest all-weather masochist knows better than to venture abroad on the links. There are no animal weathervanes at Doonbeg, unless you count a few head of cattle several fields away. Of course, it's a well-known fact that if the cattle are lying down in the grass, it means rain. If they're standing up, it's going to get heavier.

There are creatures that play a major role at Doonbeg, however. Snails. Unfortunately for Greg Norman, the course designer, this particular corner of the Four Green Fields of Ireland is the habitat of a rare breed of snail. As soon as the golf course was proposed, every environmentalist and tree-hugging mollusc-lover in the country rallied to the snails' defence. Mr Norman was very lucky to get his course built at all, and only after he guaranteed to protect the snails' environment by cor-doning off hundreds of acres. The snails were fenced in, although how you can prevent a snail no bigger than your little fingernail from sneaking out when the mood takes him, I don't know. I suppose the fencing is more to keep the golfers out than the snails in, and if you hit an errant ball into the snail reservation, don't go climbing in after it. With your golfers' feet, you'll wipe out thousands of the little blighters. Paul Walters, who would eat a baby's bottom through a wickerwork chair, won-dered if they might be tasty, but you'd need many hundreds to make a decent sandwich, and you'd be better off waiting until you get back to the clubhouse for a hamburger.

Hamburgers are big in Doonbeg, because it has many Ameri-can members. They fly in for the weekend to Shannon, stay at Dromoland Castle, and take a helicopter to the course. These are real golf-lovers, giving up a couple of weekend rounds on a sunny, easygoing American course to get sand-blasted and blown to kingdom come, with every chance of killing whole families of rare snails with a careless shot . . .

The sand dunes of Clare were the site of our Wogan family picnics. We didn't have a car; dammit, we didn't have a phone, and television had barely been invented. We had a wireless, thank goodness, that helped to mould me into the eejit I am today. Not having a car was a drawback, although I don't remem-ber any of our neighbours in Elm Park, Ennis Road, Limerick, having one, either. When I last looked in at the little avenue of semi-detached houses where I was born and reared, the cars were bumper to bumper for its entire length, which could only have been a couple of hundred yards, from the Ennis Road to the Union Wall. It seemed miles long when I was a lad. The Union Wall was too tall and pebble-dashed, even for somebody who could climb, and nobody bothered to put up a ladder because we knew what was on the other side: the workhouse.

Yes, in 1940s Ireland, a workhouse in the Dickensian tradition, for the homeless, penniless and destitute. I think I went inside once, but I can't be sure if I didn't dream or imagine it. There were other places in Limerick that disturbed me as a boy: the Blue School, from which issued the occasional small crocodile of pale little children. I didn't know whether they were orphans, abandoned or illegitimate, but they weren't like us. There was something sad about them, something pitiful. I can remember worrying about them, but none of my pals knew anything, nor did my parents. Maybe they did, but in those days, there were lots of things a growing boy would be better off not knowing. The memory of those children remains with me, evoking the sadness I used to feel when queuing with my Auntie May for an evening of cine-variety at the Theatre Royal, Dublin, and being unable to enjoy it because we'd encountered a poor, ragged creature who begged us for a penny. The compassion of childhood – just a memory, never as intensely felt again.

I suppose the Wogans could have been more mobile if we could have got my mother up on a bike, but Rose Wogan had a highly developed sense of her own dignity, and felt that the bicycle was for people in trousers. Also, it got her husband and two sons out of her way, at least for Sunday afternoon, when my father would take us fishing, my little brother Brian perched on Dad's crossbar, and me with my own trusty two-wheeler. Then, people we knew started to have motor cars, and our weekends changed. Gordon Wood, by then, I'm sure, only in his very early twenties, started to enjoy the same success in insurance as he did on the rugby field, and bought a car. A foolish extravagance, my father thought, but accepted Gordon's offer of a trip to the seaside. Almost every weekend of summer, it seemed, we'd picnic in the sand hills on the Atlantic coast of Clare. Miles of sandy beach, deserted, from where Michael Wogan and Gordon could hurl their fishing lines into the breakers, while we dashed up and down the dunes and Rose doled out the tea and sandwiches. I've never been able to resist a sandwich since, and I've been left with a lifelong passion for corned beef. Gordon Wood, a magnificent athlete, would put down his rod and hurl himself into the surf, thrashing through the waves like a dolphin. 'Wood versus the Atlantic!' my father, who couldn't swim a stroke, would shout in admiration. Gordon Wood, who gave up his weekends just to bring a family to the sea, went on to play for Garryowen, Ireland and the British and Irish Lions. His son, Keith, did the same, and became Ireland's most charismatic captain, an icon, a national hero. I'm as proud to call him friend as my father was of his father. The wheel turns full circle, and here I am playing golf in the very sand dunes where I tumbled as a boy . . .

Our friends, the Kneafseys, had a car as well, and two families would pack into that for carefree, sunny days by the sea. I hate to drag up the old cliché, but how was it that those days by the shores of Clare were invariably lit by the sun, and nowadays, whenever I go to the same place, I'm Big Chief Rain-in-the-Face? Jack Kneafsey was a bit of an entrepreneur, and had the bright idea of importing an exciting new Japanese product into Ireland. 'Aji-no-moto' I distinctly remember it was called, an additive to bring zest and flavour to even the simplest of meals. My mother sprinkled it over everything, untested, unproven. It could have killed us, for all she knew. With the wisdom of the passing years and a thousand Chinese takeaways, I know now that it was monosodium glutamate, but it could have been arsenic. That was the way it was, then – suck it and see. If some food fell off the kitchen table when you were eating, your mother would pick it up off the floor, wipe it in her apron, and stick it back in your mouth. Nobody bothered doctors with minor ailments, your father would lance that boil, your mother slap a red-hot bread poultice on that wounded knee. I've even seen an aunt take a razor blade to a cyst. Dr Collis Browne's Chlorodyne cured coughs, fevers and probably malaria, having as one of its ingredients morphine. They gave it to children as well; I remember a not unpleasant feeling of drowsiness. People on the verge of mental breakdown were given a 'nerve tonic'. Still, we mustn't scoff – look at the people today who swear by 'rescue remedies': herbal concoctions with that extra, vital ingredient that really does the rescuing, alcohol . . .

When I was a growing lad, the demon drink was Ireland's equivalent of the Great Satan. A curse upon the land, and railed at from the pulpit almost as much as sex. The lot of the Irish working man was pretty desperate, and there is consolation in drink and oblivion. Drink and its consequences were adding to the poverty and plight of families. Frank McCourt's great book, *Angela's Ashes*, paints the picture in harsh colours that the people of Limerick thought unfair, but his story was not, I think, exceptional. Stark poverty and squalor were endemic in the Ireland I grew up in, from the 1930s to the 1970s. A few hundred yards from Dublin's main O'Connell Street were slums comparable only to Delhi and Calcutta. It lifts my heart, every time I return, to see the new prosperity and the end of the grinding suffering that was the lot of the Irish for too many years.

Early in the twentieth century, a certain Father Matthew started a campaign to try and wean the Irish drinker away from his mother's milk. The abstinence movement took on, and its members became known as 'pioneers'. Pioneers wore a little enamel pin, white, with an image of the Sacred Heart, on their lapels. There was a time when it became a mark of respectability, of the upright citizen. For that reason, the badge seemed more popular with the aspirant bourgeoisie than those lower down the ladder at whom it was really aimed. The drink problem was not that of the Irish middle class; they were too busy scrimping and saving to waste money on drink. I never saw my father drink more than a half-pint of stout in the early Limerick days, and I certainly never saw him drunk! My mother never touched a drop, but she had a sweet tooth and would prefer a lemonade anyway.

The Pioneers got you early, and it would be the independent soul indeed who wouldn't denounce the Devil, with all his words and pomps and his right-hand man, the Drink. There wasn't a single boy in my class in the Crescent, Limerick, who didn't enrol. I wore the badge for a few years, but I'd abandoned it long before I had my first drink, a glass of cider when I was seventeen, on a rugby tour in Scotland. In common with every other well-brought-up child in the land, Helen was a Pioneer too, although one of the great sadnesses in her life was being rejected as a Child of Mary at fifteen, when she was caught smoking. We now know that fags will kill you, but nobody knew that then, so why it was such a terrible sin to have a quick puff is hard to fathom, unless you were brought up in Holy Catholic Ireland, where everything was a sin, particularly if you were only fifteen. It's a wonder Helen wasn't excommunicated. She clung to her faith, and when she left school, joined the Pioneer Musical and Dramatic Society. At the time, you couldn't throw a stone in a country road in Ireland without hitting a member of an amateur dramatic society. Helen, who has a lovely voice to go with the rest of her, played principal boy in panto. There's a picture of her in full fig somewhere, but she wouldn't let you see it, even if we could find it . . . I myself, having starred in school productions of Gilbert and Sullivan, went on to join the Rathmines and Rathgar Musical Society, but that's another story, and you've heard it before.

The R and R, for that was how they were known to the cognoscenti and music lovers, were unashamedly the cream of the crop when it came to Dublin's — nay, Ireland's — amateur musical scene. As usual, there were far more women applicants for a place in the back row of the chorus, which explains how the likes of me passed the audition. The thing about the R and R was that they didn't give their all in some dingy old temperance hall, but on stage at Dublin's premier variety theatre, a grand old music hall, the Gaiety Theatre. The Gaiety was where Ireland's greatest comic actor, the legendary Jimmy O'Dea, most often trod the boards in variety and pantomime along with the almost equally legendary Maureen Potter, and a very small sidekick, Mickser Reid. Whenever this winning team took to the stage, it was a full house. Television came a little late to Ireland to catch them at their peak, and on the odd occasion when they did appear on the box, it didn't really work. They were theatricals; television was too small for them. I often think that's why so many British actors don't measure up to their American and Australian counterparts in television comedy or drama series. Their expressions, their gestures, their delivery are too big. Too much RADA, LAMDA and Rep, love. Watch somebody like Anthony LaPaglia in the American series *Without a Trace*, or William Shatner in *Boston Legal*. They mutter, they pause, they scarcely move. It's television acting, acting in close-up, in a whisper. Very few British actors can bring themselves to do it. Laurence Olivier, the greatest stage and Shakespearean actor of his generation, was, at least in my humble, pure ham on film. There are still actors like him, and you can see them on television most weeks exaggerating, gesticulating, projecting, still trying to reach the back row of the stalls . . .

The legendary Bourke family ran the Gaiety Theatre, and they were larger than life, and any mere actor. The two brothers, Rick and Lorcan, had a flair for showmanship, and the tales of their doings and sayings are still told with relish in Nearys, McDaids, Davy Byrnes and other Dublin watering holes.

Rick's retort, when asked if a certain popular artist would fill the place: 'Rubber walls. We'll need rubber walls'.

Lorcan's impassioned appeal to a Variety Club of Ireland lunch, on behalf of the blind: 'I know what a tragedy blindness can be. Haven't I two blind children myself?'

Afterwards, a friend who knew the family took him aside and said: 'But, Lorcan, your children aren't blind!'

'I know,' said Lorcan, 'I got carried away.'

When Lorcan Bourke was Deputy Lord Mayor of Dublin, he welcomed Sir John Barbirolli and the Hallé Orchestra to the facility with the ringing welcome, 'And a hearty *ceadmile failte* to Sir John Barolli and his band!'

Then there was a reception for Senator Edward Kennedy at the Mansion House, Dublin. Lorcan, all bonhomie, engaging the senator in fine-sounding talk: 'How honoured we are tonight, Edward, may I call you Edward? Good man, to have you and your lovely wife—'

A small man tugs at Lorcan's sleeve and whispers in his ear.

'No!' says our hero, turning once again to his new American friend. 'And further, Senator, Edward, I know that I speak on behalf . . .'

The little man interrupts again, whispering in Lorcan's ear.

'No, I said!' this time with anger bubbling up, which he controls as he turns again to his distinguished visitor '. . . of the plain people of Ireland in whose place I stand today, to welcome you and yours to our little island—'

Another tug at his sleeve, another plaintive whisper. It's one whisper too many. Lorcan Bourke loses it.

'Listen!' he shouts, 'I've told you before! There's no f-in' stout!'

5

The Togmeister of Eurovision

―•―

In 1971, I returned to the Gaiety Theatre, Dublin, not to relive my triumphs in *The Gondoliers*, *Naughty Marietta*, *Bitter Sweet* or *Love from Judy*, but as the BBC commentator for the Eurovision Song Contest, my very first. Who would have thought that I'd still be at it thirty-five years later? Extraordinary to think too, that this little variety theatre, which could seat no more than, say, a thousand people for a Jimmy O'Dea panto, staged the Eurosong. When you remember the 35,000 that packed a football stadium in Copenhagen a few years ago, it's hard to imagine the tiny scale of Dublin, 1971. There can only have been five hundred people in the audience, to accommodate all the cameras and sound crews; the commentators were at the back of the gods, and the presenters did it all from a box overlooking the stage. There could only have been fifteen countries taking part, in contrast to the twenty-four who contested the final in Kiev, Ukraine, in 2005. And, of course, the twenty countries who took part in the semi-final, two days earlier.

I'm still astounded by the number of people who, after all these years, still ask me if I enjoy doing the Eurovision Song Contest. I'm fed up asking them to complete the question, 'Has ... Pope ... balcony?', or 'Does ... bear ... in the woods?' Thirty-five years on, would I still be doing something that I didn't like? I've always loved the Eurovision, through the long weary years of critics and reviewers who missed the point and lambasted it for its silliness and lack of musical content, through the opposition of those at the BBC (at least one of whom is still clinging to the wreckage) who can't tell the difference between popular and trendy. I even love the travesty of a contest that it has become ever since they threw it open to phone voting, and the arrival of the former members of the Union of Soviet Socialist Republics.

In 1999, to avoid what the European Broadcasting Union (EBU) saw as elements of national prejudice and the settling of old scores ruining the Contest, the voting was taken out of the hands of national juries and handed over to the plain, honest straight-voting people of Europe. It immediately became apparent that they were even more biased than the juries against their neighbours and historical enemies.

We got used to it. Every commentator worthy of his microphone could predict each country's voting on the basis of their political and national bias. I knew that the UK was going to find it very hard to win the Eurovision ever again — Europe didn't like us, we'd been too big for our boots for too long. And, of course, Britain had made the crucial error of saving Europe in World War Two. The British will never be forgiven for that ...

Over the past six years, however, it has become even more obvious that not only will the UK find it impossible to win the Song Contest, so will every country in Western Europe. The West won the Cold War, but it lost the Eurovision in the process . . .

The Eurothing of 2006 was held in Athens, Greece, since they won the title in Kiev the previous year. Ukraine, Turkey, Latvia, Estonia, Denmark were the previous five winning countries, three of them from the former Soviet bloc, which came as no surprise to even the casual observer of how the influx of the 'new' countries, from the Baltic and the Balkans, has changed the voting pattern. We'd got used to the petty national prejudices of Western Europe, but the bloc voting of the founder members of the Warsaw Pact, and those who had suffered in the shadow of the Russian Bear, caught us on the hop. Suddenly, whole regions were voting for each other, and unashamedly at that: 'And we have great pleasure in awarding twelve points to our dear neighbours . . .' The Balkans voted for the Balkans, the Baltics for the Baltics. It didn't matter about the song – keep your allies sweet.

The result depended on which group had the most representatives in the final. Denmark just sneaked in before the new order took over, but the next two winners, Estonia and Latvia, kept it in the Baltic. It's a hangover, I suppose, from the bad old days when these countries were part of an oppressive dictatorship that allowed no room for individual expression, and, indeed, only allowed voting if it was for the ruling party. All of these newly independent countries are reaching for democracy, but old habits die hard, and it will take a few years yet before they extend the democratic principle to voting for songs from countries that they had been brought up to regard as enemies for at least a half a century.

It's not without its own significance that the four countries that brought up the rear in the 2005 Song Contest were France, Germany, Spain and the UK, incidentally the four major financial contributors to the Eurovision. It helps that, because of these hefty contributions, none of the Big Four may be relegated to suffer the indignity of having to requalify in the semi-final round, a fate meted out in 2005 to Ireland, of all countries – the nation that has won the Song Contest more than any other. Mind you, the Irish entry was a far cry from their halcyon days of the nineties, when Ireland seemed to win at will. Then, they were meticulous in their song selection, picking the winner of their national contest on exactly the principles of the Eurovision itself, with regional juries. The Song Contest changed its method, Ireland changed theirs, and haven't come close to winning since then.

The UK's failure to trouble the judges has been just as abject since Katrina and the Waves won in 1996. It has to be accepted that no country is going to vote for the UK out of sympathy, or love, any more than they'll vote for any of the other 'big countries', but that doesn't explain, or excuse, Britain's shocking recent record.

'But,' I hear you cry, 'surely if there's one thing in which Britain leads the world, it's popular music?'

Calm yourselves, *mes braves*. First of all, the Eurovision Song Contest is not about popular music as we know it, but as Europe knows it. And not even Western Europe, but beyond the Danube to the very foothills of the Urals and the shores of the Bosphorus. In the not-so-good-old days, it was bad enough having to cope with the French idea of pop music (Plastic Bertrand, Johnny Hallyday) or the German (Lilo Wanders, Oompah and heavy-handed attempts at 'camp'), the Spanish (frills, flamenco and flounce), the Icelandic (blonds and black leather) or the Portuguese (sun, sea and sad sailors), but at least we knew where we stood. Well, you never quite knew with the Italians. I mind well when the contest was staged in Rome, and everybody – delegates, musicians, singers and commentators – were lumped together in a Holiday Inn-type establishment well outside the Eternal City, with a view of motorway flyovers. It might just as well have been Slough, even down to the Italian waiters. We were all bussed to the location, the Italian film studios, Cinecitta. There, we drank in the glory of the setting for the Contest. The set seemed to be constructed of rusty tin-plate, but when I pointed this out, I was reassured, 'No, on camera it will look like marble.' On the big night, it looked just like rusted tin-plate. Not to put a tooth in it, the Italians couldn't have cared less.

We had a couple of marvellous evenings in the trats of Rome, but the Contest itself looked as if it was thrown together. We queued up in our DJs in the soft Italian rain, knowing that it was going to be a shambles. So it was, but the repercussions were surprising: delegates and commentators sitting in their soaked finery vowed never to get dressed up again, and the Eurovision ceased to be a 'black tie' event. More importantly, the extraordinary performance of the male Italian presenter seemed to breathe new life into the Contest itself. He missed his cues, he interrupted, and he argued with the referee, the God-like Frank Naef, on the scoring. I personally think that he was auditioning for the Commedia dell'Arte, but the man's buffoonery seemed to strike a responsive chord, at least with the viewers at home. It was as if the shades had fallen from their eyes, and they realised that the Eurovision Song Contest was not at all what it proclaimed itself to be, but an evening of unexpected delight where you never knew what was coming next, but whatever it was, you weren't going to sleep through it. You might leave it in disdain, you might wince, you might laugh, you might even throw things at the television in anger, but you couldn't ignore it.

For a couple of years preceding the Rome event, it seemed to me that the BBC, or at least my *bête noire*, the one who could never distinguish the popular from the fashionable, was blowing cold on the Eurosong. It wasn't broken, but in the time-honoured tradition, they were of a mind to break it. Rome's popularity put paid to that, and it's true to say that the Contest has never looked back since then. The Italians themselves, however, took umbrage, and stalked from the stage in a marked manner. I don't know why; some say it was wounded pride, others that Rai, the Italian national television service, didn't want to spend the money. I favour the theory that Italy sees itself as the pre-eminent European musical nation – after all, it invented the first Song Contest, the San Remo Song Festival, and it just got fed up being an also-ran to what it considered less musical nations. If the bloc-voting of the new countries in the Contest continues, I wouldn't be at all surprised if one of the other Western countries, and possibly even one of the Big Four, took a powder.

Anybody who takes even a passing interest, and it's probably wise to take no more than that, will know that the Eurovision is an impossible dream, a fantasy that works for the wrong reasons.

How can anybody reared on the shores of the Caspian, or in the shadows of the Carpathians, possibly share the same musical traditions or taste as someone from the banks of the Seine or the foothills of the Alps? As the Contest has grown to include much of Eastern Europe, so the musical divisions have become more marked. In the old days, whined the Ancient Commentator, there was an orchestra on stage, and each country provided its own conductor. I miss those conductors – they were always good for a laugh. The Contest sorely misses the orchestra, which ensured that every performance was entirely 'live', in the musical sense. Nowadays, the backing track is all over us like a cheap suit.

Indeed, it was the sad mistiming of her vocals against the backing track that caused poor Jemma Abbey of Jemini to earn Royaume Uni the shame of last place, and '*nil points*', a few years ago. Then, just as we were beginning to grin and bear it, along came the drum-machine. And a drum-machine with a difference: a drum-machine that brings with it a whiff of the mystic East, a breath of the souk. It brought success to Turkey, and every other country jumped smartly on the bandwagon, even those who should have known better, including the UK. In 2005, we went for it with a song so full of Eastern promise that it wouldn't have been out of place in the old bazaar in Cairo. Much good it did us; we brought up the rear, again.

There doesn't seem to be a solution to the UK's decline in the Contest, but then, it's not that unusual; Italy have gone, Ireland have faded, Monaco's disappeared along with Luxembourg. Maybe they'll come back, and so may we, but it'll have to be a blockbuster of a song. So many people ask me, 'With all our song-writing talent, why can't we come up with the goods?' Well, you can't expect Elton John, Tim Rice, James Blunt, KT Tunstall or their ilk to come out fighting for Britain. What if they lose? And as we've established beyond reasonable doubt, there's no guarantee that even the most copper-bottomed sure-fire hit in the British charts is going to mean a light in Moldova. Speaking of which former Soviet Republic, it made the final in 2005, much to the distress of the French TV commentator, who said to me after the Contest, 'You know, for one awful moment I thought Moldova was going to win! Do you know where it is? Can you imagine? No hotels, no restaurants!' We were in Kiev, in the Ukraine, at the time, and a sympathetic shiver ran through me. (Incidentally, why is it that the signature dish of every city, or country, is always so much better elsewhere? As I've said before, Chicken Kiev, in its city of origin, is terrible. The duck I had in Peking was the worst I've ever had anywhere, I've been disappointed by salade niçoise in Nice, Chianti in Chianti, and Irish stew in Ireland – but that could have been my mother, and I'll give them this: only the Irish can make proper Irish coffee . . .)

Usually, my manager, Jo Gurnett, comes along for the ride to the Eurovision, and Helen comes, too, to drink in the delights of places you'd never think of visiting for pleasure: Lausanne, Oslo, Bergen, Malmo, Tallinn, Riga, Kiev. Actually, neither Helen nor Jo came to Kiev – the memory of the Orange Revolution was but a few months old, and we'd heard rumours: accommodation was so scarce that the local authorities were pitching several thousand tents on an island in the river to cater for the anticipated rush of thousands of Eurosong-mad spectators with nowhere to rest their weary heads. As it turned out, there wasn't a tent to be seen and the local population's attitude to the

Great Event seemed at best half-hearted. There was no evidence whatsoever of teeming multitudes rushing westwards from the Urals, or northwards from the Black Sea. Hotel and guest rooms were freely available, although 'freely' is the wrong word, since they were being charged at five times the normal rate. The oldest trick in the book had backfired on Kiev's hotels and guest houses: when the rest of Europe heard that rooms were scarce, they didn't rush to pay extra – they just didn't bother to come.

I didn't think that Kiev would have much to offer Jo and Helen, two of the most feared shoppers in Europe, and, stap me vitals, I was right. The gateway of the former satellite states to Mother Russia, one of the great cities of the Union, Kiev has broad, treelined boulevards, the better, one felt, to facilitate the swift movement of troops and armour than the indolent stroller or the carefree passer-by. Not many shoppers, not many shops; underground malls, full of cheap goods, although there was a Bentley/Rolls-Royce dealership with the up-and-coming oli-garch in mind. A great covered market took a whole block in the very centre of the city. Fruit, vegetables, and, everywhere, caviar. Oscietra, sevruga, beluga, in every size of tin. And the prices? Let me at it! In case your wandering ways ever take you to Kiev, a word: taste it before you buy it. The stuff I tasted was fine, the rest was like tiny rubber balls. If they don't open the tin, save your money for vodka. Although I'll have a taste of that too, first, if they let you open the bottle.

'Not coming with your wife? Ha! Careful!' they admonished. 'The most beautiful women in Europe are Ukrainian!'

A quick survey of the boulevards and the hotel lounge, which appeared to be heaving with the aforementioned loveliest women in Europe, confirmed the well-worn phrase of beauty being 'in the eye of the beholder'. On every side were skintight jeans, six-inch heels and peroxide hair. It's extraordinary, the notions that smaller, or more remote, countries have about themselves. My own country, Ireland, cannot be excluded from those others with delusions of grandeur. 'The loveliest scenery in the world,' is a boast you will frequently hear from Irish people who have never put a foot outside their country. My daughter, visiting Buenos Aires, was confidently informed that 'the best pizzas in the world' came from Argentina. My son, in Australia, was told in no uncertain terms that Australian Rules Football was 'the greatest game in the world'. Nobody else in the world plays it, but when in Sydney . . .

Speaking of small countries, Denmark, and Copenhagen in particular, was a delightful setting for the Song Contest. We ate herring by the waterside, drank our share of schnapps, and admired the *real* contenders for the title of 'the most beautiful women in Europe'. A supermodel on every corner, a Hollywood starlet on every bicycle. Denmark had won the year before with two old geezers in knitted pullovers, whose plaintive dirge was in such marked contrast to the yelling and jumping about that had gone before that every right-thinking citizen in Europe who wanted a bit of peace had voted for them.

The Danes, who fancy themselves as the entrepreneurs of Scandinavia, and think Swedes and Norwegians dull dogs, held the Eurovision in a football stadium. Thirty-five thousand people, which put Stockholm's fifteen thousand firmly in their place, vodka-sellers in every aisle, and a stage so far away that the commentators might as well have stayed at home. No matter, the atmosphere was jolly, the crowd's spirits well boosted by the passing vodka shots.

Up came the Euro-anthem, on came the presenters. It must have seemed like a good idea at the time to have the two unfortunates deliver their links in rhyming couplets, but for this commentator, at least, the quaint conceit quickly lost its charm and descended into farce. Not by any means unusual, and always welcome to the eager observer stuck for something to say. So I said, 'It's Doctor Death, and the Tooth Fairy,' struck by his cadaverous appearance and her resemblance to Rebecca of Sunnybrook Farm. They continued with their ridiculous couplets, I with my cheery ribbing . . .

The following morning I rose to my herring and croissant to find myself reviled as Denmark's Public Enemy Number One. European television is no great shakes, and Danish TV no exception, so half the population watched the Song Contest on BBC Prime TV. Obviously, they did so wishing to hear only good things about their staging of the Eurovision, and were none too pleased at my cavalier attitude. Not to put too fine a point on it, their newspapers were spitting blood. My comments were taken as a slap in the face to the Danes, nay, to all that was best in Danish life. You see, not only do small countries have delusions about themselves, they also have inferiority complexes. The Danes, like the Irish, and indeed the Australians, want to hear you speak well of them. The first question you will be asked upon arrival is, 'And what do you think of our beautiful country?' To which there is only one answer, and it had better not be in the negative. The Danes took my gentle banter as a foul slur on their fine country, and I had to be smuggled down the Skaggerak in a herring boat. Nor have they forgotten. I rarely meet a Dane, but on the odd occasion since then that I have, they pin me to the wall. 'You don't think much of Denmark, then?' A weak smile, and I'm off. My ancestors had the same trouble with berserkers . . .

Eurovision Song Contest presenters are always good for a jeer – wasn't I one myself, along with Ulrika Jonsson, in Birmingham, the year following Katrina and the Waves' 'Love Shine a Light' winning for the UK? An evening to remember, with me making announcements in French and English, then tearing around the back to the commentary position, and back out front again for the next link. I'll swear that I passed some cutting comments on myself, but you'll have to ask Ulrika – the whole evening was a blur for me. Only one thing moved slowly – the winner, Dana International. The usual form, when the winning song and singer is announced is, after the shrieking and hysteria have died to a dull roar, is for the winner to briskly make their way to the stage, take the Grand Prix, then go straight into a reprise of their winning effort. Dana International was nowhere to be seen. The cheering waned, Ulrika looked at me, I looked at Ulrika, we both looked at the camera, mouthed banalities, and fell silent. It was as long a few minutes as I've spent in broadcasting, with four hundred million people all over the world hanging on my silence.

Then Ulrika broke the spell with a fit of girlish giggles: 'She's here!'

Where had she been? Changing her dress. How I restrained myself from slapping her senseless, I'll never know . . . However, next year, in Jerusalem, fate took a hand, and Dana International got her comeuppance. As last year's winner, Dana International was to present the award to the winning singer. On she teetered in her twelve-inch heels, and, as she handed over the trophy, staggered and fell over. Thinking the worst, six members of

Mossad immediately flung themselves on top of her. The Gods of the Eurovision are not mocked . . .

When Ulrika and I presented the Contest, it was in the usual manner such things are done on British TV. Two pals together, some good-natured joshing, with never, ever, a hint of a flirtatious glance nor sexual frisson. As far as Europe is concerned, though, put a man and a woman on the stage together and it's Nelson Eddy and Jeanette MacDonald time. She flutters her eyelashes, he winks in a manly way, and within minutes they're all over each other like a rash. They hug, they hold hands, they look into each other's eyes as they speak. And how they speak. The lady in Kiev in 2005 had a voice like a plaster torn from a hairy leg, but was severely upstaged by the two guest presenters, Ukraine's most famous sons, the Klitchko Brothers. Who? you may ask; as indeed did all of Europe. Heavyweight boxers is the answer. Their job was to bang a gong, which might have worked if it had been one of the J. Arthur Rank variety, requiring a show of strength, and, perhaps, a glistening pec or two. The gong was of the small Chinese type, and nobody even removed a jacket.

I don't always keep a record of the places I've been lucky enough to visit through the auspices of the blessed Eurosong, but here's just a little taste of the capital of Estonia, which we all loved so much, I wrote this paean of prose in my diary:

For three lovely days in Tallinn, the sun shines. Way up north, on the toe of the Baltic, with nothing between us and the Urals, the temperature is in the seventies, the skies are clear. The weather forecast on the BBC World Service shows wind and rain all over the Mediterranean. Don't you love it when it's raining on everybody but yourself? And don't you hate it when you return home from holiday and everybody tells you how good the weather's been at home?

There are only 1,300,000 people in Estonia, with approximately a quarter of them living in Tallinn. Apart from trees, and the Baltic lapping up against their shoes, these people have no mineral nor natural resources, no industry. They've been bullied, occupied and oppressed for centuries, most recently by Nazi Germany and Soviet Russia. They've only been independent for eleven years, yet Tallinn is bursting with life, commerce, new building and optimism. I know that I'll never make an economist, but I don't get it. Why is Estonia on the up and up, when its neighbours, Latvia, Lithuania, and even Russia, are in the doldrums? It's not that the people are particularly sparkling. They're civil enough, but, in the shops and on the street, unresponsive, unsmiling, the old Soviet Bloc mentality still hanging on in there.

Tallinn has become a big tourist town, almost overnight. It has almost replaced Dublin as the Mecca of the stag weekend for the British. It's the girls. And the drink. What are stag weekends for? The young ladies are beautiful and leggy, but just a little too old-fashioned: skintight jeans and stiletto heels. The beer flows from early morn, and is for nothing. Everywhere you look, Irish pubs. The kind of Irish pubs that you'd never find in Ireland, and that the Irish themselves would never be caught dead in, but that's true the world over. Apart from the staggers, every weekend half the drinking population of Helsinki, Finland hops on the ferry and spends the weekend stocious in Estonia's capital. A pint is about five quid in

Helsinki ... The food's cheap and good, as well, although there doesn't appear to be any particular Estonian delicacy. The universal chip seems to play a major role, but there's a disappointing lack of indigenous fare. We've eaten rotten fish in Norway, reindeer in Sweden, but what of the local dish of the day in this little corner of the Baltic? No elf, no eagle, no creatures of the forest floor. Still, the barbecued chicken isn't bad ...

Tallinn itself, apart from the historic old town with its cobbles and thirteenth-century town hall, is a sprawling mess of old Eastern Bloc housing and most of it in poor repair – the living conditions are pretty terrible. But then, who are we to criticise? I've seen worse in Dublin, in London's East End, in Glasgow, in the North East ... These people are famously undemonstrative, untactile, yet everywhere you sense forward movement, strength, determination. These people are going to make their independence count. And they see the Eurovision Song Contest as a major step forward.

This Eurosong is the most important event in Estonia's brief independent history: a chance to let the world know of its existence, a window of opportunity to showcase itself. The atmosphere in the Saku Suurhall on the big night is electric with excitement, the decibel level bouncing off the roof. It stays up for the whole evening, the noisiest, most exhilarating Song Contest evening since the Irish staged 'Riverdance' at the Point, Dublin, six years ago. It ends up a ding-dong struggle between Latvia and Malta, right down to the wire. Actually it seemed more exciting than it really was. Neck and neck for most of the evening, Malta's chance had gone by the time the last two countries announced their votes. Latvia and Lithuania were never going to help Malta; Latvia for obvious reasons, and Lithuania because they're Latvia's next-door neighbours. I know that each country's votes are supposed to be counted and locked away until the moment of announcement, but all of us who have been around the block with Eurovision for a few years know that this splendid idealistic concept doesn't always work. Certain countries have been known to be economical with the concept in moments of high drama, or when they want to get their own back on some country that's given them a lousy '*nul points*'. Latvia gave Malta just enough points to bring the two countries level with each other, knowing full well that their next-door neighbour would give them the full '*douze points*'. So it goes; so it went.

Kiev is not yet, I would judge, a tourist destination, unlike Tallinn or Riga, who have come out of their starting blocks under the Russian Bear's shadow like sprinters after capitalist gold, yet Kiev is a lot easier to get into than to get out of. We arrived as VIPs with an amount of gratifying fussing, while at the same time being frisked and patted in a rough, but essentially friendly manner. The Contest itself went well, I think, although I can remember no more about it than any other. Only the occasion itself counts for a Eurovision; trying to recall the song or the singer the following day is futile. A few minutes' confusion in the hotel, where the porters had lost our bags, and then Kevin Bishop, Head of Delegation, or 'GB One' as he likes to be known, pushed us into a car for the airport. Unfortunately, he neglected to tell the driver to drop us off at departures, and the

The only wedding photo you'll ever see to feature a dustbin, 1945. That's Auntie Kitty who's the bridesmaid, a laughing Michael and Rose Wogan right at the back, and me, doing my Toulouse-Lautrec impersonation in front.

Michael T., Rose, the Brother and Big Ears in 1950. It must be summer holidays, the Da is wearing a beret …

THE BARON DE WOGAN.

After the defeat of the Jacobites, members of the Wogan family became soldiers of fortune in France. They didn't do too badly for themselves although obviously the thrifty family tradition of knitting your own clothes dies hard.

THE BARON DE WOGAN AT THE WAR-POST.

For some reason, the good Baron de Wogan took to the Americas, little knowing that his moustaches would infuriate the natives …

MAGPIE PUBLICATIONS
**70 Winifred Lane,
Aughton, Ormskirk,
Lancashire, L39 5DL**
Tel : 01695 423470

21·1·99

Dear Sir Terry de Wogan,

As editor of Card Times, top magazine for the cigarette card collector, I believe I have come across evidence of one of your ancestors. The Carreras card attached, from their 1934 Believe It Or Not series, tells of one **Tanneguy de Wogan** of Paris who **'travelled 2,500 miles in a paper boat'**! Apparently no other materials were used in its manufacture but compressed paper.

The only thing which puzzles me - he must have been a pretty bad navigator to miss England on his way over from Ireland, to finish up in paris. No wonder he travelled 2,500 miles. He probably went via the Pentland Firth.

Anyway, hope you like it. All felicitations.

David Stuckey

David Stuckey : Editor, Card Times

2,500 MILES IN A PAPER BOAT

Presented to Princess Margaret in 1975, I apologise for my shirt which has just exploded, a button narrowly missing the Princess but causing a nasty flesh wound to a commissionaire standing fifty yards away ...

A proud moment for a local lad, as the University of Limerick confers me with an honorary degree. They let me keep the hat and coat. I wear them at the weekends ...

The chap in front gets a gong, backs off, white with fright. This is it. Remember to bow…

The newest Knight of the British Empire, **Sir Terry Wogan**, relives his moment of glory

The thing is, nobody really cares. All they want to know is "What did she say to you?" After a hundred such queries it's hard not to answer: "Hello mush, here's your gong. Now clear off – don't want to be late for lunch…"

My loyal listeners (and Her Majesty's loyal subjects) were all concerned for my well-being at the hands of the sword-wielding monarch. One offered to tape back my ears, lest the cold steel leave a lobe on the Palace carpet, while another suggested a small but serviceable device not unlike a stair-lift that would help me off my knees.

After my dangerous moment with the blade was shown on television, a worried mother wanted to know how the Queen gets all that swordplay past Health and Safety, when it's too dangerous for her own children to play conkers? This perceptive viewer also noticed that Dr Brian May of Queen (the pop group – do keep up) who was receiving a CBE for playing his guitar on the roof of the Palace in the biting wind, had blagged a Busby as a souvenir and wanted to know if I'd managed to nick anything, such as a bottle of Blue Nun, or a couple of teaspoons.

First of all, that's Brian's hair, and second, there was no strong drink. There wasn't any tea, not to mind spoons… No time, you see. Three hundred spectators to be corralled into the Ballroom, and 110 nervous wrecks to be rehearsed in the protocol of investiture. You think you can just walk out there, exchange the airy banter with Herself, trouser the gong, and off to the bar? There's no such thing as a free lunch (although, having been up since all hours of the morning, I could

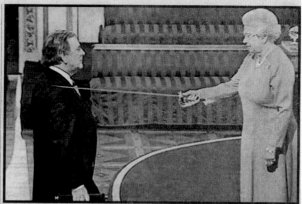

Sir Terry at the Palace 'They are very jolly when they rehearse you… but it makes you even more sick with worry'

rehearsal room at the Palace is a definite step-up in class. Huge, vaulted, hung with drapes and grand portraits, chandeliers, and a generous daubing of gold leaf, it is well calculated to reduce even the most confident and self-regarding of worthy recipients to apprehensive shivers. In case you've forgotten who you are, this will get you

All those equerries, commanders and colonels haven't gone to all this trouble for some hobbledehoy to swan in as if he owned the place

have done with a sustaining sausage-roll or two) and there are no free rides at the Palace.

All those Beefeaters with their halberds, Gurkhas, chamberlains, equerries, commanders and colonels, Hussars in highly-polished boots, haven't gone to all this trouble for some hobbledehoy to swan in and out as if he owned the place, even if he has got into a frock coat and a top hat. Then there's the Orchestra of the Welsh Guards, running the gamut from Sinatra to Bach, who haven't come all the way from the Valleys for their own amusement. Although the pianist did seem to have a mind of his own.

If you're used to draughty, empty rooms in North Acton, or some

back on the straight and narrow. A charming military man, in blinding boots and spurs, about seven feet tall, takes us through the routine. Come to the entrance; wait. When the shaking figure in front of you moves on towards Her Majesty, step forward a few wobbly paces and stand by the equerry. Chap in front gets a gong, backs off, white with fright. The man calls out your name.

This is it, forward a couple of paces, then turn to face the Queen; bow the head, not the body, kneel on the cushion, head up. Down comes the sword. Up you get, while they hand Her Maj the doings on a cushion. She hands them over. You speak when you're spoken to – not before. She's

One of the greatest, proudest moments of my life. Sir Terry Wogan KBE and Lady Wogan on the day Her Majesty dubbed me Knight at Buckingham Palace, 2005.

THE BERLIN WALL
APRIL 1990

I may not leave behind me 'footprints in the sands of time' but I made the Berlin Wall before they tore it down.

fellow set us down at the VIP entrance. They welcomed us in and left us.

We stood there, Paul Walters, Ken Bruce and I, for some time, tickets and passports in hands, before we realised that we could be there until hell froze over. It's all very well being a sophisticated polyglot, but not much good if you haven't got a word of Russian. I stopped a member of the ground staff and pressed our tickets and passports into her hand. She smiled, took them in a purposeful manner, and disappeared.

Time passed.

Paul went into another room, and there they were – tickets and passports, on a counter, abandoned. Now we're panicking. We may never see home and Mother again. Do they still have gulags?

Some shouting and sign language later, it turns out that we have no business to be in the VIP room, because British Airways have no agreement with the Kiev Airport Authority. I point out that we didn't want to be in the blasted VIP room in the first place, how do we get out? Not without paying . . . I hand over seventy-five quid; now we can enjoy the luxurious surroundings and someone may try to get us on our plane. Upstairs to the bar. Vodka and tonics; it looks as if we're going to make that run for freedom. The barmaid comes out to the lounge. I've got to pay for the vodka and tonics. But I've just paid seventy-five quid . . . Never mind. You're not in the pay of the Danes, are you? . . .

Having survived the worst excesses of the Eurovision, including Death by Drums and the Incredible Shrieking Woman, it came as something of a body-blow to find myself all over the papers a couple of days later, portrayed as a lickspittle strikebreaker: BBC staff were protesting about severe cuts in personnel. It's hard enough to pass a picket that includes friends and colleagues without the implication of being a traitor. Look, I crossed the line because I'm a freelance radio and television presenter who would otherwise have been in breach of contract. Then, to add insult to injury, some eejit in the *Daily Mail* writes, while trying to make a case against the BBC and its profligacy, on the subject of the Eurovision: 'Terry Wogan, and his enormous retinue of support staff.' That'll be my radio producer and my television producer, then. If the BBC wastes money, it's not on the likes of me. With eight million listeners every morning, five mornings a week, my programme commands the BBC's biggest audience, on radio or television. Two and a half people work on the programme: a producer, a part-time assistant and me. The producer also makes the coffee. I wash up. Some retinue.

At the beginning of March 2006, Natasha Kaplinsky and I presented *Making Your Mind Up*, another futile attempt to pick a song – any song – that would proudly fly the flag for the UK at the Eurovision Song Contest. The year before, the show had excited a deal of popular interest because of the performance of Katie Price, aka Jordan, who delivered herself of a lively routine while barely togged out in a pink rubber number, which did nothing to hide the fact that she was six months pregnant. It got a lot of votes – old Jordan can certainly pull in the punters – but the winner was Javine, wearing even less and bouncing merrily to a ditty that owed more to the mystic East than her home turf. As I've said earlier, the rhythms of the souk are all-pervading of late at the Eurothrash, but it availed Javine and the UK little as she trotted in with eighteen points, in twenty-second place.

Criticism, as ever, was rife: why had we tried to ape the music of another culture? Since when had belly-dancing been a British pastime? The ghosts of Lulu, Sandie Shaw and Cliff Richard were freely invoked (a little strange in Cliff's case, since he came second. Never mind, everybody here thinks he won). Jordan fulminated mightily at her loss, and in her highly successful book, *A Whole New World*, she says that appearing on *Making Your Mind Up* was the biggest mistake of her life. Which, when you think of what she's got up to so far, is saying something. I can't see it myself; winning or losing on that show makes not the slightest difference to a career. If you lose, at least six million people have seen you strut your stuff, which, in the case of most of the performers, is five million, nine hundred and ninety-nine thousand more than have ever seen you before. If you're a winner, three hundred million people all over the world will see you on the Eurovision. But even if you win that, they'll have forgotten you, and the song, ten minutes after the show is over . . .

The winner in 2006, picked as they only can be by the great British public, with no regard for what they're picking, or why, was a rap number called 'Teenage Life' by a gentleman called 'Daz'. 'Teenage Life', as the music-lover will know, featured the rapper with schoolgirls. One of our panel of judges, Kelly Osbourne, thought it was 'pervy', but it provoked an avalanche of mail that was greater even than Jordan's pink rubber pregnancy.

A must-win selection! Were those girls from Farnborough Hill Convent? Brought back tears to my eyes as a boy attending the

Salesian College, riding on the bus between Camberley and Farnborough – without the courage to chat the girls up . . .

From Dame Ariadne Ledinispensil, Headmistress of the Cheltenham School for Young Ladies of Athletic Prowess, Halifax:

Recently I agreed to let several of my girls act as supporting dancers to one of the acts on your show. So far, none have returned to the school, and I am somewhat concerned as they are a shy and retiring group . . .

Chuffer Dandridge, the old Shakespearean actor-manager who is permanently resting, and who enlivens most of our mornings with salty tales of life in the fit-ups, loved it all:

You and Natasha were wonderful on Saturday! Which one was which? She's a smasher! So 'Grange Hill, the Musical' won, eh? That's what comes of giving people with mobile phones a text vote, without including an IQ test! Well, look on the bright side, at least the UK won't have to host the Eurovision next year. And by the way, what was the story with Jonathan Ross's new hairstyle? Is he starring as Moe in a *Three Stooges* remake?

Admittedly, Jonathan did look as if he was addressing us through a hedge, but it was the insanely lovely Natasha Kaplinsky that got as big a reaction as the winning song:

Shouldn't Saturday's programme have carried a health warning for those of a weak disposition? My dear husband had to go for a lie-down after spotting where Miss Kerplunkski was hiding her ample supply of marbles. Just when he returned with his magnifying glass (for his newspaper, he claimed) he was taken all funny again by the sight of those schoolgirls, and a chap who seemed to be trying to hail a taxi . . .

That judges for *Making Your Mind Up* were Bruno Tonioli, Fearne Cotton, Jonathan Ross and Kelly Osbourne tells you how seriously you should be taking the thing. I'm convinced Bruno's real name is Mick O'Shaughnessy, from Cork, but his cool-Italian routine works a treat, Jonathan is always good for an outrageous remark, and Fearne and Kelly were charming, while confessing that they didn't know what they were doing there. Not their kind of music. But it's nobody's kind of music, except that of the audience in the studio, camp to a man, and *loving* it.

The column I write weekly for the *Sunday Telegraph* has a Friday deadline, but I knew that they'd want a deeply reflective thought-piece on the 2006 Eurosong Contest, so I wrote this a couple of days before the event:

Kalimera! You find me in Athens, the Edinburgh of the South, for the umpteenth running of the Eurovision Song Handicap. By the time you read this, the tumult and the shouting will have abated, the winning song been awarded the Grand Prix, and already been forgotten. I'll bet you can't even remember which country won . . .

I'd hardly be sticking my neck out, writing this before the event, if I predicted that the emerging nations of the former Soviet bloc will dominate the contest by the simple ploy of voting for each other, as was their enforced habit while festering under the Kremlin's shadow. I'll be amazed if Belarus gives anything other than '*douze points*' to Russia; the Big Bear is on their doorstep. The jolly exchange of full marks between Cyprus and Greece is as old as the Odyssey; the Scandinavians will vote for each other, Iceland and Denmark will cement their ancient ties, and nobody will vote for us. France won't give us a saucisson, and although the UK will award marks to Ireland, I'll eat the Blarney Stone if Ireland have given anything to Royaume Uni. The UK is there to pay for the thing, pretend we think it's all a bit of nonsense, and we wouldn't want to win anyway. Germany will get the usual votes from Turkey, because the Turkish *gastarbeiten* in Germany will have monopolised the phones and awarded top marks to their homeland . . .

On the basis of the previews, I know that I will find you sated this morning by a musical macédoine the likes of which even fifty years of this grand farrago will not have prepared you for: Germans in Stetsons, Finns like a cross between Klingons and Orcs, Icelanders phoning God, Latvians a cappella, Disco, Twist, Rock 'n' Roll, Torch songs, the now inevitable breath of the souk, choreography straight out of the sixties, bongos, banjos, musical saws, and I'll swear I saw somebody try to get a tune out of a sheep's stomach . . .

I have high hopes of the presenters, and look to them to flirt heavily, and possibly sing to each other, rather in the manner of the unforgettable Estonian presenters, who bellowed into each other's faces at a distance of six inches. She was an opera singer, and he was the country's leading Shakespearean actor, who also played accordion in a folk band. And you ask me why I love the Eurovision?

As it turned out, I wasn't a million miles off the mark as far as the scoring was concerned, but then, you don't have to be Nostradamus in this game. Andorra gave '*douze points*' to Spain, which caused nobody a sharp intake of breath. Cyprus, of course, did the right thing to Greece, but I was wrong about Ireland, who donated eight big ones to the UK's entry, Daz Sampson.

Finland carried off the Grand Prix with a Gothic hard rock horror show, featuring a lead singer with wings and what looked like the worst case of broken veins ever seen on television. My TOGs, TYGs (Terry's Young Geezers) and assembled Euro-fanatics reacted in their thousands with predictable panache and vigour:

To: Terry Wogan
From: Stars in their Eyes

Strewth, Terry! I nearly choked on my Sanatogen. Did you see all that hideous gothic make-up and that lumpy, scary clothing? Anyway, enough about you. What about those Finnish blokes...?
  Stars in their Eyes

To: Terry Wogan
From: Elaine Cohen-Dorf

Congratulations to the BBC for their acquisition of *Stars in Their Eyes*, which I watched on Saturday evening (admittedly with the sound turned down so as not to frighten the budgie). I particularly liked the one where Old Mother Riley emerged from the piano. Bet Lynch seemed to have spent a lot of time at the tattoo parlour since leaving the Street, but I couldn't work out how the football hooligans dressed for their court appearance had got on to the show. The best part was the Finnish.

    Elaine Cohen-Dorf

One of my regular correspondents, the resting actor-manager, Chuffer Dandridge weighed in with a theatrical word or two.

To: Terry Wogan
From: Chuffer Dandridge

Does 'Amazing' mean something different in Greek?

    What Ho Me Old Voice in the Wilderness.

    Well, wasn't the Eurovision . . . amazing? Wasn't the female presenter . . . amazing? Did she know any more adjectives other than . . . amazing? But she was right! I haven't seen a show like that since a cabaret in pre-war Berlin, where I was naked, painted in zebra stripes and sitting bareback on a horse . . . and I was in the audience! I must say Moldova was robbed! They had three changes of costume and a rapper on a scooter.

124

I've been in three-act plays with less going on! Latvia sang a cappella and brought their own cyberman! Too scary. And poor old Daz Sampson didn't win. The rest of Europe obviously don't find chav culture as amusing as we do! But the winners were appropriately named – Lordi! Because that's what I said when I saw them perform and again when they won! Nice to know the Eurovision has a 'Best Make-Up' category. You always suspected it wasn't about the song, didn't you? It means next year we'll be inundated with fire-eaters, tightrope con-tortionists and people juggling accordions! The gimmick's the thing! And did you notice the deliberate error in the interval act? How could you have a celebration of songs from *Grease* without anything by John Travolta and Olivia Newton-John?

I must congratulate you on your stoical reserve throughout the show. You were . . . amazing! Well done, you were so enter-taining you should have won! Less said about the voting the better. I'm beginning to think it's strategic. Say nothing!

Cheery Pip.

Chuffer Dandridge

P.S.: I think you've found your next holiday stand-in in that chap who read out the Netherlands vote. He's a raw talent, isn't he?

The British public will never grasp with what pride other coun-tries regard a Eurosong win.

To: Terry Wogan
From: Asa Sandberg

Good morning, Terry!

Are you back from Athens yet? Just wanted to write in because I'm a Finn and am sitting here beaming with a glorious grin, since Finland went home with the win.

It's amazing, isn't it?

In my almost forty years on this planet (the last eleven in sunny Morecambe) it had never entered my head that Finland stood a chance in the Eurovision Song Contest.

And here we are. Finland's small ethnic sub species 'The Lordis', who until a few decades ago lived in caves in the far north of the country and hunted polar bears with their bare hands. Flushing the meat down with raw vodka has done it!

It is amazing! Maybe now this tiny ethnic group will be allowed into the Finnish school system. And by the way, all you TOGs out there, Finland is not situated close to Switzerland and we are not that close to China either. The capital of the country is Helsinki and I'm sure the Hartwall Arena in the capital will give everybody a great spectacle next May.

And Terry, Helsinki normally has very warm and sunny days in May.

I'm sure you'll find that amazing!

Asa Sandberg

The 'amazing' reference is to the show's Greco-American co-presenter, a feisty baggage named Maria, whom I had pegged as a loose cannon from the first rehearsal; and so, mercifully, she proved. She found everything 'amazing', and said so at least twenty times, on one occasion four times in the same sentence. She was supported in this by the UK's spokeswoman, Fearne Cotton, who also found the whole business 'amazing'. 'Amazing' was the word for it, but a thesaurus wouldn't have come amiss for a few alternative epithets.

The Greeks had been waiting to strut their stuff again after the triumph of the Olympic Games, and the opening sequence was the most stunning I've seen in thirty-five years. 'Terry's Chocolate Orange', with gold-painted nymphs, cherubs and possibly dryads clinging to its sides, swung over the 18,500 raving flag-wavers in the Olympic indoor arena, while dolphins frolicked on the stage, and a very loud soprano sang a hymn to life. I was expecting the presenters to swim on, but they flew in from the rafters on kirby-wires. A far cry from the Gaiety Theatre Dublin, 1971.

The interval took us through four thousand years of Greek music, starting with Aristophanes' 'Frogs' and 'Birds', and ending up with a giant 'Zorba's Dance' to a bouzouki. 'Riverdance' it wasn't. Still, it didn't detract from what, to my rheumy old eye, was the best staged and produced Eurovision ever. It reflected the confidence that has pervaded Greece since the country staged the Olympic Games with such panache and success a couple of years ago. Athens is a city transformed – a new airport, new motorways, by-passes, flyovers, tunnels, trams, a magnificent Olympic stadium. It made for a wonderful trip, particularly the sunny day we went to Glyfada, thirty minutes from the city by the shining Aegean, and ate fresh fish by a beautiful beach, while sirens and naiads frolicked in the waves . . . Roll on Helsinki! Anyone know the Finnish for 'amazing!'?

I used to joke that the good old Song Contest would be my pension; that it would eventually grow into a massive creature like the World Cup, with preliminary rounds, first rounds proper, then quarter-finals and semi-finals before exploding into a Grand Finale. It would take all year, and involve some lucky commentator in endless foreign travel, staying in luxurious hotels and eating for Britain. How we chuckled at such a pre-posterous prospect. Nobody's laughing now, as the monster swells before our very eyes. A couple of years ago, the EBU, reflecting, they said, the growth of the European Union and the ever increasing number of countries wishing to join what they obviously saw as the gravy-train, decided to expand the remit of the Song Contest. 'Everybody In!' was the cry, and so they came, from the Adriatic to the Black Sea, from the Urals to the very shores of Asia – Albania, Macedonia, Moldova, Slovenia – and surely only a matter of time before Azerbaijan, Uzbekistan, and with a little tolerance, Outer Mongolia, join the merry throng. The more the merrier? Not for this curmudgeonly commentator. As I've said earlier, the influx of countries, new to our decadent democratic Western ways, have cocked the Contest up. It'll never be the same again, but hey! Let's go with the flow. I just think it's all going to be a bit too much for the British viewer, an over-egging of what is already a very rich pudding. The semi-final, or qualifying round, with which the Song Contest has been saddled for the past three years is simply, as they say in Ireland, going to the fair with the story. The Eurovision stands alone, straddling the world of television like a colossus. The last thing it needs is another contest in the same week, with twenty-four more countries taking part, ten of whom hope to qualify for the Grand Prix on the Saturday. It's overkill and it diminishes the Contest itself. The British viewing public will end up not watching either, if we show both. Which is why it's a mistake for BBC 3 to have jumped on the bandwagon and transmitted the semi-final. BBC 3's coverage of the Big One scarcely adds to the gaiety of nations, either. Camping up the Eurovision Song Contest is leaning on an open door. If you leave it alone, it sends itself up – let's not beat the thing to death.

6

They can't all love you

⟋⟍⟋

I see no reason why, if the Middle East and Asia are to be welcomed into Europe, Australia cannot be invited to participate. The great majority of the Lucky Country are of British and Irish stock, and the Eurovision has a sturdy following there, and increasingly includes immigrants from Europe who desperately miss their yearly Festival of Fine Music. Also, they like *me*! A couple of years ago, the Australians sent their own commentator to cover the show, an unfortunate named Des Morgan. Obviously, old Des didn't quite cut the mustard: 'When will SBS realise that the reason for the popularity of the Song Contest is Terry Wogan's brilliantly humorous and politically insightful commentary?' That was a shrewd observer from Murrumbeena. Ferntree Gully, Wantirna and Princes Hill all wanted to be associated with the remarks of the last speaker.

I could be big in Australia, given half a chance. However, it appears that I'm the only person in British showbiz for whom there is no demand Down Under. When I last heard, Max Bygraves is still touring there, and Val Doonican continues to knock 'em dead. I shouldn't be surprised if the Krankies go down a storm in Alice Springs. Yet, for me, the call of the distant didgeridoo never comes . . . Still, who needs to swim in a sea full of killer sharks and box jellyfish, or scour the dunny for a deadly red-back spider before you sit down?

People are forever asking, 'Why do you do the Eurovision Song Contest?', as if it were somehow beneath me; then, in the same breath, 'And you still do the early morning radio?' as if I'm somehow desperate for work and will get up at all hours just to get my face in front of a microphone. I gave up explaining years ago that I do the Eurothingy because I love it, and it loves me, and ditto the early morning radio. I used to take people aside, in the same way as I once saw Sir Clement Freud do to explain why he didn't give autographs, and try to make it clear to them that in my sad old game, popular broadcasting, popularity is what counts. The Song Contest is one of the high spots of the viewing year, with eleven million viewers watching and cringing long past their bedtime. If it didn't get the audience, it would have been consigned to the waste bin long ago, and me with it. Forget *Wogan*, *Blankety Blank*, *Auntie's Bloomers*, *Points of View* and the hundred and one other flawed epics with which I've been associated, the Eurovision Song Contest is *the* television show by which the public identify me, more so even than *Children in Need*. It's probably something to do with the fact that they don't have to look at me . . . which is undoubtedly at least one of the major reasons for the success of *Wake Up to Wogan*.

For the benefit of those who don't watch the Eurovision, and who can't be bothered to listen to a lot of ould talk on the radio, the reason I get up at half-past five every morning, eschewing the full Irish breakfast in favour of a mango (eaten, of course, while standing naked in the sink, otherwise every stitch of clothing is covered in juice) and a cup of instant coffee, is not *just* because I love the fun and frolic, the jolly bonhomie of my underlings, the rebuilding of the studio after Johnnie Walker has dismantled it the evening before, the muffins from catering, of which I never get a taste, since the producer seems to think they belong to him, and distributes to passing females in a desperate attempt to curry favour; nor even the delights of sitting in the traditional traffic jam that is the Marylebone Road. No, if you're still with me, I'm doing the blasted thing because if you're a presenter on a 'popular' radio station, breakfast-time is the only game in town. It's where the audience is. Mercifully, whether it's because most people don't have a TV in the kitchen, or because British breakfast television is either tedious or terrible, upon rising from their trundle beds the public reach for the radio. Every radio station in Britain's biggest audience show is their 'breakfast' programme. If the breakfast show is a bust, there goes the network. Radio 1's steep decline over the past few years can be directly attributed to its unfortunate choice of early morning presenters. (As I write, Chris Moyles seems to have halted the fall, but from where he started, the only way was up.)

Any presenter worth their salt should want the network's flagship programme; why else are you in the game, if not to be the biggest and the best? I didn't join up to be an also-ran, and when the day arrives when they take away my locker-key, don't look for me on the graveyard shift or a Christmas Special. I'm where I've always wanted to be, just as with 'Hospitals' Requests' on Irish radio all those years ago – where the audience is.

My fellow early-morning men and women tend to sniff a bit when my dear little show is referred to as 'breakfast-time'. Most of those other hobbledehoys have been moiling and toiling long before I rear my ugly head. God knows what time Chris Moyles gets up, but then he always looks like he's never been to bed, anyway. Many of these unfortunates start as early as six o'clock in the morning, and often gabble wearily on until ten. When I returned to BBC Radio 2 for my second incarnation in 1993, my start time was 7 a.m. Whether I'd still be doing the thing if this madness had persisted is doubtful, but luckily the then Controller of Radio 2, Frances Line, and her cohort, David Vercoe, who had never really wanted me back in the first place, decided to start Sarah Kennedy at 6 a.m. and extend her to 7.30 a.m.

This was to be the thin end of the wedge for me – I could eventually be eased out and the network returned to the form that everybody knew and loved with, say, Derek Jameson returning, and lots more organ music and songs from the shows. Unfortunately for everybody, instead of withering on the vine, *Wake Up to Wogan* prospered. There was no getting rid of me. Obviously, if the programme were to be extended by a half, or even a full, hour, then the listening figures would be even better. But I'm content – all right, pleased with myself – that each successive year shows a bigger audience for Radio 2 and my show.

When I took over again in 1993, I'm quoted somewhere as saying that if I could add a half-million to the audience, I'd consider it a job well done. The journalist expressed considerable doubt: hadn't I just been 'axed' from the television – would the public bother to listen to old washed-up Wogan? It was a valid point, but I hope he was still around in 2001 when the penny really dropped for the print media. If I may trouble you with a modest quote from the *Daily Telegraph* editors five years ago:

> The supposed king of the media, television, has suffered a body-blow: for the second time in a year it has emerged that average daily radio listening has exceeded the number of hours the nation spends watching television. And the most popular presenter is neither young, nor married to a pop star. Radio 2 has drawn in a million new listeners for the real master of the airwaves – Terry Wogan.

And so it has gone, year on year. In 2001 the listening audience was over five million; as I write, it's over eight million. By January 2005, the *Daily Express* was calling me the 'most popular man in Britain'. And you and I and everybody else with even a tittle of wit will know that as soon as there's even a suggestion of a slippage, they'll be on to me like a pack of ravening wolves: 'Is Wogan finished?', 'Woe-begone Wogan' – we could all write the headlines now. It's happened before, and they were wrong. Next time, they might be right, but when, and if, I quit, it'll be my decision. And you can tell 'em I told you so . . .

All that kind of stuff, while burnishing the ego to a high-gloss finish, should never be taken seriously. The media are obsessed with themselves. Journalists read every newspaper, editors every other editorial, the print watches the television, the television laps up every word in print. Everything in the media, for those intimately involved, assumes a far greater importance than it does for the man in the street. Piers Morgan, former editor of the *Mirror*, turned television presenter, is rarely out of the newspapers. A passing foreigner might imagine him a major media figure, yet I would suggest that, to the great mass of the public, he, and his name, are completely unknown. Rageh Omaar, dubbed 'the Scud Stud', following his TV reports on the Iraq war, was lionised in the press. Hundreds of thousands of pounds changed hands for his war diaries in advance of their publication. The British book-buying public, being unfamiliar with the name, ignored the book . . .

Hard to believe that they would also ignore Greg Dyke's book of dirty doings at the BBC. After all, the papers and the TV had been full of it for weeks. Once more, a large advance was repaid by public indifference. Jon Snow, who takes both himself and his news very seriously, had a similar chastening experience. Meanwhile, Jordan, who is famous for an enhanced embonpoint and reality television, has had two books ghosted for her that sold like hot-cakes. People decide for themselves who, and what, is important, worth watching or reading about. And it's been my experience that the media are always behind the public when it comes to knowing what's popular. Not that anybody is as popular as they think they are. For most people, you're just a face or a voice that's vaguely familiar. They think they've met you somewhere, at a party or in a pub. Only recently I went into a post office. The man selling me the stamps smiled, then turned to his workmate.

'Look who it is!' he said, obviously hoping that his partner would know who it was.

'Yes!' the other man smiled, completely in the dark.

I thanked them civilly and went downstairs to the card department.

'Hello,' said the man at the counter, smiling vaguely. He called to his wife: 'Come, look who's here!'

Out she came, smiling brightly. 'What are *you* doing here?' she asked.

'Buying cards,' I replied brightly.

'Oh, good,' she said, and retired.

As I was looking at the cards, a voice behind me said, 'We don't see much of you these days.'

My smile was becoming a real effort.

'I'm still on the radio and television.'

A puzzled look:

'Oh, really? What do you do now?'

Don't talk to me about eight and a half million listeners. There are fifty-two million others out there who couldn't care less . . .

It's undeniably flattering when people say, 'You're not going to retire, are you? What'll we do when you're gone?' Listen to whoever takes my place, is the answer. It's only about being there. When you're gone, you're gone. Nobody on radio and television leaves footprints on the sands of time. It's debatable whether any 'great' man or woman does, outside of the history books. How often does Alexander the Great crop up in conversation these days? People for whom I've been a steady drone in the background of their lives from child to adult may miss the familiarity of my voice for a week or two, at most, then it's onwards and upwards with the next incumbent. Film stars survive their movies repeated again and again, their charisma, star quality undimmed by time, but television and radio is a much more mundane business. The public become familiar with you, you share their sitting rooms, kitchens and bedrooms. If you're any good, you might even become their friend; but it's distance that lends enchantment to the view. Film stars are unreachable, an impossible dream; television and radio personalities are a face or a voice in the corner, forgotten long before they're gone. Still, Tom Cruise never got a letter like this from a lady in Cirencester to the *Telegraph*:

Sir, I note that Terry Wogan's popularity continues to increase. I believe the Government should try to analyse why its citizens are tuning to him in their droves. I believe they are driven by a variety of factors, including: bill demands from electricity companies which have already been notified by phone, fax and letter that no money is due; the requirement that empty paint tins and empty Cornflake packets be disposed of in separate bins; advice from the Food Standards Agency that floors that are going to come into contact with food should be kept clean. In my youth, I used to watch *Star Trek*, and hoped that humans would learn to embrace the ideals of the Federation, who had done away with greed, and respected diversity. Instead, it appears we more closely resemble an outpost threatened by assimilation into the Borg. The inhabitants of the outpost know that their only champion is Terry Wogan.

I'm sure I could add to that those whose bins remain

unemptied because they're not full enough; the lonely travellers, sitting, even as we speak, in a newly built bus shelter in a Midlands town which is not on any bus route; and the many thousands, nay millions, of people of a certain age who are deprived of nourishment by their bumptious offspring who demand that all foodstuffs past their 'use by' date are thrown out. I am ready to serve. I await the call . . .

And just in case you think it's all braggadocio, let me assure you that the title 'Ireland's Greatest Living Entertainer' rests lightly on my shoulders. You're not dealing with hobbledehoy rubbish here. It was a glittering evening in Dublin in 2005, when Gay Byrne, a little-known, elderly Irish television presenter, handed me the award, cursing and swearing like a sailor under his breath. It came as a shock and a delight that my own people had not forgotten me, thirty-odd years after I took the immigrant ship and arrived barefoot and in rags at the door of the BBC. The commissionaire told me to be on my way in the kind of language that's all too familiar these days, particularly on the Jonathan Ross show, but I survived, striking up a warm friendship with Lord Jimmy Young, as he then was, by dint of plying him with drink and licking his boots. There was never anything remotely sexual between us, which is a disappointment to the publisher, and means that you're never going to read racy excerpts from this in your favourite red-top. Other people with whom I've never had sex are Joanna Lumley, Sophia Loren and Sir Sean Connery. As for the drugs, the closest I've come is Dr Collis Browne's Chlorodyne. They took it away some time ago, and I shall miss that floating feeling.

The Irish award left me with a warm glow, which was immediately vitiated by the, as ever, begrudging tributes of my listener, who wrote that there was no need for me to get all hoity-toity, Iceland was a tiny country with only 300,000 inhabitants, most of whom were too cold to care about anything, and anyway, he had voted for Björk. Another go-be-the-wall wondered if my new status in Iceland meant that I would meet and greet the customers as they entered the supermarket? It was ever thus . . .

Nothing I've done, nor ever will do, on television or radio, gives me more pride than *Children in Need*. It's a classic example of a show that only the public love, for the critics have always looked upon it with a rheumy eye. It reminds me of the critical reaction to the Eurovision Song Contest, right up until the nineties, when the penny finally dropped for the hacks, and they realised that criticising the Song Contest for its lack of intrinsic merit was not only flying in the face of public opinion, but completely missing the point. It took them about thirty years to cop on, and with *Children in Need* merely in its twenty-sixth year, it'll be a couple of years yet before they realise that they've yet again been barking up the wrong tree!

Children in Need raised over £34 million last year, its greatest total to date, and the gross amount contributed by the public over twenty-six years is close to £400 million, every penny of which goes straight to the children. All costs are paid from interest earned on the capital, something no other charity can claim. That's why it's become Britain's most popular, and Pudsey Bear the country's best-loved icon. Through the seven hours of the telethon, the viewing figures rarely flag, while the public in their millions make their contributions, big and small. It's family viewing, not cutting-edge, nor trendy. It's not smart, it's not stand-up, it's not 'yoof'. (That's *Comic Relief*, and magnificent that is, for catering for its audience and raising millions for the world's starving.) It's a critic's job to carp and cavil – he's being paid for his subjective opinion, and the more pungently he puts it, the more attention he attracts. But where do you leave a twerp in *The Times*, who wrote in 2005: 'November is short of ersatz national days, except for the annual BBC *Children in Need* atrocity, an event better calculated than any other to make me contemplate self-harm.' Don't contemplate it, chum, do it. Start with your heart, if you can find it.

How in heaven's name can anybody be so crass? There are innumerable other channels this moron could watch on the night with a light heart and no compulsion for self-abuse. Nobody's forced to watch *Children in Need*, but millions do from choice, and, unbelievably, they seem to enjoy it in their simple, unsophisticated way. I've been privileged to be a trustee of the charity for some years, and it's been a chastening experience. It's the trustees' responsibility to distribute the immense amount of money raised, but if all the worthy applications for help were to be satisfied, we'd need at least five times the money raised in 2004. To be a trustee is to have a heart-rending education in the seemingly innumerable ways in which children may be deprived, abused, ill-treated; but worst of all are the diseases and afflictions, most of which I'd never heard of, that make life almost impossible for these children and their families. I say 'almost', because these children and their families do not countenance impossibility – they struggle; they do not yield to what those of us who are more fortunate with the health of our children would deem insurmountable odds. All over this country there are hundreds of small charities formed by the parents of children with rare, unheard-of diseases and conditions. They can't afford publicity, and since the disease only affects the lives of a tiny minority, they're ignored by the media. These are the people and the children that I'm most proud to be helping. There is no glow of pride, however, for we can never do enough. For all that the public contribute more and more money every year, the mountain of need grows higher and higher.

Not that that is going to stop the thousands of good people who want to help. No day goes by that I don't receive news of a school, a council, a golf club or just a good-natured group of friends who have rallied round to raise money for *Children in Need*.

Contributions come pouring in all year for *Children in Need*. It's significant that whatever is raised on the Big Night in November is inevitably doubled by the time the grand total for the year is announced – witness 2004, the record year: £17 million on telethon night, over £34 million as a total figure. The build-up starts in earnest in October, when the fun packs are announced; they're free to whoever wants to help, full to bursting of ideas, suggestions and fun ways in which individuals and groups can raise money and have a laugh into the bargain. The TOGs start to flog their calendar, which raised £80,000 the last time I looked; then there's the special TOGs Pudsey T-shirt, which went flying off the shelves as soon as I mentioned it. Photographic sessions (pretty rough work, with Natasha Kaplinsky and Fearne Cotton, but it's all for the kiddies), TV and newspaper interviews, recordings for every BBC local radio station. Local radio is a great supporter now, a far cry from the early days, when some stations looked upon the Appeal as unwanted interference from Big Brother at White City.

As I've said elsewhere, although *Children in Need* night got off to a great start in 1980, it wasn't with the wholehearted support of the BBC. Recently, Sir Bill Cotton, who was Managing Director of Television at the time, told me that the Director-General, Alaistair Milne, didn't like the idea at all when it was first mooted. Many producers resented having their programmes interrupted, and I suspect the general view was that it was worth giving the thing a try, but perhaps not quite what the BBC should be doing. Ridiculous in retrospect, it was a view that quite a few mandarins and apparatchiks on the upper floors of Television Centre held for many years.

Indeed, it hasn't been entirely stamped out yet. We seem to get a great deal more support from some ITV programmes than we ever do from some of our own. *Coronation Street* and *Emmerdale* have been particularly helpful, and at a considerable cost of money and time, have produced features that have been among the highlights of the night. *Children in Need* might have poodled about indefinitely after its tentative beginnings, scratching around and pleading for support from BBC programme-makers, if Michael Grade, then Director of Programmes, hadn't given everybody a kick in the pants five years in and told the laggards and the begrudgers to get their fingers out and support what, even then, was manifestly the most important, and, as far as the Corporation was concerned, the most cohesive, programme that the BBC produced every year. Hard to believe that it's still not trendy enough for some, who seem to think that *Comic Relief* will carry more kudos, even if it's only on every second year.

And why anybody – producer, presenter, comic or actor – would imagine that helping one should preclude you from helping the other can only be guessed at. *The Royal Variety Performance*, which, every year, alternates between the BBC and ITV, in 2005 was ITV's baby. Anybody who appeared on it was excluded from helping us out on 18 November. Now, whether this exclusivity was at the behest of ITV or the BBC, I neither know nor care. But in the name of all that's holy, who gives a rattling damn whether a star who graces the boards for Her Majesty turns up the following week on *Children in Need*? Appearing on the television is what these people do for a living, quite often more than once a week. Who is it hurting, that they should do both shows? Don't tell me that the Queen cares . . .

Not that we've ever had any support from Buck House or elsewhere in the realms of royalty for our appeal. It does seem a little strange that one of the country's major charities, and probably its best-loved, which raises millions every year for the common good, our most precious resource, our children, never gets a word of praise, nor even a passing glance, from the monarchy. Princess Anne rallied round one year, I remember, to help Riding for the Disabled, but apart from that gracious gesture, from the Palace has only come a great silence. Every year I ask Nick Vaughan-Barrett, our Executive Producer, and also the BBC's man at the Palace, whether we may expect, if not an appearance, any sort of endorsement. As ever, there are only two alternatives: either he's not asking, or they're saying 'no'. Which latter, frankly, I find impossible to believe, don't you? Tony Blair helped last year by holding a tea in Downing Street, which was much appreciated, but Margaret Thatcher actually appeared on the programme when she was Prime Minister. It didn't seem to affect her, electorally . . .

Nor will it do any harm to Mr Blair. In 2005 he shone in a

send-up of himself by Jon Culshaw, who does a frighteningly good Tony B. Culshaw doesn't do a bad Terry W., either, and remains the only impressionist who doesn't make me sound like the late, lamented Eamonn Andrews.

In a wildly misguided effort to whip up uncontrollable waves of enthusiasm for the 2005 Children in Need Appeal, it was thought a superwheeze to have me make an even bigger eejit of myself than usual and star in the 'commercial'. Break-dancing. Naturally, I leapt at the chance. The Wogans have always been big in Terpsichore. I only gave up ballet because I grew too tall, so boogeying, twisting, rocking 'n' rolling, and, lately, break-dancing was the only way to go, bro'. I spent a day strutting my stuff in front of an appreciative crowd of fellow ravers, and when it hit the screen, people couldn't believe it. The main reason they couldn't believe it was because, just before the 'commercial' was transmitted, the *Radio Times* blew the whole thing out of the water in a revealing double-page spread of 'how it was done'. Computer wizardry and photographic chicanery, apparently. I retired, exhausted and not a little hurt. Wilting Baz, who thinks he's Lewis Carroll, showed no mercy:

Wilting Poem

'You are old father Wogan,' the young man said,
'And your hair is fast turning to grey
'And yet you continue to spin on your head
'Tell me, how do you do it that way?'

'In my youth,' said Sir Wogan, 'I'd dance and I'd sing
'And spin till I'm all of a tizzy,

'But now that I'm old, I'm not quite so bold,
'And watching it makes me feel dizzy.'

'You are old,' said the youth, 'and to tell you the truth
'You just shouldn't be spinning like that
'If you do it again, try protecting your brain
'And spin on your head in a hat.'

'In my youth,' said Sir Terry, 'I used to be merry
'And dance every night until three.
'But now that I'm old, the truth must be told.
'The one who is dancing's . . .not me!'

Wilting (with apologies to Lewis Carroll)

I'm supposed to have no feelings, of course . . .

Everybody played a blinder again in 2005, and the grand total on the night broke the record yet again, comfortably over £17 million. If it's anything like previous years, we should double that — I predict another record-breaking total. Certainly, we broke all records with Radio 2's contribution of £1,066,000. It was presented on the big night of Friday, 18 November by the extraordinary Osbournes, Sharon and Kelly, who both pledged £10,000 each as they handed over the cheque.

In the four days, Monday to Thursday, in the run-up to *Children in Need* night on the Friday, my Auction for Things that Money Can't Buy on Radio 2 raised £440,000. My early training in the Royal Bank of Ireland, Cattle Market branch, Philsborough, Dublin, enables me to calculate that that's £110,000 a day. And that's from five past eight to quarter to nine in the morning. When I came back from the wilderness of *Wogan* on TV in 1993, all the Radio 2 presenters participated in the auction, and for the first few years after my return to the stained carpets of Broadcasting House, I joined in. In a good year, we barely raised £30,000 between us. For the past ten years, they've left it to me. Well, me and Paul Viney, gentleman auctioneer, who abandons his lucrative wheeling and dealing in antiques to join me with his mighty gavel, and spur the bidding listener on with word and gesture. Paul gives his time freely and generously, like thousands of unsung heroes up and down the country.

In the Auction for Things That Money Can't Buy, the bidders give freely of their hard-earned cash ever more generously with every passing year. In the first year that Viney and I ran solo with the auction, I'm sure we made less than £40,000. In 2004, it was £300,000, and we thought that simply couldn't be topped. But with Mark Hill pulling some extraordinary strokes, the items on offer have got better, more extravagantly unattainable every year. And it's marvellous to get feedback from the successful bidders. Mary and Alex Seldon paid plenty for a trip to Ascension Island, and Mary wrote to tell me all about their time at this unique outpost of one of the last British territories. The island dentist, scoutmaster, hotel operator and much more, Johnny Hobson, catered for their every whim, from green turtles to land crabs to feral sheep. They had tea at the administrator's residence, and the RAF flew them there and back from Brize Norton.

The Young family outbid all comers for a day on the set of *Doctor Who* in Wales, and were enthralled, not only by the day's shooting, but by the kindness of everybody on the set, from director to stuntman, from clapper-boy to Billie Piper. The great

Doctor himself, David Tennant, came in on his day off to greet the Youngs. It was the same on the set of *The Archers* at the BBC studios in the Mailbox, Birmingham. It was a rest day, but they turned up. David Hunt had paid handsomely for his wife Christine, an avid *Archers* fan, to play a part in a special scene of the story of everyday country folk. And despite the fact that I stuck my nose in, Christine Hunt repaid her husband's faith (and money) and played a blinder. I transmitted the scene on my morning show to loud applause from all lovers of finely wrought radio drama. Mind you, they weren't dealing with some johnny-come-lately in my case. I'd been to Ambridge before, when declaring the then new Country Club open. Dame Judi Dench turned up as well, in the role of Pru, gamekeeper Tom Forrest's wife, who had never opened her mouth previously. She never spoke again either, a cruel blow to a great actress. At least I got asked back, even if it was in the guise of charity.

Talking of work for charity, any praise would be too faint for Helen Bach and Norm, also far-famed as the Bushes, Anita and Tudor, of Exotic Films Ltd, the makers of doubtful movies for the discerning gentleman, starring the TOGs' favourite sex symbol and stud-muffin, John 'Boggy' Marsh, as freely discussed elsewhere in this motley tome. Helen and Norm, who found romance at a TOGs convention, traipse up and down the country, begging and cajoling the great and the good, the famous and the infamous to pose with Pudsey for the TOGs calendar. A loyal band is ever at their side – Edina Cloud, Dora Jarr, Cocktail Clare, Mick Sturbs, Antonious the Anonymous and the Willowy Iris. It's thanks to their charm and dogged persistence that the calendar roused £120,000 for *Children in Need* last year. And it's not just persuading people to put their famous faces beside a one-eyed teddy-bear — Helen, Norm and the geezers and gals design the thing, get the sponsors, persuade W.H. Smith to sell it. Not only that, they package and post thousands of calendars to those who order by post or internet. And just as not a penny donated to *Children in Need* is spent on anybody but the children, so every penny spent by these good people comes out of their own pockets as they travel the country.

This year, they haven't left it at that: Pauly Walters and I had been talking for some time about putting the 'Janet and John' stories on CD and selling them for *Children in Need*. John, a BBC engineer also known to those who love him best as 'Mad Dog', put together a series of the charming kiddies' tales, and with the cooperation of 'Punxsutawney' Phil Hughes, and the gracious blessing of Dame Lesley Douglas, finest BBC Controller of this or any other century, the CD became a reality, with sleeve notes from myself, Pauly and the hero himself, John Marsh. Pauly has even thrown in a few arpeggios on the guitar to further lull the innocent. Guess who is collating, posting and packaging? Helen Bach and Norm. I mentioned the website at the beginning of April — by the middle of the month, they'd sold £12,000 worth. Hang on, it's the middle of June, and they're past 60,000! That should be £600,000 for *Children in Need*, but of course VAT has to take $17\frac{1}{2}$ per cent — thanks, Gordon.

As a postscript, Helen and Norm had John and Janet Marsh cavort on the back of the TOGs calendar with a cool ad for Exotic Films Ltd (with the discerning gentleman in mind . . .). You'd be surprised at the number of people who wanted to know where they could be bought . . .

On the Friday before the Big Night in 2005, we launched what was hoped would be a major money-spinner for *Children in Need – The Great Big Bid*. Like many television ideas, this seemed a good one until it made the studio floor, where it smartly, no, slowly, fell apart. A slow death over five hours of recording, it made a limp show even when edited to less than an hour for Sunday night viewing. The idea was Lorraine Heggessey's, and before she left the BBC for pastures new, she handed it over to Tiger Aspect, a highly successful and respected independent production company. We had a jolly lunch together and several meetings, and all seemed set fair to get the Appeal off to a multimillion-pound start in 2005.

Unfortunately, no one spotted the fatal flaw in the idea: a studio full of multimillionaires bidding for exotically desirable lots was entirely against the spirit of *Children in Need*, which has always had its core support from the common people. I've called it the 'Widows-Mite' Charity for years, and although the big battalions of the banks and supermarkets contribute mightily, it's the ordinary people's efforts that give real worth to the charity. Every day, for weeks, they write to tell me of their efforts to help. A mother speaks of her two sons, aged twelve and ten, who swam over three miles between them and raised over £500; a child of five has a sale at her garden gate of her unwanted toys, and raises £10; I play a record in the Music Marathon on Radio 2 for £50, and the next one for 50p; a children's therapist who has ME and has been unable to work for a year holds a forty-eight-hour sponsored silence and raises £80 . . .

The Great Big Bid for Millionaires sits uncomfortably in this context, and we should have known that from the start. Still, we did raise £400,000 on the night, but the four nightly shows that followed only added £350,000, despite the valiant efforts of Eamonn Holmes. So, back to the drawing board for 2006 . . .

The Big Night itself of 2005 was thought by many whose opinions I respect to be the best yet. Certainly it got off to a roaring start, with an early appearance by Madonna, and the hectic pace was sustained through the evening, as were the viewing figures – over eleven million at the peak, and handing out a sound hiding to all comers, including *Coronation Street*. Gaby Roslin having decided that, after ten years of propping an old geezer up, enough was enough, I was joined on stage by Natasha Kaplinsky and Fearne Cotton. You wouldn't expect me to say anything against them, nor will I, even if I could, but Natasha is beautiful, cool and charming, and Fearne, whom my son Mark recommended for this, having seen her on *Live 8*, was all gamine warmth, and perfect for 'live' television. If ever a girl has got a future, it's Fearne – just so long as hanging around the likes of me is not the kiss of death. Will they risk it again this year? Will we top the 2005 total? Every year we make a rod for our own backs by going for more and more, but win or lose, I'm not giving up. Will someone please tell me when it's time to go – because I'll never do it of my own accord.

When I left Radio 2 at the end of 1984, it was to the sound of weeping, wailing and gnashing of teeth, at least according to the national press. 'How will we wake up without Wogan?' bemoaned one headline. 'Mornings won't sound the same, now that Wogan's jacked it in,' as another put it, less felicitously. It went on: 'Wogan can be excruciating at times, but you can't help liking the feller'. The *Daily Mail* had me saying, 'It's time I gave listeners' ears a rest. The days of the huge mass radio audience are over. Since breakfast TV started, I've lost between a quarter- and a half-million listeners . . .' Which just goes to show that I know no more about this great imponderable business than anyone else.

It's extraordinary how we latch on to trends and extrapolate them into far-fetched predictions for the future that inevitably turn out to be 'pants'. When television really got going in the sixties the wise pundit sounded the death knell for radio. At the turn of the new millennium, the audience for radio began to outnumber that of television, and by now, there's a considerable amount of blue water between them. Television was to be the death of magazines; currently you can hardly keep up with the number of new titles on the market. Books were going to be banjaxed by the box; the reverse is true. In America *The Oprah Winfrey Show* has boosted book sales by millions, and, shrewd enough to jump on the bandwagon, over here Richard and Judy have done the similar decent thing by the written word.

On the day after my final radio show on Friday, 28 December 1984, the *Daily Mail*, in a centre spread, splashed: 'Wogan – The secret of the magic that has left our mornings'. It went on, 'After 13 years, breakfast time will never be quite the same again. It's the end of more than a decade of unique broadcasting.' The writer, after several thousand words of unstinting praise, went further: 'On television, his future arena, he is emerging as a nigh-perfect people's surrogate. He doesn't smarm like Parkinson, he could never be as irritating as Harty.' Once again, prediction bites the dust. Six years later, according to the same worthy publication, when it came to smarm and irritation I was in a class of my own, with added smirk. It was the *Guardian*, in a long editorial, that delivered the ultimate imprimatur, with a headline, 'The end of good morning'. Written a couple of months before my departure for pastures new, it went on, alarmingly: 'The impending demise of the Terry Wogan morning show on Radio 2 gets more and more like Marie Lloyd's final tour every day, each show heaping fresh wreaths of fragrant national epitaphs upon a particularly ebullient corpse . . . The fact that he has turned up at all has continually verged on the miraculous. How could one frail figure cram so much quiz show and chat show and disc jockey and Eurovision into a working day? Devoted listeners over the twelve years have long awaited the moment when the gags and banter ran dry. He couldn't, surely, keep rabbiting on, for ever?'

You see: another prediction gone West.

I remember Jimmy Moir, then the Head of Light Enter-tainment, Television, saying that the *Guardian* editorial was the greatest tribute to a presenter he'd ever read. This is the same Jimbo who got the elbow from BBC TV about the same time as I got shafted by *Eldorado*, one of the very few soap operas to have failed. *Neighbours*, *Home and Away* and even more mind-sapping daily serials survive, why not *Eldorado*? I'm convinced that if they'd persisted with it, it would be now enjoying the same success as, say, *Emmerdale*. Not up there with *Corrie* or *Enders*, but pulling in an audience far bigger than anything that's replaced it. Would *Wogan*? I doubt it, in the deadly time slot in which my chat show was placed. Dear Bill Cotton, who was the begetter of the show, is still convinced that had it been scheduled as a late-evening show, like every other talk show on either side of the Atlantic, *Wogan* would be still there, chatting endlessly on, like a Letterman or a Leno. It's hard to imagine, and I'm bound to say that I'm glad it isn't.

The 'axeing', as the press had it, of *Wogan* in 1992 was the best thing that could have happened, in retrospect. At the time, of course, it didn't seem much of a boon. BBC TV gave me dinner and a specially bound book. Jonathan Powell, then Controller of BBC 1, thanked me for taking the blow so gamely, and promised me more television work. Indeed, the press, who, as ever, had a keen eye for a man down, saw another chance to resume the kicking. The BBC apparently was paying not one, but two executives an enormous amount of money to find a programme, any old programme, for 'Worn-out Wogan'. Somehow, I doubt it, but we did end up with *Friday Night with Wogan*, which had an interesting format that included Danny Baker and Frank Skinner, and might have succeeded if anybody had cared, but as far as some people were concerned, I was a busted flush, and after a season or two the show was suddenly not there any more.

The 'axeing' of *Wogan*, however, again turned out to be a blessing in disguise. Again, not one that Mystic Meg would have predicted. David Hatch, who'd always been a fan as well as a friend since the days when we'd worked together on *Late Night Extra* in the sixties, and was now Managing Director of Radio, suggested to Frances Line, the Controller, that I be brought back to breakfast on Radio 2. David Hatch was not a man whose suggestions were to be trifled with, and in 1993 our hero was back. 'Terry Wogan gives Radio 2 another spin'; 'Tired Terry is Back'; 'Air I Go Again' the headlines trumpeted. The critics were welcoming: 'Welcome back to the breakfast bunker, weird and wonderful Wogan'; 'Return of the Prodigal Wogan'. Inevitably, comparisons were drawn: 'The television Wogan is wooden, cumbersome, awkward. The radio one is a cascade of quirky verbal felicities, meaningful pauses and throwaway wit . . .' 'His television show was sunk by his lack of interest in his guests; incuriosity killed the chat. Now the only person he has to talk to is himself.' If ever there was praising with faint damns.

Frances Line's doubts about the wisdom of returning a ghost to his haunts was endorsed by at least one columnist: 'Hitler's invasion of Russia, Kennedy's visit to Dallas and Wogan's Return to Radio 2, all have one thing in common – they were mistakes.' How do you like that? And he wasn't alone. The *Daily Mirror* of August 1993 reported: 'Pensioner Gwyn Shaw wanted to listen to the radio while she had a hip operation. But she switched off when she could only get Terry Wogan.' It seemed as if my return was being received with the enthusiasm of one hand clapping, and the listening figures were no improvement on the previous incumbent, Brian Hayes, so, more in hope than in anger, the BBC launched a series of newspaper ads. At first, these didn't seem to be having the required effect: 'As a licence holder, I am incensed at the vast sums of money the BBC must be paying out for full-page newspaper adverts promoting Terry Wogan's early-morning radio show. If he can't pull listeners without this expensive plugging then it is high time he was pensioned off.' The expensive plugging worked, thank goodness, because, despite the earlier publicity, a large section of the potential listening audience were not aware that I had returned to the old homestead. Figures started to move upwards in a marked manner and have been doing so ever since, leaving the show at the present time with nearly eight times the audience when I took over . . .

By 1995, there were still those to whom I was anathema: 'I fully agree with readers who complained about Terry Wogan; they endorse the feelings of many thousands of others. Wogan must go.' 'I'm glad somebody else as well as me is fed up with

Terry Wogan's stupid banter.' 'I wonder how many people can stand listening to Terry Wogan's idiotic burbling?' All of these from the *Birmingham Evening Mail*. I think we can safely say that the Letters editor wasn't a fan. And thank heavens for him. It is a vital lesson for everybody who sticks their head above the parapet in showbiz, theatre, radio, television, politics, football and any allied trade, to learn: for every person who worships the ground you walk on, there'll be another who can't abide you. And another, representing the great majority, who couldn't care less one way or the other . . . Then, just when you think 'they're all agin me', a heartening word from about the same time in the *Daily Express*: 'BBC Radio 2 is spending a small fortune on newspaper ads – *Wake Up to Wogan*, The rest of the day can only get better. A woman I met last week takes that quite literally. She told me that she had been suffering from depression following a serious operation. "Honestly," she said, "if it wasn't for Wogan, I don't know what I would do. I switch him on for therapy. They'll be prescribing him on the NHS next."' There was even a cartoon to go with it, by Hector Breeze; it's in this mighty tome somewhere . . .

7

Can you hear me, Mother?

⟍⟋

Two years on from my reincarnation on Radio 2, things were looking up sufficiently for Frances Line to invite me to deliver the Radio 2 Lecture. This misguided venture had started in 1992, when Richard Stilgoe gave a talk on 'Popular Culture: The Endangered Oxymoron'. I titled mine 'Radio Two – The Slumbering Giant Awakes', and on 4 April 1995 delivered it to a select audience in the Council Chamber, Broadcasting House. The marvellous Duke Hussey, the beloved Chairman of the BBC, was there, the Managing Director who had lately taken over from David Hatch, controllers of programmes, heads of departments and producers, among them Paul Walters, who had just rejoined me as producer of *Wake Up to Wogan*. He told me that for the first couple of minutes, the Managing Director was laughing along with the best of them, but slowly, inexorably, the laughter stopped, and the smile was like a rictus on her lips. All around, taking their cue, senior management shuffled uneasily, while dear old Dukie chortled throughout, along with most of the creative people.

The gist of what I had to say was against the Birtian ethos of the day, but I don't think that, these days, many would disagree.

I started with a couple of illustrations of what my listeners enjoyed in the way of music:

K-Tel, in association with Paltry Productions, are proud to present:
The Greatest TOGs Album in the World — Never!
Come with us as we shuffle down memory lane to enjoy some Toggie tunes of yesteryear. Give your hearing aid a treat with much-loved favourite melodies, such as:

Waking Up Is Hard to Do
Zimmer Holiday
It's My Cardy, and I'll Cry if I Want to
Do You Know Where I'm Going to?
Hit Me with Your Walking Stick
Wake Me Up Before my Cocoa
Dewdrops Keep Falling Off My Nose

This limited edition offer is not available in the shops, so order now to ensure disappointment. Send cheques, postal orders, pension books, Green Shield stamps to:
  Tel & Wally Enterprises
  Box 222
  Cayman Islands.

Followed by how to identify them:

Good morning, Terry and Pauly,

I thought that I would like to check with you if I yet qualify as a TOG under the following conditions:

You're asleep, but others worry that you're dead.

You can live without sex but not without glasses.

You are proud of your lawn mower.

You constantly talk about the price of petrol.

You enjoy hearing about other people's operations.

People call at 9 p.m. and ask, 'Did I wake you?'

You have a dream about prunes.

The end of your tie doesn't come anywhere near the top of your pants.

You get into a heated argument about pension plans.

Then I turned on the assembled crowd:

And where does *that* leave the distinguished audience gathered here in the gloom tonight?

Apart, of course, from the majority – a clique, paid by myself at considerable expense to laugh hysterically and applaud enthusiastically at appropriate moments. I can only assume that they're saving themselves for a big finish . . . Don't forget, I have all your names and these cheques are post dated . . .

But to return to the rest of this audience: some of the

best and brightest of the BBC are gathered here: managing directors, controllers, executives, producers. The very people who *appoint* the megalomaniacs! These people who even now are feigning indifference, or trying to hide under their chairs, are the ones who decide what you're listening to, when you listen to it and who you're listening to. 'But these people can't be mad also,' I hear you cry. These are people in charge of the greatest broadcasting organisation that the world has ever known. They must perforce be of high intellect and the product of rigorous training, who, by an almost savage process of elimination and cull, are finally selected as being qualified to decide to what and to whom the Great British Public may listen. Well, that's as maybe, but I'm here to tell you that they know nothing. *Nada*. Worse than that, *nobody* knows anything. Oh, you can train technicians, sound engineers, camera crew, floor managers, directors, lighting men, scene shifters and even producers, but if any one of them ever comes up to you and tells you that they know the secret of *popular* success, have them gently taken away to the nearest Home For the Bewildered. Or Channel Five, whichever is the nearest . . .

You see, this is not brain surgery – this is the radio. Like television or theatre and the movies, nobody knows what's going to work until they've tried it. Oh, you can do sequels, of course, but eventually it's one Bond too many, or a Die Hard too far, and even Arnold Schwarzenegger has been known to fall on his gluteus maximus. You see, there's no master plan, no previous form, no breeding data, no formula, no recipe for success. You can put all the correct ingredients together: Ace producer/director/scriptwriters, with a proven record of success, the most popular artists or presenters in the country, throw all the money in the world at it, and still come up with zip. The entire length and breadth of this fair land there is only one person who can make a popular programme, or, more correctly, make a programme *popular*. It's you. Yes, you. Half listening while you're waiting for the kettle to boil or the phone to ring or the lights to change. You, gentle listener, you decide with a careless flick of the button whether we succeed or fail. And by the time you've decided, it's too late for us. Which is why we're out there with charts and graphs, projections and questionnaires trying to find out what you think before you've even thought it. I'm not big on all this focus group, survey and poll stuff – as Messers Gallup and Mori will readily agree, there's a hell of a difference between what people tell you and what they actually believe. Most people tell pollsters and researchers what they think is *expected* of them, not what they're *really* going to do. It also depends on how you ask the questions. I could produce charts and figures within a week that would prove convincingly that what the Radio 2 listener *really* wanted to hear was a diet of brass band music and religion:

'Hello, I bet you like brass bands, don't you?'

'Well yes, actually, I *do*.'

'Do you like listening to brass band music on radio?'

'Yes, I *do*.'

'Do you think there's *enough* brass band music on the radio?'

'Well no, actually, I *don't* . . .'

'Would you like to hear *more* brass band music on Radio 2?'

'Yes, you know, I think I would . . .'

'Do you believe in God?'

'Yes!'

'Do you think there's a place for religion on radio?'

'Yes! Why not?'

'Would you listen to religious programmes on Radio 2?'

'Certainly.'

'Do you think a half an hour's programme every day would be too much for people?'

'Certainly not! We're a Christian country, aren't we?'

Or – on a more mundane level, I think of the man who compliments his wife at dinner:

'Do you know, dear, this cabbage is wonderful!'

'Oh, do you like it?'

'It's delicious!'

Six months later, at dinner, he complains:

'Oh no! Not cabbage *again*?'

'But you said you *liked* it . . .'

As any well-worn politician will tell you, the only poll worth its while is the 'exit' poll, when they come out of the booth and tell you how they voted. As I've said earlier, nobody knows *anything*, and nobody can *predict* a thing in this business, until the fat lady sings . . .

Not just because people tell you one thing in public, and in the privacy of their homes do something completely different; not just because the whole business of radio listening is entirely subjective. We talk of a radio audience as if it were a group, as if it moved in blocks. There are millions of people out there – but they're all *individuals*. When people are listening to the radio, a ripple of laughter does not run around the stalls. Nobody chortles in Chorleywood because somebody chuckled in Cleckheaton. Every single radio listener makes up their own mind. My postbag over the years is full to bursting of letters from loyal lady listeners whose husbands leave the room in a marked manner whenever they turn me on. And vice versa.

Radio is the most individual, the most personal medium. Which is why it's a terrible mistake for broadcasters to cat-egorise their listeners. 'Radio 2 is for the fifties and over' ignores the basic precept of radio listening. It's *personal*. What pleases one fifty-year old won't please another, but may delight a forty-year old. Many of my listeners are in their twenties and thirties. I tell 'em to get lost, of course, but they won't go away. When you say 'Radio 2 is for the fifty-year old and over', what you *really* mean is this network is for the 'old geezer', and as a fifty-six-year old, I resent that. It's politically incorrect for a start – it's *ageist*!

So, I take it, when you claim to broadcast to fifty-year olds and over, you mean you're going to play music to suit that age group. Music from fifty to fade-out. I've news for you – it's impossible. Because every day, hundreds, perhaps thousands, of people become 'new' fifty-year olds. Because in five years' time a couple of million forty-five-year olds will be fifty and a similar number of fifty-year olds will be fifty-five; and believe me, their tastes in popular music will not be the same. Not to even mention the disparity of taste between the new intake and those at the other end of the spectrum who were seventy and are now seventy-five . . .

I'm sorry – you cannot lump your grown-up listeners into age groups. God Almighty Himself could not devise a music policy to satisfy a national age group as broad as fifty to Curtain Time. And a *computer* certainly can't . . .

Luckily for Radio 2, you don't *have* to . . .

Because, and let me break this to you gently – Radio 2 is *not* a music network. It never has been. The vast majority of the people who listen to Radio 2 – that is, the people who tune in every weekday from, say, seven in the morning until seven in the evening, the most loyal, the most consistent group of any in the country – do *not* listen for the music. I realise this will cause confusion, nay, panic, among songwriters, musicians, producers, middle management and even, mayhap, a frisson at controller level. Perhaps I should nail this thesis to the door of Western House.

Radio 2 weekdays is a 'personality' network.

People don't listen to Sarah Kennedy, Jimmy Young or even *me* for the *music*. They listen because they've become attached to the person presenting the programme – and, because of the personal, very intimate nature of the radio, far more deeply attached than they would ever become to any presenter on television. An indication of this is the listeners' need to fax, to email, to write to their radio favourite to contribute, to establish a dialogue. I've often said that I can present a television show to eighteen million viewers and not receive a letter from one of them. I do a radio show for five and a half million, and get three hundred letters, emails, faxes and cards a day. So . . . where does the music come in? The music only matters when it's wrong. When it jars, when it's inappropriate, when it sits uneasily with the personality of the presenter.

Radio 2 music should be selected to complement the personality of the presenter and the content of the programme. My programme differs from Sarah Kennedy's as much as hers differs from Jimmy Young's, and Jimmy's from Ken Bruce's.

Self-evidently the music should reflect that difference. Radio 2 music is the mortar between the bricks we make . . . or drop. It should be as different as the personalities who present it, and reflect these personalities.

A draconian music 'policy' is a mistake for a national radio station. Opt for a specific type of music, and you are opting for a 'niche' audience. Now a 'niche' audience is fine for a commercial radio station that doesn't want to compete in the mass marketplace and attract advertisers to its specific audience. It's fine for Channel 4. Radio 3 is another good example. But 'niche', by definition, means small – a little corner of the market.

No national, popular radio network should be looking for a 'niche'. Least of all BBC Radio networks funded by the public. If each BBC network seeks its own 'niche', trust me, each BBC network will end up in its own little corner, and the whole mass of the middle ground, the popular audience, will be swallowed up by commercial independent radio. And then, how will anybody justify a licence fee for BBC national radio?

I believe in Corinthian Casual broadcasting. Strolling out at Wembley to play the Arsenal in the cup final with hands in the pockets of our baggy shorts, having nonchalantly flicked away a careless cigarette . . . Lord Burghley training for the Olympic high hurdles with a glass of champagne balanced on each obstacle . . . C.B. Fry and the crown of Albania . . . Broadcasting without the strain showing, broadcasting without effort, without tedious training, without mind-numbing, spontaneity-killing rehearsal. Broadcasting without a safety net! Broadcasting that relies on wit, intelligence, but, most of all, on talent. Broadcasters that can do it without thinking about it too much. Broadcasters that can open the microphone without a thought in their heads, and rely on whatever it was that put them there in the first place to get them through this time . . .

Let me have presenters about me that rely on their own invention, rather than newspaper cuttings; that don't have to write it down before they say it; that don't have to fill up their air time with phone calls from the obsessed and deranged. Let me have ad-libbers, the ones who make it up as they go along. The finely chased, minutely sculpted, meticulously delivered prose is fine if you're Alistair Cooke, but has it got warmth, has it got heart, passion? Popular radio should be peopled by risk-takers, arm-chancers – stone-brave broadcasters who teeter on the tight-rope but never quite fall over.

It's not about research and figures and futures and focus groups, memos and papers and polling; and worrying yourself sick whether you're super-serving the bourgeoisie and under-cutting the ethnic minorities. It's not about planning – you can't work it out by logarithms and graphs. It's about what comes out the other side of the microphone or the camera, and that's about talent and instinct and creativity and spontaneity – all the very antithesis of planning and polling.

The problem is, the BBC's never been very good with the Talent. And I don't mean the normal producer/performer jealousy. With some honourable exceptions, the attitude of BBC senior people to the poor old hobbledehoys who actually keep them in their jobs has been, to put it at best, supercilious. 'Who does he think he is?' 'He'll come crawling back.' 'Nobody is bigger than the BBC.' These are the historic watchwords, the leitmotifs of the Reiths, the Sloans, the Wyndham

Goldies. Sentiments that ring around upper corridors of BH to this day.

'I see Wogan's put on another half-million listeners according to the latest Rajar figures.'

'Yes, but that's due to the weather, and our insistence on a clear Greenwich Time Signal at 8 o'clock . . . anyway, don't tell him, he'll be unbearable . . .'

'Yes, bit too big for his boots as it is.'

'Absolutely. *And* he's talking far too much anyway. He'll need to speed up his links if we're going to get that five-minute social action piece in every morning at quarter past eight . . .'

The message still hasn't got through – indeed the forest appears to be growing ever fainter through the hectares of trees that are needed to produce the miles of BBC papers and the morass of meetings: *this is a broadcasting organisation.* Its most important asset is its presenters, performers, producers, directors – its programme people. Is it really necessary to say that if you don't value your programme people, if you don't encourage them, cherish them, and continually challenge them, then you've missed the point – lost the plot. The BBC produces television and radio programmes. That's it. That's what it does. That's what it has done incomparably better than any other broadcasting organisation since the whole rigmarole began. The BBC has been, and remains, the benchmark by which all other radio and television, both national and international, is judged. Its loss to the British public, and the world, would be incalculable, and unthinkable. Its slow erosion would be indecent. As it was in the beginning, so it will be, for ever and ever. But only if you damn the torpedos, keep the faith – and for heaven's sake – trust the talent.

It's a measure of how 'those who must be obeyed' took the lecture that no tapes were issued to the critics for review, and the Radio 2 Lecture was never broadcast again in the land.

From the late seventies until the early nineties, the British press and I had what could only be described as a love affair. The 'Wonder of Wogan' was, by all accounts, a delight to eye and ear. Tabloids had 'Wogan Weeks', broadsheets extolled my virtues in long-winded articles on 'turning non-stop trivia into an art'. It seemed that *Blankety Blank* would have been irredeemable rubbish in lesser hands, but by dint of coruscating wit and ineffable charm, I had turned the dross into gold. Series such as *You Must Be Joking*, and *What's On Wogan*, although not much cop, never got the kicking they deserved, because of my ongoing honeymoon with press and public. *Wogan's Guide to the BBC* in 1982 was received with the kind of plaudits normally reserved for classical music programmes, ballet or David Attenborough – 'as hilarious and entertaining a programme as you're likely to see all year'; 'the temptation to snap Auntie Beeb's garters is irresistible, and Wogan and his producer had a go at both legs. The twang of elastic was exhilarating'. The awards came thick and fast – *TV Times* Personality of the Year for ten years running; Best-Dressed Man in Britain; Variety Club Showbusiness and Radio Personality; Television and Radio Industries Club Radio and Television Personality on seven occasions; then, to put the tin hat on it, 'Terry Wogan's named today as the all-time favourite man on television'. Clint Eastwood was second . . .

In view of the barrage of contumely that came my way as *Wogan* petered out, it's instructive to dip lightly into the earlier reviews of the chat show: 'A spectacular success'; 'easily the best chat show'; and so on, enough to turn a chap's head. Compare and contrast that with the dog's abuse of the final year, when 'boring' was the least offensive epithet. I was self-obsessed, I smirked, and where I used to twinkle charmingly, I now smarmed oleaginously. 'Woebegone' took over from 'Wonderful', executives publicly questioned the wisdom of persisting with 'cheap' shows such as *Wogan*. 'Wogan is past his sell-by date,' a BBC insider said, 'he's a quintessentially seventies figure' . . .

(Ah, 'sell-by' dates. Terry's Old Geezers and Gals have a thing about them, and even more about 'use-by' dates. They pay no attention to them; in fact my mailbag is full to bursting with tales of young limbs returning home for the weekend and throwing out perfectly good food from their parents' larders and fridges, on the grounds that the stuff is past its 'use-by' date. Those of us well-weathered by the passing years, and wise to the ways of commercialism, take these arbitrary dates with the pinch of salt we're not supposed to have any more, and providing the foodstuff smells all right and has no furry growths we'll dive in. Even the furry growth may be scraped off if the larder has been left bare by the over-cautious young . . . Maybe that 'BBC insider' – a famous euphemism for when the reporter can't get a quote from anybody – was right about my 'sell-by' date, but I'm ignoring my 'use-by'; I'm showing very little signs of fungus, and my loved ones tell me that my smell is hardly noticeable.)

I wouldn't remember a damned thing about my television

and radio past if it wasn't for newspaper cuttings, and sifting through the tonnes of printed matter that has accumulated in sideboards, drawers and files has been no labour of love. How many supermarkets, dress shops, fêtes, fairs and charities have I opened; how many public appearances, concerts, corporate events; how many film premieres, opening nights, record receptions and glitzy parties have I attended? And how many of them do I remember? The fading pictures in the yellowing cuttings stir no memories, apart from vague recollections of openings that went too well, in terms of public attendance, and too badly when the impatient crowd came through the plate-glass windows. But then, I used to find it difficult on *Wogan* to remember who I had chatted to a couple of days previously. I suppose it's my attitude: I've never put any great stock on what I do for a living; it's just what I do, and I know that I'm lucky to be doing it, although any self-respecting young person would have thrown me out of the larder years ago.

I sometimes wonder, but not for long, what I would have done if Radio Eireann hadn't beckoned to me. Probably stayed in the bank and moved up steadily by annual increments through the ranks, even to the dizzy heights of manager. I'd be long-since retired by now, probably with a part-time job looking after some convent's financial affairs a couple of mornings a week. I'd be playing a lot more golf, of course, and probably bridge. I might occasionally think, with a twinge of regret, of what I might have been, had I been brave, nay, reckless enough to leave my permanent pensionable position with the bank to chance my arm at the radio. I'd be happy because, luckily, that's my nature, and anyway I could never possibly imagine the good fortune that would have come my way. Would I have married Helen? I doubt it. A mere bank clerk would never have the gumption to approach such a beautiful creature. Would I have married and had a family? Probably, but I can't envisage any state of wedded bliss approximating the sheer joy that Helen and our children bring me. Life turns on an instant, and everything changes on a single throw; if I hadn't answered that ad in the Irish paper for radio announcers; if I'd been sensible and accepted that I didn't have the qualifications required; if I hadn't lied about a dentist's appointment, or the bank manager had refused to give me time off and I hadn't attended the audition; if RTE hadn't given me the job; if Mark White had thrown my back-to-front tape into the wastepaper basket when I applied to the BBC . . . So many lucky breaks – and if only one had failed, a different life. And people think that I'm being falsely modest when I put it down to luck!

8

A citizen of no mean city

In late 2000, the first, and some would hope, last, volume of this mighty autobiography was published to universal acclaim.

'Love the book! Great stuff! I've been reading it for two weeks now and I'm still only on page 49. It's the funny bits that keep slowing me down. As soon as I start slapping my thighs, crying with laughter and rolling about on the floor, what happens? Yes! The bookshop's security chap marches up, grabs the book off me, sticks it back on the shelf, and turfs me out . . .'

I've never read *Is It Me?*. Why would I? I wrote the thing. It's the same reason I never watch myself on the television, nor listen to myself on the radio. As I've said before, I'm easily embarrassed, particularly by myself. Having been brought up in a culture of repression of virtually every natural instinct, if I listened to, or watched, myself, I'd never be able to bring myself to do either again. It's 'showing-off', and so's this book. I'm often accused by discerning critics of false modesty, of self-denigration that is merely a front for a rampant ego. Maybe they're right, maybe there's a touch of Nietzsche lurking behind the façade, but I'm inclined to think that it's a bit simpler than that. I'm just getting my retaliation in first, in the best Munster rugby tradition. I'm apologising before anybody accuses me of anything, particularly self-regard, cockiness, or vaunting ambition. I was brought up not to rock the boat, to be one of the crowd; and there's no 'i' in 'team'.

We were a conventional lot, we lads of Crescent College, Limerick. No arts and crafts, no drama and culture. Lots of cinemas in the town, but I'm damned if I can remember a theatre. If there was, I certainly never went to one. There were the 'fit-ups' – the travelling players who toured Ireland with their repertory of Shakespeare, Yeats and Synge. Their caravan must have rested in Limerick every year, but it was only the inside of circus tents that I ever saw. 'Fossett's' and 'Duffy's' turned up in a field off the Ennis Road on a biannual basis, and were required viewing for any young fellow who wanted to be part of what the in-crowd were watching. Look, this was long before television, and the radio was something for grown-ups. (I was the only one of my age group who listened to the wireless.) There weren't too many people with whom I could have a literary discussion on the merits of *Just William* or *Billy Bunter*, either.

Young and all as I was, I knew a terrible circus when I saw one: tacky costumes, scruffy people, poor sad animals. 'Stand well back there, and let the lady see the monkey!' Mind you, I had the advantage over my schoolmates – I'd been to a proper zoo, Dublin Zoo, with my Auntie May. I knew what well fed, cared-for wild animals were supposed to look like, even if they were behind bars. The touring circuses were cheap and nasty, and I've never been to a circus since, although I knew Billy Smart personally . . . And clowns? I wouldn't thank you for a clown, while I'm sure the art and practice of clowning is steeped in history. They just don't make me laugh, any more than a jester hitting the king over the head with a pig's bladder would provoke a smile.

Humour dates, even the knockabout stuff — except, of course, at the Eurovision Song Contest. I mind well one such in the seventies, where the organising country (it had to be somewhere in Europe, the only place where they still had circuses, even in the seventies), decided that a capital turn for the interval would be a clown act. And guess who was doing the commentary for BBC Radio? Ten minutes of silence to fill. It doesn't sound much, but trust me, it's a lifetime in front of a microphone when all you have to describe is a crowd of capering eejits in baggy trousers, huge feet and red noses falling over each other. There are probably still circuses in Europe, just as there are still mime acts. Sorry again — I'm sure it goes all the way past the Commedia dell'Arte — but mime also leaves me cold. Only the French could think that Marcel Marceau was hilarious. What's all that about, pressing against an invisible pane of glass or walking into an imaginary gale? And if you really want to know, even as a boy I thought Charlie Chaplin was as funny as the plague; and now you're going to agree with me and say, 'Ah, yes — but Buster Keaton?' Sorry. If it comes to that, Oliver Hardy was funny, Stan Laurel wasn't, and the Marx Brothers were awful, apart from Groucho. See? I'm a curmudgeon when it comes to knockabout. I blame the circus; send out the clowns . . .

Somebody in Limerick who did go to see the 'fit-up' touring players was a young man a few years older than me named Dickie Harris. Dickie was something of a hero to little lads like me – a fine rugby player, good at tennis and, by Limerick and Crescent College standards, a bit of a wild card. Even in his late teens Dickie Harris was a recognised character in our town, and, surprisingly in a parochial setting in which individuality was generally regarded as the mark of Cain, he was well loved. Then he ran away to join, not the circus, but the strolling players, the hobbledehoys. In a very few years he had made his mark on the London stage, married a titled lady and changed up from Dickie to Richard. I met him in London in the mid-seventies, a big Hollywood star by then, but still the wild, mercurial big boy that I remembered from Limerick and Kilkee. He kept the table entertained with his memories of youth: stealing an extra drop of cordial when Mrs Hough, the little woman who kept a shop near the Pollock Holes in Kilkee, was pretending she wasn't looking; mad priests; the savage nature of Limerick rugby and its noble camaraderie. That nobility, that Corinthian attitude, combined with fierce aggression, still characterises Limerick rugby and its people. The rest of Ireland calls it 'Stab City' because of a reputation for gang violence, but anybody who has ever seen a rugby match at Thomond Park, Limerick, will tell you that it is the last bastion of the true spirit of fair play and sportsmanship. Let the crowds in the Stade de France whistle and jeer when opposing sides enter the arena; in Thomond Park, they are applauded on and off the field. Let them hoot and holler in Melbourne, Jo'burg and Auckland when an opponent runs up to take a penalty kick; in Limerick, there's silence . . .

Richard Harris loved his Munster rugby, and dragged Peter O'Toole along with him to cheer them on. 'Hellraisers' is the well-worn phrase, probably more true of their youthful days together, making their breakthroughs in the West End. I meet Peter O'Toole every year at the *Oldie* magazine's prize-winners' lunch, and a cheerier chap would be hard to meet. If 'raising hell' is falling about with laughter, then he's the real deal. Spike Milligan was another who frequented the 'Oldie of the Year' lunches when he was still with us. More of a laughter-maker than a laugher, you never knew quite where you were with Spike, but he too, like O'Toole and Harris, was a rugby player from way-back-when. On the wing for London-Irish actually, my own rugby club. I never had the pleasure of seeing Spike scamper down the wing, but I'd give anything to have seen it. 'Like a startled deer' was how an older member described it to me.

Limerick rugby has produced more than its share of char-acters, many of them swapping the jerseys of young Munster, Shannon or Garryowen for the green of Ireland – 'Musty' Clifford, Gordon Wood, his son Keith, Tony Ward, Anthony Foley, Clohessy the 'Claw'. Such is the enduring reputation in a hard town for its hardest man that the 'Claw' is reputed to be the only man in Limerick who can leave his car door unlocked. Gordon Wood used to recall his fellow Garryowen men with great humour – in particular a nuggety front-row who had lost most of his front teeth, and, since he was playing rugby every week, saw no sense in replacing them only to have them knocked out again the following week. After a game in Dublin against the rather more patrician Trinity College team, the little fellow was placed at the dinner table beside the Provost of Trinity, a Protestant clergyman. The meal progressed in a rather more stately fashion than the boys from Garryowen were used to, until the coffee and cakes. Then, our toothless hero, having hurled a huge lump of cake through the yawning gap where his teeth should have been, turned triumphantly to the provost. 'Aha!' he shouted, 'you has me with the mate, Father – but I has you with the buns!'

He would have had no idea that there was such a thing as a Protestant clergyman – anyone with a collar was a Roman priest. Limerick was a *very* Catholic town, not just priest-ridden, but under the thumb of the lay organisation, 'The Arch Confraternity' as it was known. This unelected body held itself responsible for the morals and behaviour of the town's citizens, and was the power behind the throne of the mayor and councillors. That power was never more ardent than in the mid-forties, when Shannon Airport had become the most important international airport in the western hemisphere, a staging post between America and newly liberated Europe. Limerick, the closest big town to the airport, had what a friend of mine from Mayo used to call a 'bozana'. Americans came and lived in our midst, chewing gum, drinking Coke, eating chocolate that tasted like chocolate. They threw parties, which my mother and father attended. Extraordinarily, for a town that had been wrapped up in itself for hundreds of years, these parties had people of all nationalities: the displaced, the fleeting, the conquerors, the conquered. Feelings sometimes ran high in the aftermath of a terrible war, and my mother told us of an occasion when the party was at its height, with music and dancing. A striking blonde, who had been a dancer, was asked for a solo performance. 'I vill dance for you,' she announced proudly, 'as I danced for my Führer.' Skin and hair flew in all directions. 'It was such a good party, too,' said my mother.

There was a thriving black market. Men would hop on a plane in Shannon with a side of ham and return from Stuttgart with a bag of Leica cameras. Limerick was alive with foreigners, with money to spend. Inevitably, this was brought to the attention of certain entrepreneurial elements in Dublin, and pretty soon the trains from there were disgorging a disproportionate number of young ladies. These fun-loving girls and, indeed, some right old boilers were, within the hour, on the arms of the aforementioned well-heeled foreigners, parading up and down O'Connell Street as if they owned the place. The Arch Confraternity knew its duty, both to God and the moral well-being of innocent Irish men and women. Swiftly and silently the fallen women were 'disappeared', never to be heard of again in the City of the Broken Treaty. The foreigners were allowed to stay; they had the money, if not always the affection of the locals. At another dinner, my father observed another one of the town's timeless characters, Steve Coughlan, who was the mayor at the time. An American made the mistake of asking the mayor's lady to dance. But this was Limerick, not Massachusetts, and Steve the mayor was across the table like an avenging angel, his hands around the unfortunate's throat. Another party gone West. 'I didn't mind,' said my mother, 'they were a boring crowd . . .'

In case you need it, I've included photographic evidence – proof, if proof were needed – that all those aunties, great-aunts

and grannies were not figments of my over-wrought imagination. There's one of the wedding of Auntie Enda, who wasn't
my aunt at all, but beloved Auntie May's best friend, who shared
her love of laughter and of fags, and who I thought would remain
May's spinster-chum for the duration. The fellow with the rictus
grin in the front is the groom, having separated Enda, on the
left of the picture, from May, on the right. The little chaps are
the brother, Brian, on the left, whose angelic looks belied his
nature, and a young shaver on the right, who, although he has
the ears, is no relation of mine. Seated on the right are the
angelic Muds, and my mother, Rose. See the identical set of
their heads, and smiles, and then look over Muds's right shoulder
at her youngest daughter, Dinah. Exactly the same slight inclin-
ation to the right, exactly the same smile.

The eejit with his mouth open and a headful of buck-teeth
behind Muds (the Granny) is our hero, and directly behind him,
his Da, Michael Thomas Wogan, victualler of O'Connell
Street, Limerick. Auntie Dinah's clinging on to Uncle Eddie
Cunningham. They're recently wed as you can see from the
excessive body contact. Beside Eddie is his sister in a pork-pie
hat, and, slightly overshadowed, as she was all her life by her
sisters, Auntie Kitty. A further couple of heads to the left and
there's Great-Aunt Mag, Muds's sister, proprietor of 207 Clonliffe Road, and, typically, with her head inclining in the opposite
direction to the rest of her family. The smile's there, though,
and one that shouldn't be discounted; this was not a woman to
waste a smile. On her right, and far left, the two Nellies: the
taller, Nellie Nolan, the smaller, my Auntie Nellie. Looking at
myself and the brother, I would say the date is around 1949–50,
and that's 207 Clonliffe Road in the background, although why

**First, we got them looking.
Now, we've got them listening.**

B B C   R A D I O   T W O

Created by Arc Advertising · February - March 1994

Some call 'em 'the crew', others 'the team'. To me, they are the underlings — Pauly, Deadly, Boggy and Fran. (© *BBC Photo Library*)

Edward Scissorhands lives. Paul Walters frightens the elks on Sheeprock Mountain, British Columbia, 2001. Later that day he was downed by a buzzard ball.

Eurovision 2006 — and another British hopeful prepares to bite the dust. (© *BBC Photo Library*)

Lordi — Finnish winners of the 2006 Eurovision Song Contest. If you think they look odd, you should see them without their make-up. (© *Rex Features*)

Fearne Cotton, Natasha Kaplinsky and A. N. Other. Shortly after this I broke into a break dance that stunned the nation. (© *BBC Photo Library*)

The NEW Wogan – Pink Socks at Karate. (© *BBC Photo Library*)

The present Lady Wogan and myself, at one of the very few grand occasions to which I'm invited these days. (© *Rex Features*)

It's not only the listeners he sends to sleep … (© *Mirrorpix*)

Auntie Enda should get married from my Granny's house, I don't know.

It may not look much to you, but I thought 207 Clonliffe Road, Drumcondra, Dublin, was huge. And so it was, compared to 18 Elm Park, Limerick. An entrance hall with a large grand-father clock, and a living room to the right, with a large fireplace, a cabinet for the best china, and, against the opposite wall, a piano that nobody in the family could play. At least two wedding receptions were held in this cluttered room, including Michael and Rose Wogan's. Next on the right was the dining room, with a big circular table in the middle that was exclusively used for playing cards at Christmas. All the dining was done in the kitchen. The room had two armchairs on either side of the fireplace, Auntie May and the usual packet of Player's in one, and Muds in the other, under a picture of the Sacred Heart of Jesus, whose eyes followed you around the room, like all good pictures. The kitchen was down a small flight of stairs, and a longer flight took you upstairs to the bedrooms.

My brother Brian, who has been an invaluable aid to these recollections, tells me that in a desk on the second landing were bound copies of minutes of the first Daíl, or Irish Parliament, and all my Grandad's military medals, including those of the Boer War. On leaving Clonliffe Road, Auntie Nellie dumped them all, including some incriminating pictures of herself and Nellie Nolan enjoying the attentions of some SS Officers in a Hofbrauhaus in Berlin, *circa* 1938. While not exactly blaming Nellie for the outbreak of hostilities, my father, with whom she shared a mutual distrust, always felt that things might have been different if Nellie hadn't made her fateful visit to the Third Reich. The 'Magpie', he called her, and although in retrospect it was a touch unfair to the woman, much of what she touched turned to dust. She always overcooked the Christmas turkey, for instance, which infuriated the Da, who wanted to cook it himself, and there was a major falling-out one Christmas when she cooked somebody else's ham, rather than the one my father had lugged up all the way on the train from Limerick. When Nellie would bid at cards, my father would always say, 'Dearly bought, Nell,' which infuriated her.

My brother, the fairest of men, put no store by my father's estimation of Nellie as the harbinger of doom until one night, during severe flooding which had banjaxed the bus services, when Auntie Nellie's taxi had broken down, he offered her a lift home, and, halfway there, watched the front wheel of his car, having inexplicably taken on a life of its own as he slowed for traffic lights, roll past his car window. In view of my brother's own record, I'm not entirely sure that this incident can be laid at the Magpie's door. This, let us not forget, is the same Brian Wogan who, in a moment of boyish high spirits, tried to push his ageing granny down the stairs, having a little earlier failed in a game attempt to set the house ablaze by lighting matches under the curtains . . .

Talking of Auntie Nellie consorting with the enemy reminds me that Auntie Enda (friend of May's, no relation) was one of the very few people living in neutral Ireland at the time to have suffered the parlous dangers of World War Two. She was buried in the wreckage of her house on Dublin's North Strand for forty-eight hours, after the Germans made their one and only bombing raid on Dublin, mistaking the fair city for Belfast a fair bit up the road in Northern Ireland, which, as a part of the United Kingdom, was a legitimate target. Enda had all our sympathy. If it had happened to Nellie, of course, no one would have been surprised.

Let it not be thought, however, that the Byrne sisters knew nothing of war and its dangers: on the morning of the Easter Rising in 1916, my mother, who was six, and another sister, probably Kitty, were staying with their Auntie Maggie (my Great-Aunt Mag) in her house in Rutland Street, Dublin. When the shooting started and news of the doomed revolution reached Mag, she immediately decided that the safest place for the two little girls would be back with their mother and sergeant major father in the British Army barracks at Beggars Bush on the other side of the Liffey, miles away. She crossed twenty blockades with the children, and it took nearly twelve dangerous hours, through a city full of snipers and trigger-happy soldiers. Rose never forgot the sight of a sniper falling from a roof-top on to the pavement close to her. They made the safety of the barracks, and then Mag turned again for home, through the bullets and the shelling. It took her twenty-four hours . . .

Although my Grandad's Boer War medals are no longer with us, my brother still has the bronze medal that my mother won for Irish dancing at a *Feis Ceoil*, a major competition. Although the children of a British Army soldier, no one questioned the right of my mother and her sisters to call themselves Irish; but things could have been very different for Brian and myself, according to Rose. Warmed by a nice cream sherry, she would tell the tale of a Christmas at the barracks, the commanding officer and his lady dispensing good cheer to the men and their families under the Christmas tree. Rose, a pretty little handful, asked to touch the angel on the top of the tree, and the commanding officer lifted her up to do so. He took an immediate shine to her, and as he and his wife had no children, asked Granny and Grandad if they might adopt Rose. Although money was scarce and they had five mouths to feed, they turned the offer down. As Brian says, that's how we were both lucky enough to miss Singapore, Aden/Burma and who knows what other theatres of war.

Another wedding photo, this time from the early forties and something of a collector's piece. How often do you see a dustbin in a wedding photograph? The happy couple centre-stage are Michael Nolan and Patricia Nevin, and it was sent to me out of the blue by their son-in-law Eugene Shannon. The scene is Rutland Street, North Dublin, where my mother's family lived before moving to Clonliffe Road, Drumcondra. Way up at the top right-hand corner are Michael T. and Rose Wogan, both looking younger than I ever remember them, my mother with a careless arm over some gay blade's shoulder, and a girlish attitude that was never captured in any photograph before or since. Yer man with the tie in front is already displaying the ears that were to become such a major feature of British life and a source of merry ribaldry to so many, but at least he's kept his mouth shut and spared us the buck-teeth. Dublin hadn't changed much in fifty years, and this photo could have been taken in O'Casey's or Joyce's time. The faces, the suits, the hairstyles, the attitudes epitomise a city that was still a village, and would remain so for at least another twenty-five years.

The bridesmaid is Auntie Kitty, always the odd-one-out of the Byrne sisters. It's interesting, at least to me, that there's no sign of Nellie, May or Dinah, or, if it comes to that, Auntie Mag. After all, she owned the house in Rutland Street in which Granny, Grandad and their girls lived after Grandad left the

British Army. Kitty had followed her Auntie Maggie into the French-polishing game, but Brian and I grew up thinking of her as somehow different from her sisters. We learned that by observing how the others treated her: not as an equal, but someone to be nurtured and treated with a kindness and gentility that they never displayed to each other. All of the Byrne girls had sharp wit and tongues to match, but Kitty was never part of the general banter. My brother Brian, whom she particularly loved, remembers her as kind, strange, childish – always the one to join in our games while the others sat about chattering like jackdaws. He remembers the crushing nature of her embrace – she was always the most affectionate and tactile of the family – and my own children remember the horror of her enthusiastic, hairy kisses. My brother can keep a small crowd entertained for some time by recounting the tale of the naked fear that showed on my face when, during *This Is Your Life*, in the seventies, he whispered to me, 'Kitty's on next' . . .

The innocent, gentle Kitty might have strolled through life under the strong, protective wings of her family had she not been hit by a car while on a pedestrian crossing on the main Drumcondra road. She barely survived, and after a considerable time in hospital received a ludicrous sum by way of compensation, which, nonetheless, enabled the remaining sisters to move to more manageable accommodations in Iveragh Road, Whitehall. They were north-side Dubliners through and through; the south side of the Liffey was another country. It was ever thus, and still remains, in the city that was so lately a village.

The terrible accident had its effect on Auntie Kitty. From being the quiet, uncomplaining, cheerful and gentle soul, overnight she became, at least according to Nellie, who had taken charge, as she always did of everything, being the elder sister, 'difficult'. Timid Kitty demanded her place in the pecking order from the bed she rarely left. Brian remembers the little lady that thought the sun shone from his every pore disagreeing vehemently with everything he said in her later years. She took on the mantle of the invalid, and with strong, reliable Nellie doing everything for her, she remained in bed. And that's my last memory of dear, sweet Kitty: propped up in bed, the pretty, round smiling face now aged and a little drawn, and over the coverlet the French-polisher's delicate hands now milk-white, their perfect nails painted a bright crimson . . .

Next we have Michael T. and Rose Wogan, otherwise known as the Ma and Da, pictured in their prime – well, certainly the best time of their lives, at the opening of the flagship store of the Peter Dominic wine shop chain, on Grafton Street, Dublin, about 1952, I'd say. The Da was general manager of Peter Dominic, and had masterminded the conversion of the Leverette & Frye chain of grocery stores into wine shops. Not bad for a young fellow who had run away from home at fourteen years of age after a fight with his father over the old fellow's mistreatment of the Da's adored mother. He used to say that he was 'apprenticed' to a grocer's in Bray, Co. Wicklow, but I'm sure he just got a job and a roof over his head by dint of living in the cellars by the wine vats. He learned his trade there, and although the very name 'Bray' was anathema to him for the rest of his life, he learned enough to get a job behind the counter of the finest grocery store in Dublin, Leverette & Frye, Grafton Street. Which is where you find him and the woman he loved all his life in this picture where the wheel has come full circle. For it was in that very shop that he met Rose, who worked in the cash office. Shortly after their marriage, in 1936, he took her to Limerick, where he had been made manager of the branch. Nineteen years later they were back in Dublin with two sons, and Michael T. was the general manager. And so we find them ten years on, plump, successful, healthy and happy. When people compliment me on my career, I always think of my father. Compared with his extraordinary rise, I'm only in the ha'penny place . . .

A man called Frank Dolan, who knows a thing or two and writes an erudite column in the *Irish Post*, a distinguished publication that keeps the Irish in Britain up to date on Hibernian happenings in perfidious Albion, put it forcibly in 1997: 'What I object to about Terry Wogan's inclusion in the New Year's Honours List is the modesty of the thing – only an OBE, for God's sake! An OBE is the most lowly national or international honour ever bestowed on the noble Wogan family. Previous Wogans have been recipients of Europe's most splendid honours – from France, Spain, Italy, and, indeed, Britain . . .'

Up to then, I'd been beside myself that Her Majesty had graciously bestowed an Honorary OBE on my unworthy head. Because it was honorary, I didn't have the pleasure of a visit to Buck House, and the privilege of some light banter with the monarch as she pinned the medal to my heaving breast. Chris Smith, then the Minister for Culture, handed me the gong with grace and charm before an audience of friends, colleagues and family in the old council chambers of Broadcasting House, 'neath the portraits of various Director-Generals. (The very spot where Paul Walters sent an entire tray of chipolatas flying, most of them over the forbidding countenance of Lord Reith, who was minding his own business over the fireplace. But that was another do, another story . . . Suffice it to say that Walters' career never really recovered. You can make a mess of a programme, and turn up drunk as often as you like, but throwing snorkers around the Council Chamber gets you noticed. You won't get fired, of course – nobody does, in the BBC – but a little black mark goes on your file. Responsible employer that it is, the BBC keeps a file on all its employees. They're usually dragged out as a source of sneering merriment on retirement. They can also be a revelatory source: the late Charles McClelland, when he was Controller of Programmes, Radio 2 (he had come from the BBC's Middle Eastern Service, not an easy leap to make), told me that while idly flipping through the file of his Head of Music Programmes before an annual interview, he'd come across the fellow's startling promotion through the ranks of the British Army. He'd joined the BBC after National Service as an acting corporal; twenty-five years on, he'd been promoted to major, according to his latest file. He'd been upgrading himself at every annual interview, as he went along.

Anyway, back among the branches of the Wogan family tree, the bold Dolan went on to say that, in the beginning, the Wogans were Welsh 'Gwgan', meaning a frown, or a scowl. Here he was not telling me anything I didn't know, because hardly had Helen, myself and two-year-old Alan arrived by steam packet from across the Irish Sea, but a large scroll arrived at our simple bothy – from whom or where I have no record – which spilled the beans on what it called 'the Wogan Pedigree'. Now, you know me: plain-spoken, honest yeoman broadcaster, no airs or graces, call a spade something else, no need for any great fuss or palaver, up off your knees, for goodness' sake – yet when your family tree kicks off with 'Cradog of the Strong Grin, Lord of Gloucester, Knight of the Dolorous Tower and the Round Table', there is a tendency to lift the chin, straighten the back, and look down the nose at the passing peasantry.

Old 'Gwgan' makes his appearance midway through the eleventh century, trading up, by marrying the daughter of the Lord of Wiston in Pembrokeshire. Suddenly, there are Wogans everywhere – Sir Walter Wogan, then Sir Mathew, then several Sir Johns, one of whom became Sir John Wogan of Picton Castle, and another who, in 1295, became the Lord Chief Justice of Ireland and founder of the Wogan chapel in St David's Cathedral. The early fifteenth century has a Sir David and a Sir Henry, but by the close we're back into the Johns again. The female name that is most prominent is Katherine – which is why we called our daughter by that name. I suppose we should have called our second son John, but certainly not after the Thomas Wogan who, in 1646, was one of the judges who signed the death warrant of King Charles I. Mind you, there was a Sir John who got beheaded at Pontefract in 1483.

The founder of the Irish branch was, apparently, another Thomas, in the early fifteenth century. Now, distinguished and all as the Welsh line is, it can't hold a candle to the swashbuckling Irish Wogans. They fought for James Stuart at the Battle of the Boyne, at Aughrim, and, paradoxically, at the last heroic stand in Limerick. After that, in 1691, the Wogans joined the Wild Geese, soldiers of fortune, fighting in the pay of France, or Austria, for generations. The brothers Charles and Nicholas took part in the Jacobite insurrection of 1715; Charles was captured, escaped and rejoined the Irish Brigade in France. Three years later, James III, still aspiring to be King of England, asked Wogan to find him a wife, from among the Catholic royal families of Europe.

The dashing Charles came up with Maria Clementina Sobieski, granddaughter of the King of Poland, who had saved Western Europe from the Turks. All he had to do was get the lady to Rome. Unfortunately, the English, hearing of the plan, imprisoned the princess in Innsbruck Castle. With three members of his Irish Brigade, one of whom Peter O'Toole claims was an ancestor of his, the gallant Wogan breached the battlements and carried off the princess, over the Austrian mountains and beset by danger at every turn, to her wedding with James III in Rome. After a decent interval she delivered the Old Pretender a son, Charles, better known to history as Bonnie Prince Charlie.

By then, Charles Wogan was a chevalier de France, a senator of Rome and a hereditary baron of England. However, disappointed with the Stuarts and their lost cause, he fought for the Spanish king and became a brigadier general, and then governor of La Mancha. Charles Wogan died in Barcelona in 1754. His younger brother, Nicholas, however, was with Bonnie Prince Charlie in Scotland in 1745, limping back to France the following year after the disaster of Culloden. The French made him a chevalier as well, and he died in Paris in 1770. The proud tradition was carried on by a nephew, Francis, who joined the Irish Brigade and, like old Gwgan long ago, married well, into the aristocratic du Chastel family. His last direct descendant, Baron Tanneguy de Wogan, died in Paris in 1906. Charles Wogan's portrait hangs in the National Gallery, Dublin, and his brother Nicholas's in Malahide Castle, Co. Dublin.

Some years ago, somebody sent me two pictures of yet

another fearless adventuring Wogan. I don't know where he got the outfit, or why the Injuns tied him to a totem pole. I don't even know what a Wogan is doing in America in the eighteenth century, but I know that the chevaliers would be proud of him . . . And have a look at this:

Dear Sir Terry de Wogan

As editor of *Card Times*, top magazine for the cigarette card collector, I believe I have come across evidence of one of your ancestors. The Carreras card attached, from their 1934 Believe It Or Not series, tells of one **Tanneguy de Wogan** of Paris who '**travelled 2,500 miles in a paper boat**'! Apparently no other materials were used in its manufacture but compressed paper.

The only thing which puzzles me – he must have been a pretty bad navigator to miss England on his way over from Ireland, to finish up in Paris. No wonder he travelled 2,500 miles. He probably went via the Pentland Firth.

Anyway, hope you like it. All felicitations.

David Stuckey:

Editor, *Card Times*

I hope that the old ancestors might be happy, too, and even Frank Dolan satisfied, that in June of 2005 Her Majesty the Queen appointed me an Honorary Knight Commander of the Most Excellent Order of the British Empire, in recognition of my services to broadcasting. I was even more honoured when, in November 2005, Her Majesty appointed me an Additional Knight Commander, allowing me the title of Sir Michael Terence Wogan, KBE, and Helen, Lady Wogan. Whatever Charles and

Nicholas might have thought, Michael and Rose Wogan would have been mightily pleased, although my father would have been slightly puzzled, as he always was, by my success. Helen's mother would have been thrilled for her, and the old Tim Joyce, her blustering dad, would have pretended that he'd hardly noticed, but would have spent the rest of his life boasting about it to his cronies in the pub.

The family, my friends and the public were enthusiastic and generous in their praise when the news broke on the morning of Saturday, 11 June. We were in Fowey, Cornwall, with our friends the Smiths, Temporals, Hugheses and Saads, to celebrate the wedding of Kits and Hacker Browning's lovely daughter Grace, Helen's godchild. Of course Helen and the family had known about the honour for weeks, but you're not supposed to tell anybody until the Honours List is published. On Friday night we all had dinner together, eagerly anticipating the wedding. The following morning, Helen and I were woken by the phone and a tirade of abuse from Michael and Lorna Smith, who wanted to know what kind of friends we thought we were, keeping a secret like that to ourselves. The sun shone, the wedding went beautifully, and the bride looked gorgeous, just as her mother had done all those years ago in Dublin . . .

Unusually, the press were as kind as the public. David Jason had also received a knighthood, and as his most famous role was as 'Del Boy' in *Only Fools and Horses*, the headlines were, almost inevitably, 'Arise, Sir Del and Sir Tel!' A wonderful editorial in the *Daily Telegraph* enthused: 'Tony Blair has frequently been accused of abusing the honours system . . . today we acquit him on all counts . . . we rejoice at Wogan's knighthood. When that voice is on the radio, as mellifluous and soothing as the shipping forecast, we know that the world can't be all bad. If anyone deserves an honour, he does . . .'

So on Tuesday, 6 December 2005, I presented my radio show like Alvar Liddell in the 1930s, in full fig, frock-coat and all. Sarah Sands, the then editor of the *Sunday Telegraph*, asked me to relive my moment of glory for her paper. My recollection of the day, written while it was still fresh in my memory, is in the picture section – take a look.

And by the way, Her Majesty didn't say, 'Arise, Sir Terry'. She never does, which will come as a blow to whoever it was who brought out a book to exploit my Great Day, in time to catch the Christmas rush, in October 2005. They called this cheap bit of opportunism *Arise, Sir Terry*, and got it on the bookshelves without so much as a 'by your leave' from me. I've never read it, and I don't know anybody else who has, either. So let's hope that this tacky bit of cut-and-paste hackery has sunk without trace.

Many years ago, an Irish journalist, Gus Smith, wrote an unauthorised biography, and at the time I was furious and ready to drag old Gus before the courts for invasion of privacy, exploitation of my good name and anything else an 'Injury Lawyer for You' could throw at him. Then I met Eamonn Andrews at a drinks party, and the wise man set me right: the names of people in the public eye are in the public domain. It's one of the so-called 'prices of fame'. If your name's up there in lights, anybody unscrupulous enough knows that the law is not going to bother its bewigged head if they use said name for their own fell purposes, as long as they stay just the right side of the law. Some smart alec tried it on once for Virgin, when they were trying to break into the lucrative London–Dublin flight market.

Something along the lines of 'Getaway from Wogan to Dublin'. I confess that I had a humour bypass and rang Sir Richard Branson, who gave the ad the sharp elbow.

It *is* a bit much to see somebody trying to make money out of your name without asking permission or, indeed, offering to cross your palm with silver, but as dear Eamonn said, it's not worth the hassle. You just have to ignore it – paying attention, jumping up and down, is playing into the exploiter's hands. And as for going to court; my great friend, the distinguished solicitor, the late Sir David Napley, told me never to do it. No matter how watertight your case, no matter how much you know yourself to be in the right, warned Sir David, don't take it before a judge and jury. This former president of the Law Society, one of the most respected solicitors of his generation, said that you could never tell which way a jury, and even more so, a judge, was going to jump. Cases are not always won on rights or wrongs – all too often they are lost on the personal prejudices or the minor likes and dislikes of jurors and judges.

So what are you supposed to do if some fly-by-night is bruiting your name abroad? Starve them of the oxygen of publicity. Don't comment, don't react, rise above it. It worked with *Arise, Sir Terry*, and also in 2005 when Chris Moyles started a campaign on BBC Radio 1 to 'Stop Wogan'. The idea was to convince the younger radio listeners to wrest control of the family wireless, or car radio, from their parents and tune in at breakfast-time to 'Moylesy', rather than me. Like any good tabloid, the *Sun* jumped at the idea of a 'Battle of the Networks', and, even better, a personal ding-dong between Chris and me. Banners, posters, badges were printed and sent all over the country. I even saw the legend 'Stop Wogan' written in the dirt on the back of a filthy van. The great campaign lasted about a week because I refused to rise to the bait, apart from commenting that things must be more desperate at Radio 1 than we had suspected. It withered and died, and culminated in ultimate shame for old 'Moylesy' when his supporter, the *Sun* newspaper, held a poll to find out which of us was the more popular, and I won, by a large margin. Recently, they backed the boy once more, on *Celebrity X-Factor*. Wrong again.

The knighthood was welcomed by all and sundry, at least by all whose opinions mattered to me. I replied to everyone who had been kind and gracious enough to write to congratulate me. I've kept all their letters, including one from Mary McAleese, the President of Ireland. My knighthood was first promulgated as an honorary one because I am a citizen of the Republic of Ireland. An honorary knighthood is a very great honour indeed, and rarer than the usual knights bachelor award, but it was suggested to me that I might be entitled to a 'regular' knight-hood, and the right to call myself 'Sir' and Helen 'Lady', because, having been born in Ireland while the country was still part of the British Commonwealth, I was entitled to dual citizenship, both British and Irish. I made inquiries, and then an application, and in no time the Foreign and Commonwealth Office wrote to confirm that Her Majesty was pleased to make me an Additional Knight Commander to add to my honorary title. In the end, I've got two gongs for the price of one: Sir Terry Wogan, KBE. You can call me Terry (even better, 'lucky' . . .).

Somebody sent me a cutting from an Irish newspaper – one owned, interestingly enough, by my fellow Belvederian and dual Brit/Irish citizen, Sir Tony O'Reilly – which said: 'There will be those who argue because Ireland was occupied by England,

and because our ancestors fought a long and bloody war to win our independence, it must therefore be a shameful and treasonable offence against our ancestors if an Irish citizen accepts an honour from the Queen of England.' The final few words put the tin hat on the begrudgery: 'It is acceptable, such people argue, to accept honours from foreign powers, not just ones we were at war with'. So no Englishman has the right to accept the légion d'honneur from France because of the Hundred Years War? No Spaniard the right to accept an English award because of the Peninsular War, no German the right to accept any award from anyone, because of World Wars One and Two? As I've remarked elsewhere in this homely tome, my own ancestors gave their all in the fight for Irish freedom, and at least two of them were knighted. To hell with small-minded begrudgers; I'm proud to join my knightly Irish ancestors.

9

Trying not to count my chickens

~⸻

The last couple of years have been pretty damned good in the way of what an old Radio Eireann favourite of mine, Seán Bunny, used to call 'prizes'. Not Seán Bunny himself, of course, because he was merely a figment of his author's imagination. It was his author, who, when recounting the little chap's weekly adventures on the radio, had trouble with her 'Rs', so Seán used to 'wun' rather than 'run' and 'pwesent his pwizes rather than . . .' Well, you know.

Deadly Alancoat and Pauly Walters were immediately taken with Seán Bunny, just as they were intrigued by Curly Wee and Gussie Goose, more cartoon figures from my innocent youth. Poor souls, they'd been brought up on a meagre diet of Rupert Bear and some early Noddy. But there are no 'prizes' on *Wake Up to Wogan*, and it's a sore point. All over the country, on a thousand ramshackle commercial radio stations, prizes are scattered daily like confetti. Free skiing holidays, a lifetime's supply of snorkers, sports cars, private jets, and £10,000 a week for the rest of your life are offered, if you'll only listen to Capital, Kiss, Kerrang! and a million others.

They don't get it. There are no incentives to listen to me, and precious few to listen to anyone else on Radio 2. So why do millions do it? Why, as the redoubtable Catherine Tate might say, 'ain't they bovvered' by the promise of untold wealth and luxury? Because until some commercial radio station can put together a combination of presenters and music to rival Radio 2, 'we ain't bovvered'. In twenty years of independent radio, run, presumably, by smart people with sharp commercial brains, the penny still hasn't dropped. It's not about giveaways, television commercials, or the 'right' music. It's about getting some decent presenters with whom the daily listening public can identify. Forget doctrinaire playlists, mid-week chart positions and the other false gods of popular music; identify the real music that your core audience want to hear, blend it in so it sits easily with your presenters, and you have half a chance.

This is not the USA. British and American radio grew up with more than just the Atlantic between them – the habits of listening are poles apart. In America, radio sprang into the air unrestricted; overnight there were a million stations clamouring for attention. Little towns would have ten, twenty stations, the bigger cities, hundreds. They still do. There just weren't enough presenters who could put two words together to go around. There still aren't. So Americans sped around the dial until they found the kind of music they could listen to, and there they stayed. If you go to America today, you'll find yourself doing the same thing.

In Britain, under the severe presbyterian mantle of Reith, radio grew up in a straitjacket; well, a dinner jacket, anyway. It wasn't until the sixties, and the pirates offshore, that anybody had a choice of listening to anything other than the BBC. Yes, there was Radio Luxembourg, but it never worried the estab-lishment, although it must be said that present-day commercial radio could learn a thing or two from old '208'. They got the music right, and the presenters – Jimmy Young, Pete Murray, Keith Fordyce, Barry Alldis – or their equivalents today, if you could find them, would certainly challenge Radio 2. The rascally radio pirates got it right as well, and in the space of a couple of years, Tony Blackburn, John Peel, Ed Stewart, Johnnie Walker, Pete Brady, Emperor Rosko and many others were household names. The habit of listening to people first, of identifying with the presenter, had become ingrained in the British listening public through the years of BBC dominance of the airwaves, and that's the way it is to this day.

And just as the listening habits of Americans and ourselves differ, so, as far as presenters are concerned, radio and television are poles apart. You can be a star overnight on television; on radio it takes longer. It takes years. Years for the listening public to grow to know and warm to you. The idea that you can take a shining star from television and turn him overnight into a radio broadcaster is beyond foolishness. I think we're at the core of why commercial radio is finding it so difficult to compete with BBC Radio: it just doesn't have the time, the patience or the money to nurture a promising presenter over, not weeks, not months, but years. I came to the BBC from Ireland entirely unknown, they gave me a daily radio show because they thought I had potential, they let me grow into it, and my faithful listeners grow with me. After a couple of years, people began to recognise me, although there's still a hard core who believe that I am Eamonn Andrews and Val Doonican's love child. I grew, and brought an audience with me. That's the only way to success on the radio. It takes time and faith, and until commercial radio can find those two qualities, they'll struggle for a loyal audience.

In January 2002, Charlotte Green of Radios 4 and 2, and I graced the cover of the *Radio Times* (other listings magazines are available, as if you cared . . .). We had been selected by several thousand discerning, possibly cloth-eared, listeners as the most attractive voices on the radio. It scarcely came as a surprise to the bold Charlotte or myself, since we'd had our photo taken for the cover a couple of weeks before. You always take your life in your hands when you submit to a photograph for half the world to sneer at, but after a sneaky glance, I thought mine was OK, until Paul Walters said it made me look like Jack Nicholson in *The Shining*.

I got off lightly. A fragrant nosegay from my diary of April of that year:

12 April 2002
The *Sun* has a picture of David Beckham's foot on its front page. It asks all its loyal readers to place their hands on the picture, and pray. Pray for Beckham's foot and England, for how can we win the World Cup without him?

And just in case we think we're in the final throes of tabloid populist insanity, GMTV's *Breakfast Show* has Uri Geller on board, asking every one of their loyal viewers to do the same thing, like a spoon. It was an Argie that did it while playing in the vital Europeans Champions League tie between Manchester United and Deportivo La Coruna. It's not without its own significance that England and Argentina are drawn together in the same first round of the World Cup. It's a plot. The Argies have hated us since Sir Alf Ramsey called them 'animals' in 1966; never mind the Falklands . . .

Becks is England's hero, ever since he saved the country's football bacon with a last-minute goal against Greece in the World Cup preliminaries. They've forgotten the last World Cup, when, with a typical display of petulance, dear old Becks got himself sent off, and England were knocked out. Guess who were the opponents? Who else but those dastardly Argies? Beckham was reviled and cursed the length and breadth of this sceptred isle, booed every time he touched the ball. For months he and Posh were subjected to disgraceful abuse. Now, all that matters is Becks' foot. A less secular society would be rubbing relics and sprinkling holy water . . .

My listeners' sense of irony and the rightness of things do not desert them: 'All is not lost. Put him in goal. They'll never get the ball past his crutches.'

13 April 2002
Poor old Beckham; the cynics are up and running: a TOG in a dog collar, Father Gerard Quigley of Bury St Edmunds:

As you may have seen in a national newspaper, the *Sun*, has asked us all to place a hand on a picture of David Beckham's injured foot and pray for it to heal quickly.

Anxious to do my bit for good old England, I purchased a copy of said newspaper, placed my hand on the picture and prayed thus: 'Please restore this broken appendage to David's body in time for the World Cup game.'

You can imagine my alarm when I looked down and saw to my horror that I had actually placed my hand on a picture of page three of said publication, which showed a picture of a well-endowed lady in the Bristol area.

Whoops!!! OK, well, if it works . . . they will go well with the sarong.

And a Carl Ott, from Solihull:

On Saturday we were in Solihull town centre when we came upon a young lad dressed in Man U strip. He was bouncing a ball pretty competently and I asked him who he wanted to be. He answered, 'I want to be just like David Beckham.'

So I gave him a swift kick on the ankle and walked on. I still cannot understand his mother's protests or his ear-splitting screams.

Is it me?

Is there anybody out there with even the dregs of human kindness?

With the World Cup 2006, history repeats itself – only now it's Rooney's foot. The curse of the metatarsal strikes again.

In January 2004, one of the proudest moments of my life was when I was to be conferred with an honorary Doctorate of Letters by the University of Limerick. It was on that happy weekend in my hometown, too, that my daughter Katherine and her delightful husband, Henry Cripps, announced that she was pregnant. 'He shoots, he scores!' as my son Alan put it; it could have been more elegantly expressed, but it summed up our joy. Freddie Cripps emerged into the welcoming arms of his family in October of the same year, turning the most beautiful girl in Ireland, whom I'd married it seemed like only a couple of years before, into a granny, and someone who'd never had a proper, grown-up job into a grandfather. It's strange, but I have only the most fleeting of memories of my children as babies, so little Fred is an all-new, constant source of wonder and love. Gimme more! . . .

Limerick University is relatively new, certainly when compared to Trinity, Dublin, founded by Elizabeth I, but the Irish have always made education a priority, and Limerick has already built a huge reputation in the groves of academe. Professor Kevin Ryan delivered my citation, a paean of praise which I received blushing hotly and sweating lightly under my robes and quaint bonnet. The President, Professor Roger Downer, conferred the doctorate, and we all repaired for a reviving drop. There was a dinner in the evening at the university, to which the family were invited, and it was typical of my brother Brian and

his Pauline to come all the way from Dublin. The other doc-
torates were awarded to Mary Davis, who had masterminded
the Special Olympics in Ireland in 2003, and the ever youthful
and still dazzling author, Edna O'Brien. It was Edna who said:
'Ireland has always been a woman, a cave, a cow, a Rosaleen, a
sow, a bride, a harlot, and, of course, the gaunt Hag of Beara.'
She doesn't spare the horses, Edna, but they love her for her
eloquence and fearlessness.

As ever, when you return to the places of your youth,
everything that seemed so big now seems small, and Limerick
itself, like all Irish towns since the Celtic Tiger emerged
from the bog, has expanded, grown so that its outskirts are
unrecognisable. Some things remain: the Treaty Stone, in
memory of a great siege that ended in my ancestors fleeing
to serve a foreign king, King John's Castle, the mighty
Shannon, the Da's shop . . .

In September 2005, an old friend from the ill-fated Century
Radio days in Ireland, Enda Marren, rang me from Dublin to
tell me that I had won the award as 'Ireland's Greatest Living
Entertainer', the presentation to be made on a live RTE television show. I'm not big on showbiz, radio or television awards;
I've had more than my share, and doubt whether I was worthy
of most of them. I presented the Variety Club awards for years
on BBC TV, with voiceovers by my pal, Ray Moore, and every
few years they'd give me one to keep me from feeling left out
of it. I must have presented it for the best part of ten years, and
then Ken Griffin retired, a new producer came in, and I was
out. And following the well-worn BBC principle, the new guy
broke the mould, and the show. From prime-time weekday, it
was relegated to early afternoon Sunday. It has been replaced in

the schedules by the Comedy Awards, a scary evening, particularly if Johnny Vegas is around, and brilliantly compèred by Jonathan Ross. And then, of course, there is the BAFTAs. I presented the BAFTAs once, with my friend Stewart Morris producing and directing. I've never been invited to another one, not to mind winning a BAFTA. It hardly hurts at all . . . Anyway, I've got roomfuls of Carl Alan Awards from the palmy days of *Come Dancing* and other ballroom extravaganzas to make up for it. I even had my picture taken at some Lyceum or other with Princess Margaret, as you can see in the picture section.

The Princess and I were no strangers; low down on the royal totem pole, she got stuck with more than her share of award ceremonies, and since for much of the seventies and eighties I was either winning or presenting, we shared many a prawn cocktail and breast of chicken. She liked to light up early on these occasions, and many's the time we'd rise to our feet, at her behest, for the royal toast, just after the prawn in Marie Rose. She tended to ignore women, when she wasn't frightening them to death with a basilisk stare. I remember the formidable Joan Collins being intimidated and whispering to me, 'She doesn't like me, you know.' I had to reassure Joan that looking the way she did, she had no chance with Princess Margaret. At a Radio Industries Club Awards do, Margaret ran through the award-winners with me during lunch. She hadn't a clue who anybody was, and those whose names she recognised were dismissed with a scornful click of the tongue. I met her again, many years later, at Sunday lunch with the Marchioness of Reading. Princess Margaret had invited herself to drinks after church, and we engaged in airy banter. Distracted, I turned away for a moment, and when I turned back the Princess had disappeared.

No sign of her – and then I looked down. There she was, on her knees, tidying Margot Reading's grate . . .

So off I went across to Dublin, and there, in a great barracks of a hotel, thousands were assembled in their finery for dinner and live television awards. On came Gay Byrne, the doyen of Irish Radio and TV, and on they came, the award-winners of the year, each one more remarkable than the next for outstanding achievement in every field of Irish life. By the time they got to me, 'The Greatest Living Entertainer', I was looking for somewhere to hide. A film of tributes had been assembled, many and warm-hearted from my BBC radio and television friends, and a couple from Ireland that majored on amused puzzlement, which came as no surprise as I had been greeted at the door of the hotel by an Irish newspaper reporter who, in place of congratulation, asked me how I felt about those who thought I shouldn't be getting the award. Later, I learned that an entire radio show on RTE had been given over to blunt discussion on my right to call myself an Irishman, not to mind an entertainer. And people still ask me if I'd fancy going back to Irish radio and television . . .

Actually, I'd gone back to Dublin a little earlier in the year to take part in a tribute by the music industry to an old pal, Ireland's premier radio disc jockey, Larry Gogan. Larry has always been that *rara avis* among presenters of all races: modest, unbegrudging, happy with his own success and that of others. So it was no hardship to join him and his family in another huge barn of a hotel, and lead the cheering for a good man. Apart from that, the remarkable aspect of the evening was that, smartly after the tribute, and with the coffee still as lukewarm as when it had arrived, the great dining hall was almost entirely empty.

Nobody had said goodnight, but we did, with a plane to catch the following morning. As we exited into the soft Irish rain, we saw where the missing hundreds had gone: every one of them, in the car park, in the rain, sucking desperately on a cigarette. No smoking anywhere indoors in Ireland. It's working. Everybody's outdoors.

I've been pretty begrudging myself about the annual award-fest for radio, the 'Sonys', which might be regarded as ungrateful, in view of the fact that I've won a few in my time. And it's got nothing to do with the debacle of the one I was awarded a couple of years ago. Rising gracefully from the Radio 2 table, I received the award and prepared to deliver a succinct homily to the assembled throng, by now well sauced, if not well fed. Why can no supposedly five-star hotel in London deliver a decent meal to more than twenty people? Anyway, as I launched into my address, up on stage came a large, overdressed woman who proceeded to follow me around, as I dodged about, trying to avoid her and say my few well-chosen words at the same time. It was an unequal contest; I cut it short and got off before she laid a glove on me. She wandered about for a while longer before the ever alert security led her gently to her table, where she sat down again on the dessert which had decorated her backside throughout the spectacle. No hard feelings; it could happen at any award ceremony, where people are so bored by endless presentations and speeches that they find consolation in drink.

Despite my pleading, Radio 2 submits my name and show every year for a Sony Award. I don't like it because, in my view, these awards are not presented on merit, but rather on a rotational basis – Buggins' turn, as they say. Come second this year? You'll be OK next year. Your radio station got nothing last year? Don't go away . . .

My main objection, until a couple of years ago, was that local radio, with its lesser resources, was pitched up against the might of the BBC networks. It was an unequal contest. The Sonys should be about rewarding the talents and efforts of local radio, both BBC and independent. Let the big boys play on their own and pick on somebody their own size.

I'm sure it seems like biting the hand that feeds me, criticising the Sony Awards, in view of the fact that this year they presented me with the ultimate accolade, the Gold Award; and because, in fairness, they have made considerable efforts to make the awards more inclusive: there are now gongs for the stations that, because of their size or geographical location, have only small audiences. These are the very heart and soul of radio, and to see the enthusiasm and the elation of the winners lifts the heart. It was these sentiments that were in my mind when I drafted my speech of acceptance for my Gold Award for Achievement:

Here I stand, a shining example of the old showbiz maxim: if you hang around long enough, they're bound to give you something. Mind you, this honour, combined with the knighthood, makes me wonder if the powers-that-be are not trying to tell me something as well . . .

But radio takes time. Television is the medium of the quick fix, radio is for the long run. You can walk through the doors of the Big Brother House completely unknown and, a week later, be one of the best-known faces in the country. Of course, it involves being interviewed by Davina McCall, but that's a small enough price to pay for fame and fortune. You can't do that on radio; it doesn't take days or weeks, it takes years. Years to build a relationship of trust and affection.

I came over here from Ireland in late 1969, unsung and unknown. The British public had never heard of me, yet the BBC, or specifically, Mark White, Assistant Head of Gramophone Programmes, gave me a daily show on Radios 1 and 2. Could that happen today? I don't think so. You see, radio has become infected with the television culture of instant fame, instant success. Give that television star a radio show! And it'll work for a few weeks of public curiosity, but unless that person has the necessary ingredients of voice, warmth, wit, intelligence and ability to identify and relate to his audience, in the long run, they're doomed to failure.

The success of Radio 2 is built on the familiarity, the very predictability of its presenters. They know us, we know them. And I hate to say this to the advocates of playlists, but my friend Paul Walters — sadly not with us tonight and sorely missed, and indisputably the finest music programmer in popular radio — has always said: 'The music is only important when it's wrong.' This is not the USA. Popular radio success, indeed all radio success, is built on presenters. Even classical music radio needs people with whom their public can identify. This is how the British public grew up with radio, and how it will always be.

So, forget the instant fix; it's not going to work in the long run that successful radio requires. Go out and find the voices and the personalities that are making radio work all over this country. Listen to local radio, commercial and BBC. Try hospital radio. They're out there, the ones with the gift. Find them, give them their own shows, have faith in them, and your judgement. And give them time. Time. Radio takes time. And mine is up . . .

Thank you, you do me great honour . . .

I like to think that it would have gone down well, if I had ever had the chance to deliver it. However, once again I was sandbagged by a woman. Not a tipsy woman who had sat in her dessert, and not really a woman, but Dame Edna Everage. The grande dame of the Antipodes made her entrance from the very top of the sweeping staircase that leads into the great ballroom of Grosvenor House. Acknowledging every hurrah, and pausing freely to bow and graciously smile, she made her regal way to the stage. It was like the arrival of the Queen of Sheba, and took about twenty minutes. Once on stage, the Dame was once again accorded her due accolade of praise, and milked it like a good 'un, with many a barbed quip. This took another two minutes, before she was kind enough to mention my name. I rose, and so, it must be said in due modesty, did the crowd. It hardly helped quell the apprehension gnawing at my very vitals at the prospect of having to follow one of the world's funniest acts. Things didn't get any better. As I arrived on stage, the Dame announced that she would read a poem that she had written in tribute to me. It was funny, witty, clever, and took another ten minutes while I hung about trying not to look like a lemon in front of thousands of my fellow broadcasters.

So I didn't deliver my speech, and I can't repeat what I actually said, but it was the kind of situation for which only forty years of experience can prepare you. I do remember saying that I wanted to share the award with dear Paul Walters, sadly not with us as he fights a grievous illness with courage and humour, and it was gratifying to hear the loud applause for a great producer and a lovely man. They stood up again when I left, but maybe it was because it was the final award and they were getting up to go anyway . . .

Naturally, my listeners were sparing with their enthusiasm in response to my triumph:

To: Terry Wogan
From: Ellie

Dear Terry *et al,*
  Surely 'outstanding achievement' suggests that there is still some achievement outstanding? It's celebrating the fact that you still haven't managed to do anything really impressive.
  Just a thought,
  Ellie
  P.S. Is it wrong that I'm 22 and listen to the show? Love the show. x

Don't ask how this slipped under the wire – I only encourage abuse.

To: Terry Wogan
From: Liz

Dear Terry
  Congrats on the latest award. Could this be linked to your

return from the recent hols, the outstanding achievement being that you turned up for work?

Liz (forever youngish)

That's more like it.

And this manages to combine both praise and blame, compliment and brick bat . . .

To: Terry Wogan
From: Katie Mallet

Dear Terry,

Congratulations for whatever.
Sir Terry's got a gold award,
But can't tell why he's got it,
Perhaps he knew, but like a Tog
Immediately forgot it,
But I can tell you what it's for –
For simply being there,
As like a warming duvet
He comforts us on air.
His voice wraps all around us,
And though it's getting old
It manages to stop us
Becoming tired and cold.
Byeeee.
Katie Mallett

There are far too many 'awards', and as a consequence they lack credibility. Who decides the winner? A panel? Who picked them? Are they entirely independent and unbiased in their judgements? In your dreams. Was it the public? Who counts the votes? Are there impartial observers to make sure it's all above board? Come on . . . As long as everybody knows that it's just a bit of fun, and the results are tomorrow's fish-and-chips wrapper, fine and dandy. But spare me the 'awards' that are based on the arbitrary, subjective opinions of a 'panel of judges'. You're not talking to a know-all know-nothing here; I've sat on panels, I've judged. All right, they've been beauty contests, but the same rules apply when you've got more than one judge: everybody thinks a different girl is the most beautiful, so the contestant that most of the judges thought was third best, wins. Eye of the beholder. As William Goldman said about Hollywood, and anybody who knows anything about radio, television and the theatre knows all too well, 'Nobody knows anything.' I always thought the emphasis was on 'anything', but my friend, the extremely bright producer Tom Webber, maintains it's on 'knows'. Either way, never a truer few words were spoken.

Of course, the public are even more quirky in their judgement of winners and losers, than panels of experts, juries and the Lords of Appeal. Just look at the bummer that they regularly select to represent the United Kingdom at the Eurovision Song Contest. I'm the spokesman, the cheerleader who's supposed to 'big-up' our song's chances, but every year at the end of *Making Your Mind Up*, the cold fingers of reality clutch at my vitals, and I know that the Great British Public has voted in their thousands yet again for some repetitive, imitative tosh that will rightly be dismissed out of hand by the discerning music-lovers of Moldova and the former Yugoslav Republic of Macedonia. Admittedly it's no easy task to pick something even remotely musical from the six songs preselected by the dead hand of another panel of 'experts', but at times it does seem that there are darker forces at work. Or at least a bloody-minded public resolve to have it their way.

Years ago, that fine singer, Michael Ball, put his tonsils on the block, where no other of his musical standing and ability was prepared to chance their reputation, by agreeing to sing the regulatory six songs for Europe and bellow the winner for Britain at the final, in Malmo. It's not without its own significance that no artist of Michael's stature has risked their neck for the old country since. As befits the Broadway and West End star that he has become, Ball gave his all to every last note of every one of the six contenders. But Stewart Morris, the producer, and the acknowledged maestro of musical television, knew the song that was going to win the UK the Eurovision. Paul Walters, no sluggard at picking a winner himself, agreed. As ever, my opinion counted for nothing, but I echoed the choice of the two great men. We were long overdue a win at the Eurosong, and this was the one – and, just as importantly, we had the singer to do it.

The trouble was, could the public be trusted to pick what was clearly the best song?

Despite decades of exposure to the Eurovision, watching little girls on stools singing to a guitar, or grey-beards from Denmark, or a couple of geezers round a piano from Ireland all win the thing, the British public still thinks a Eurosong is 'Puppet on a Boom Bang Making Its Mind Up'. Stewart Morris was worried; there was a headbanger in Michael Ball's six that they might go for. He tried to get me to praise it with faint damns, to emphasise that what we were looking for, the one that would knock 'em dead in Malmo, was a romantic ballad. We were whistling into the wind. Unerringly, the great British public voted with their feet, the ones that they could thump up and down on the floor. We took the 'Boom-Bang-a-Puppet' to the Eurovision final and came second. I swear that with a lesser singer than Michael Ball we would have brought up the rear.

Music is a matter of taste, subjective; so it's possible that our views on what song should win might be interpreted as elitist, and we've no guarantee that our choice would have won anyway, and we must bow to public opinion. Although . . . Is it only me, or has anyone else noticed a certain mischievous note that has crept into public voting since the growth of the 'reality' show? Time and again, on *Celebrity Big Brother*, *I'm a Celebrity, Get Me Out of Here!*, *Strictly Come Dancing*, *Just the Two of Us*, the meritorious, the intelligent, the sympathetic, the decent get turfed out by the public in favour of the coward, the whinger, the bully and the downright disgusting. And, of course, the mediocre, whom they inevitably pick as the winner. These pro-grammes are a slap in the face for anybody who thinks that they can define public taste. They are also a hard lesson to those television executives who imagine that they know about popu-larity – who the public likes, and who they don't.

It was particularly instructive to watch the first run of *Just the Two of Us*, in which, inexplicably, some established television presenters linked up with established pop singers for a vocal version of *Strictly Come Dancing*. As with that, so with the singing contest: it didn't matter what the judges said, it didn't matter whether they could sing, the public voted for the personality they *liked*. Or, in at least one case, for somebody without a note in her head, just for the hell of it. The old saw that 'nobody ever got poor by underestimating the public's taste' might possibly be true if you're running a supermarket, but if you want to do anything on television or radio, you'd better keep an eye and an ear out for the wit, the sense of the ridiculous and the subversive humour just below the surface that characterises the British public.

Éamon de Valera, like all great Irish leaders a hero to some, a villain to others, used to say: 'Whenever I want to know what the Irish people want, I look into my own heart,' condemning at least a couple of generations to his vision of Sinn Féin (ourselves alone), a ridiculous fairyland of whitewashed cottages, turf fires, comely maidens dancing at crossroads and relentless piety. People like me, with a daily audience of millions, thousands of whom communicate with me every week, must constantly be on our guard against falling into the trap of thinking that a passing glance at our own prejudices will give an insight into the public's frame of mind.

For reasons that escape me now, in 2002 I kept a diary. (Prince Charles kept a 'journal', which we all were privy to this year; what's the difference?) No more than the present tome, it's unremarkable stuff, but a salutary lesson in never trying to second-guess the public:

30 March 2002
Easter. Flowers, a card and an Easter egg from Patisserie Valerie on Marylebone High Street for Helen. Alan comes to play golf at Stoke Poges. Katherine and her boyfriend, Henry – and the almost human Spike – will be here at Hitcham Close tomorrow, and Mark and his partner Susan,

with eccentric schnauzer, Pop – will keep me company on Easter Monday, while Helen and Alan play Mixed Gruesomes at Stoke. That's OK – Mark's cooking.

As we watch a movie on Saturday evening, up flashes a message that the Queen Mother has passed away. Television and radio clear the decks for the obituary tributes that they have been planning, rewriting and rehearsing for forty years. Trouble is, the event still seems to have taken them all by surprise. Sky Television's reporter is a stumbling embarrassment; we switch to the voice of the nation, the BBC. It swiftly becomes apparent that handling an on-the-spot crisis which requires quick thinking and spontaneous responses is not Peter Sissons' forte. It's a hesitant coverage, with a lot of 'filling' from reporters. The woman reporting from outside Windsor Castle promises to talk with members of the public, who are flocking to the environs to pay their respects. Sissons returns to her after a few minutes, but she's alone. The mourning public are there, claims the reporter, but are being held back by police. Even as she speaks, a couple of passers-by stroll by the camera. It's obvious that there's nobody there, apart from a couple of tourists . . .

2 April 2002

The newspapers, the rabidly anti-BBC *Daily Mail* in particular, are having a field day. Prince Charles has pointedly recorded his tribute to his beloved grandmother with ITV, snubbing the BBC. This is grist to the *Mail*, and all of the rest of the print media, who would love to kick television and radio, and the BBC in particular, to death. It appears that the Prince and his mother, the Queen, have been deeply offended by the BBC's coverage of the Queen Mother's death. (Not true – it was just ITV's turn.) They apparently echo the *Daily Mail*'s view that her sad passing was not accorded sufficient time or dignity. The last straw appears to have been Peter Sissons' choice of tie colour: red. He says he was told not to wear black. Hanging, drawing and quartering is not good enough for him. Let him rot in the Tower! Lorraine Heggessey, Controller of BBC1, had better reserve a place on the nearest tumbril while she's at it – it was her decision to return to normal programming after two hours. And while the print media foam at the mouth, it appears that there were 100 phone calls of complaint to BBC TV about their coverage of events. And 700 more complaining that the evening schedule of programmes had been changed . . .

The newspapers have been preparing for years: the tributes to the Queen Mother, the special editions, with their photographs of the lady from her birth, the nostalgic supplements of the last 100 years, all will go on for some days yet, right up to the final tribute of her funeral. So, who's got it right, the papers or Lorraine Heggessey? There is a great sadness, I sense, at the passing of a great queen; nobody in British life was held in greater affection or esteem. But it's nothing like the outpouring of real grief that I remember gripping the nation at Diana's sudden tragic death. We still have to wait for the funeral, but I will be surprised if the Queen Mother's cortège brings weeping crowds to the streets in their thousands, as did Princess Diana's.

Some time ago, I was told that the Queen Mother had planned the route that her funeral would take. She had one unshakeable proviso: 'The procession must not pass that *awful* man's store . . .'

9 *April* 2002

Well, I was wrong, and so was everybody else who thought the nation largely unaffected by the old queen's death. Hundreds of thousands queued for hours to view her catafalque, a million lined the streets to mark her final passing. And it wasn't middle-class, middle England either. It was young and old, black and white, every stratum of society. And they cried: not the hysterical grief accorded Diana, Princess of Wales; more a genteel, discreet, British sobbing. The funeral was a magnificent spectacle, staged with extraordinary precision and discipline – and yet moving, particularly when the plaintive pipes rent the air. The Queen had asked that it be as much a celebration of her mother's life as a lament for her death, but there weren't many smiles. Prince Charles has taken his grandmother's death badly; nine days on he still looks on the point of bursting into tears.

Charles wears his emotions on his sleeve – the British expect imperturbability, if not stoicism, from their once and future King. Charles expresses his emotions and opinions freely: politics, architecture, farming, the environment. Nobody has elected him to speak on their behalf, and he has no qualifications, but he expects to be listened to. He wants to be one of us, but as the first among equals. His problem, and indeed that of his siblings, is that nobody has ever disagreed with him. Surrounded, as he has been all his life by sycophants and courtiers, who has ever sayed him nay? Whether he will ever mount the throne is doubt-ful; his mother looks as if she could outlive *her* mother, and it would be a brave prime minister who agreed to her abdication. It would be a shame if Charles doesn't accede; he is intelligent, concerned deeply with the country and its people and, in his Duchess, has a warm and supportive partner.

10

Home and away

In the early eighties, our friends Derrick and Mina Russell invited us down to stay in the house they'd just bought on Villamartin Golf Course, near Torrevieja, south of Alicante on the Costa Blanca of Spain. I've always loved the sun, and it was typical of Helen, who has always sheltered from it, that she was as enthusiastic as I was about the place. North of Alicante was Benidorm: 'English tea served here', 'full English break-fasts', real ale, Irish pubs, discos, all the cheap vodka and Spanish brandy you could drink, and, day and night, all the charm of an English country town on a Saturday night: lads and ladettes, drunk, doped and disorderly. I'd spent a holiday there myself in the sixties with my friend Mick Heary. And yes, the drink was cheap and plentiful, and we had plenty of it. And yes, we slept off our hangovers on the beach and boogied until dawn – but then the place had a charm, a still-Spanish innocence about it, enforced by Franco's Guardia Civil, who had a short way with anything or anybody who seemed to be undermining all that was best in Spanish life.

South of Alicante in 1983 were miles of deserted beaches, undeveloped land given over to agriculture, the kind of Spain that I remembered from twenty years before – small towns, a gentle, unhurried way of life, and, even better, in Villamartin, an empty golf course. A friendly clubhouse, a few villas on the first fairway, just turn up, pay a pittance of a green fee, and play. Within a year we had bought a place overlooking the sea, with a garden, a pool and a maid, Josefa, who took at least three years to get over the loss of the previous owners, a Spanish doctor and his family from Murcia, the main city of the region. We had a gardener, Bartolo, full of charm, who never lifted a finger in the garden until he heard on the grapevine that we were coming over, then he'd put in a team to cut the grass, trim the hedges and clean the pool. And every time he'd have an excuse for the reasons why the fruit trees had perished and the flowers had died. It was the wind from the sea, the red dust from Africa, and in no way due to the fact that the trees and the plants had not seen a drop of water since we were last there.

Our friends, the Clancys, also bought a place in Villamartin, and they were followed by many of their friends from Lahinch, Co. Clare. In a very short time, Villamartin became Lahinch-by-the-Mediterranean. Our children loved it, and because Cabo Roig, where we lived, was almost entirely populated by Spanish families swapping the intense heat of inland Murcia for cooler sea breezes, they soon picked up a working knowledge of colloquial Spanish. Later on, Alan taught English in Murcia, and Katherine's university degree is in Hispanic Studies. She spent a year in Complutense University in Madrid, which knocked all the regional dialect out of her, and she still looks down from her dizzy Castilian heights on the rest of us and our rough country Spanish. Mind you, my grasp of the language was, at best, tenuous. I'm a mimic, another way of saying I've a 'good ear' for languages. It's why I'm doing the job I'm in. I'd never have passed that audition all those years ago at Radio Eireann if I hadn't been able to fake the Gaelic, French, Italian and German. Spanish I learned by a process of osmosis — all my verbs were in the infinitive, with scant regard for tense, all my nouns were singular, and careless of gender. I didn't know much, but what I knew I could pronounce correctly, and the Spanish will tolerate a lot from a foreigner who tries to speak their language.

As the children grew older, so our little deserted corner of Spain began to grow up too; almost overnight there were bars and discos, and they became creatures of the night, sleeping during the sunlit days to the annoyance of their parents. A story as old as time . . .

As the years went by, Josefa, our maid, began to warm to us. We learned to pay her a little more than she expected, and *olé!* she began to display her skill with skillet and pan. I never order paella or tortilla now, not since Josefa. She would spend a whole day cosseting the paella pan, clicking her tongue at what she saw as the inordinate amount of chicken we asked her to put in it. She grew to love our children, and when Alan was teaching in Murcia and living at the weekends in Cabo Roig, she would invite him to join her family for dinner in her little house in San Miguel de Salinas.

The changes came gradually, and then with almost breakneck speed. We first began to notice the developments on the hitherto deserted fields between Alicante airport and Torrevieja. Every couple of months, new apartment blocks, rows of villas of every colour, shape and size; Torrevieja, a charming coastal town with a pretty marina, where you could stroll and take a dry sherry with your tapas, became a forest of cranes. The traffic became so bad they built a bypass, and the jerry-built little houses and ugly apartments staggered along beside the road. Villamartin Golf Club acquired a new owner and what seemed like a thousand back-to-back villas. In a year, the course was crowded every day. The owner of our little promontory, Cabo Roig, sold much of the land to a developer with the usual results – houses and apartments squeezed into every available space.

Still, for a couple of years, we were happy enough – we could sit in our garden, surrounded by hedges and trees, and ignore the changing face of our Spain. Then our trees and hedges began to die, and when we began to taste the salt in our showers and swimming pool, we understood why: in order to keep up the water pressure to cope with the enormous increase in demand, the local council had hit upon a cunning plan – they had introduced sea water into the domestic pipes . . . Now, the flowers and fruit trees had no chance, and the grass was going the way of the trees and hedges. Then an empty building on the cliffs just in front of our house, a former jail which had been deserted for years, became a barracks for the Spanish equivalent of the Special Boat Squadron. *Apocalypse Now* came to Cabo Roig. I remember sitting in our garden with our friends, Hacker and Kits, watching the military helicopters whirr deafeningly overhead while their occupants abseiled into the sea. A noise matched only by the din of the rough soldiery every evening. Only the Spanish would carry out dangerous military operations in a residential area, yards off a marina and beach crowded with holidaymakers . . .

It was time to go, and not only because the area was going to hell in a handcart. Our young people had outgrown the urge for all-night bars and music and were seeking more mature pleasures. I love the Spanish, for all their lack of civic pride, their carelessness, the corruption that was endemic, at least when I was there. For all their foolish pride, they're a friendly, warm, hospitable people. The entire Spanish coastline, from Barcelona to Cadiz, has become a monument to greed, but the cities and towns of the interior retain the dignity and splendour of the old Spain. Burgos, where they carve the lamb with a spoon, Zaragoza, where the morcilla, the black pudding, is 'historic', to plagiarise another man who loves his food . . .

We put the house in Cabo Roig on the market with the same agent who had sold it to us twelve years earlier, and in a remarkably short time he sold it to a Dutchman who didn't seem to care about salt in his water, houses all over his golf course, and soldiers in his back yard. We'll never go back – we probably wouldn't recognise the place anyway – but there will always be memories: the *gambas rojas*, the huge grilled prawns, in a little restaurant named 'Moderno' in a village called San Javier which had a lemon-coloured church; 'Moderno' was always deserted when we ate there, only when we were leaving, at about eleven o'clock, would the locals begin to drift in. That's another thing I admire about the Spanish: their digestion. They don't eat breakfast, have a sandwich or a cake at about eleven in the morning, lunch at three in the afternoon, and, at least in Madrid, dinner at anything up to one o'clock the following morning.

I bought a boat in Spain – always a mistake. Little boats are like lawnmowers: no matter how much care you take when you're putting them away in the winter, they never start in the spring. Still, when we did manage to get the thing going, it was fun to chug around to deserted bays. Then, one hot day, as we lolled about, once again with Hacker and Kits Browning, the damn boat inexplicably stalled and stopped dead. There was nothing for it but for the ladies to stay aboard while Kits and I waded through the shallows up into a little place where we hailed a taxi, whose driver obviously didn't mind his back seat being covered in sand and sea water. Back we went to Cabo Roig marina, where everybody was out to lunch. We waited impatiently, ever conscious of our wives slowly sizzling to a frazzle in an open boat in the Spanish sun. Eventually the boat men turned up, and we set out in one of theirs for our becalmed craft, with two ladies done to a turn.

You hardly need me to tell you what happened when we got there. The Spanish boatman stepped aboard, fixed the key on to a lock from which it had slipped, turned the key, and started the boat. They had explained this 'dead man's lock' thing, or whatever it was called, when I'd bought the boat, but I'd for-gotten. The boatman looked at me pityingly, and I'd rather draw a veil over the comments of my wife and friends. I sold the boat shortly afterwards; I was never so glad to get rid of anything. Have I mentioned to you already about me and inanimate objects? We're incompatible . . .

For the next year or so, Helen and I took our holidays else-where. We went for a golfing holiday, to the marvellous Boulders Resort, near Phoenix, Arizona, where they clean your clubs before every round and remember your name. The *casitas*, little pueblo-type cottages, are delightful, unobtrusively scattered in the *arroyos* of this green oasis in the middle of a desert. If only some Spanish developers had taken a look at this before they did their worst . . . The food was delicious, the room service impeccable, and every morning, as you drew the blinds and stepped out on to the little patio, a wildlife experience: quail, wild boar, coyote, deer, chipmunks, strolling by as if they owned the place, even stopping graciously to taste a little of our breakfast. And that's the only cavil I have about the place – breakfast. Not just Boulders' breakfasts, American breakfasts in general. The coffee tastes of nothing, you eat bacon with your fingers, grits are an inedible mystery, the sausages are an insult to a proud tradition, there's fruit all over the plate, and are they really expecting you to pour that maple syrup over everything? OK, I *do* like that Canadian bacon you eat with your fingers . . .

When the children were young, we took many a holiday in the States – to Florida, where they lost our luggage, Key Biscayne, and then, in a big old air-conditioned gas-guzzler, across the State, to Walt Disney World in Orlando. As we trundled along, suddenly a sunny day went dark. I pulled in off the highway to find the air alive with insects, and the entire car covered in the little blighters. The windscreen wipers couldn't cope, and we limped slowly into a nearby garage. The air was still thick with these creatures, their millions blotting out the sun. I asked the attendant hosing down every car that came in the reason for this biblical plague. 'It's the love bug,' he said. 'Every year, 'bout this time, those good ol' boys get to matin', and they just don't care who knows it.' The clouds of love soon passed, but long after we've forgotten Walt Disney World and its delights, my family will remember those gallant bugs, giving their all for love, even as they crashed to oblivion on our windscreen.

Another year, we all went to the West Coast, to San Francisco, where we stayed in a hotel on the Embarcadero. The same hotel where Mel Brooks shot his movie about fear of heights, *High Anxiety*. He'd picked his location well: the hotel had a dizzyingly high glass dome above the atrium lobby, from where a glass-walled lift whizzed you vertiginously to the bedrooms. Ours was on the twentieth floor. In *High Anxiety*, Mel Brooks can be seen gibbering with fear in that self-same elevator, and then edging his way to his room facing the wall, with his back to the huge drop to the atrium floor. For Mel Brooks, read Helen Wogan, whose fear of heights easily matched that of the movie's character. A little later, we moved to the second floor and took the stairs to our room . . .

From 'Frisco we took the Pacific Highway to Pebble Beach, then on to Lake Tahoe and, finally, Yosemite National Park. Helen and I often wonder how we did all this with a car full of children and not a care in the world. And then we burst into our Maurice Chevalier/Hermione Gingold duet: 'Ah yes – I remember it well . . .' Ah, me lost youth . . .

The wilderness is all the Americans have in the way of ancient history, and they attempt to preserve it in quaint ways: my children were incensed to discover that there were no radios nor television in the hotel. The scenery and the wildlife dissolved the disappointment soon enough, and we went riding on cow-ponies, the one and only time I've ever been on a horse in my life. Why do people always imagine that, if you're Irish, you have a natural affinity with horse flesh? They've seen *The Commitments*, with the kids keeping the horses on the waste ground outside the terrible Dublin Ballymun flats now flattened, thank the Lord and they've been to Cheltenham, with the Irish being more Irish than they'd ever dare to be back home, but when I was growing up in Limerick, close to some of the greatest horse-rearing country in the world, nobody I knew had ever been on a horse, nor wanted to. Anyway, this little ol' cow-pony trotted, cantered and walked just as if I was in charge. Somebody helped me off the critter and I walked away like John Wayne; I know now why he walked like that . . .

While we were in Yosemite, it was Katherine's fifth birthday. We'd got all her cards and presents, but for some reason, which in retrospect seems a cruel joke to play on a little girl, we pretended we'd forgotten. Nobody mentioned the birthday all day, and the poor girl became more and more silent. We'd booked a table on the terrace for dinner, and, on cue, in came the waiters with a huge cake, ablaze with candles, singing 'Happy Birthday to You'. I can still see her face – the surprise, the joy and the tears of happiness. We fed some of the birthday cake to the racoons, and although I've had more than my share of happy memories, that was an evening that I can conjure up without even closing my eyes. Looking back, I see that I have bored you with this story before, and indeed there may be one or two more in this sturdy tome, but as you get older, most memories fade – only the very special ones remain, and they're the ones that old geezers tell again and again . . .

People often ask if we've kept a home in Ireland, and the answer is no. We spent four idyllic years in our little bungalow on Killiney Hill, Co. Dublin. It was where our first son, Alan, was born, and we've only happy memories of the place, but we had to sell it to buy our first home in Britain. So having sold our hacienda in Spain, we thought it mightn't be a bad idea to refresh our Irish roots, and Helen and I flew into Cork, and then on to

Kenmare. It's a lovely town, its shops and houses every colour of the rainbow, every second one a pub or a restaurant, and the location of, at least in my opinion, the two best hotels in Ireland, Sheen Falls Lodge, and the Park. Just outside town is the Ring of Kerry Golf Club, which surely can challenge any in the world for the sheer beauty of its location. Look across the still waters of the broad Kenmare River estuary to the blue hills of Gougane Beara, with the Atlantic beyond, and even a three-putt won't take the beatific grin off your face.

On Helen and I went to Waterville, another great golf club, where, if the wind is up, you can hit the best drive of your life and the ball will still come back to your feet. Then to Killarney, still beautiful in its lakes and mountains, for all the tacky commercialism of the town itself, and Tralee, where I introduced the first 'Rose of Tralee' International Beauty Contest all those years ago. It's still going. Irish Television gives it prime-time coverage every year, in the face of accordionists from Kerry, nose-flutes from Paraguay and banjos from Mississippi. No swimsuits, of course – this is County Kerry, not Las Vegas, Nevada.

We crossed the Shannon and stayed at Ashford Castle, a former pile of the Guinness family (the riches an ould pint of stout can bring . . .) and sailed across Lough Corrib into Joyce country, so called because every second person there bore that name in a previous century, and not in honour of the birth there of Helen's father, Tim Joyce, although he stoutly declared it so, and indeed would fight any man who denied it. Up to Westport and more golf, this time in the shadow of Croagh Patrick, Ireland's penitential mountain, up which thousands climb, some in bare feet, for all sorts of reasons apart from the glory of God and to pay for their sins. They do it for special intentions: the health of a loved one, the birth of a child, the passing of an exam.

There's another pilgrimage in Ireland, Lough Derg, where, again, thousands flock every year for their own reasons. Three days and nights of prayer, privation and starvation on an island in the middle of a lake. Some of the most unlikely people I know have 'done' Lough Derg: rascals, rogues, lechers. And Helen Wogan, just to tip the balance in favour of the good guys. She said that the pepper in hot water that they give you at the end of the ordeal was the finest dish she's ever tasted. Faith . . . it's a gift.

We flew back from Shannon with our hearts full of Ireland, but somehow we never pursued the idea of having a place there again. I suppose it's because the months we'd enjoy most in Ireland are the times we enjoy best in Britain. Although Ireland, its people and their attitudes are different, we needed a more marked contrast in life and culture. And then, one Sunday, I found it: an article on south-west France, the old Gascony. It talked of tranquillity, rolling hills, sunflowers, vineyards and space, lots of space. In an unprecedented move, at least for me, I followed it up, and in July 1996 we travelled to the capital of the department of Gers, the lovely town of Auch, with its magnificent cathedral. We were ready to stay there and look around the region, but the agent, an Englishman named Ian Purslow, persuaded us to try instead a bed and breakfast, a *chambre d'hôte* that he knew, deep in the heart of the countryside. A lovely house, in a beautiful park of magnificent trees, with vineyards on all sides, and a church.

The hosts, a charming English couple, Jean and John, had not only refurbished, but rebuilt the little chateau, restoring the plumbing, the heating, the electricity, and had built a lovely swimming pool in their spare moments. Then, after a delicious *déjeuner sur l'herbe*, they told us that they were returning to England, to be closer to their first grandchild, and the house was for sale. We looked at other places; indeed, we returned later that year to look at some more, but it was no contest. I knew I would never have the time, or the patience, to restore an old ruin of a farmhouse, or rebuild a crumbling chateau, and this place had everything in working order.

Helen and I flew into Toulouse, just after that Christmas, for our first stay in our very own French chateau. It was snowing, hard. After a perilous drive, we arrived in six inches of snow to our freezing French dream, which looked like turning into a nightmare, with no heating and a sudden plunge into utter darkness as we attempted to plug in an electric heater and fused every light in the place. That first night in our new home, lit by candles and sleeping under six layers of blankets, is another memory that I'll carry with me to the grave. The following day, I found the fuses, a helpful farmer brought us the necessities on a tractor, and ten years on, although we had our doubts on that first night, Helen and I don't regret a thing.

The Gers retains its languid, unspoiled beauty, the people are courteous and friendly, the sunflowers bloom, the vineyards march in their precise lines up and over the gentle hills. The fruit, the vegetables, even the fish, from the Atlantic, an hour and a half away, are a world away from the supermarkets of Britain. The Gers is famous for the heartiness of its cuisine, although I'm bound to say that if you're not a fan of our feathered friend, the duck, you might go hungry. Foie, confit, magret, aiguillettes, rillets, gesiers — that one small bird could do so much. The French get their money's worth out of the duck. For instance, last year we went with friends to one of the innumerable fêtes that every French village and hamlet throws every year. This was 'Demoiselles' night — melon, duck, cheese, dessert, wine and armagnac, ten euro per person. The 'demoiselles' were the carcasses of duck, after all the aforementioned delights had been taken away. No prizes for finding any meat on them, but there should have been. Still, everybody chewed and gnawed, the bones went into huge bags, and, given the thriftiness of the French, were probably recycled for pebble-dashing. Next year we'll go to the same village for the 'Escargot' festival. Just so long as they don't take the snails out beforehand and expect us to eat the shells . . .

A couple of years ago, a native of the south-west of France, having given the vin du pays a severe thrashing the night before, clambered unsteadily into his Deux Chevaux to go and collect his morning baguette at the boulangerie. Some time later his little car was found wrapped around one of those magnificent trees that line, so graciously, the little roads of France. The car was a write-off, and so, unfortunately, was he. The driver was subsequently found to have the alcohol from the night before still lapping up against his back teeth. Not to put too fine a point on it, the poor fellow was still drunk when he left the road and hit the tree. The car/tree confrontation is one that is not that unusual on the bosky routes of France. A local deputy, however, came up with a solution: cut the trees down. If the tree hadn't been there, he shrewdly reasoned, the car could have continued its erratic way until coming to a halt in a field of waving corn, or a vineyard, with little chance of loss of life. It's a tribute to the French way of life that when I last looked, this solution to drunk driving was still being considered by the local department. Can't a man have a drink without some blasted tree leaping out on the road to kill him?

What put me in mind of this was a conversation with a television cameraman who told me that he had just completed a film on a new Swedish invention, a collapsible lamppost which not only caves in when hit by a car but, by some Nordic trickery, also slows the careering vehicle down. 'Splendid!' I hear you cry, 'let's hear it, for the clever, caring Swedes.' Not everybody feels that way, least of all in Sweden, where there have been protests that the invention interferes with the inalienable right of every Swede to commit suicide when the mood takes him. Lampposts and trees – they'll be the death of us all . . .

2003 was a great year for the Wogans: two weddings, no funerals; although the present Lady Wogan might have been excused for buckling under the strain of organising a summer wedding in the Gers, and a winter one in Bucks.

Mark, our second son, and Susan Acteson, his beautiful fiancée, decided that they wanted to be married from our house in France. It was all the vindication we ever needed for buying the place. There was much to be done, most of it from a distance, but Helen Wogan had the energy and determination of ten. She visited traiteurs and restaurants before selecting someone who would cater for the reception, which was going to be held in the garden for about 150 people. Then there was the marquee and the band for dancing, and the string quartet for the church, hotel rooms to be reserved in every surrounding town and village, and, finally, the church itself. It's a beautiful little church, at the top of our parc, but it hadn't been used for years.

We asked the parish priest, Abbé Commenge, for help. He's everybody's idea of a French priest – rotund, apple-cheeked and kindly. And without a word of English. It was to be an ecumenical service, Susan being Church of England, and Mark, Catholic. I doubt if we'd have got to first base without the help of our great and good friend Father Brian D'Arcy, but after a lot of toing and froing, bishops on both sides of the Channel were placated. It was then that Abbé Commenge came into his own. Although he was committed to another wedding on the same day, he arranged for the reconsecration of the church. Not only that, but the local commune refurbished, restored and repainted the little church, just for our wedding, without being asked, and without payment. It's a constant source of pride and joy that it has been revived as a place of worship, and Mass is once again celebrated regularly there.

Susan and her family arrived a couple of days before the Big One, and stayed with our friends Nicky and Michael just up the little road. Mark and Alan arrived a couple of days early too, having driven my car, the bridal limousine, all the way from home. Abbé Commenge came to dinner, with the con-celebrants, my two friends from *Pause for Thought*, Father Brian D'Arcy and Canon Roger Royle. The guests rang to confirm their arrival from every *relais, ferme d'auberge, chambre d'hôte* and hotel in the region.

As the sun rose on the morning of the wedding, we knew it was going to be a hot one. The guests began to arrive, reflecting the glorious summer day, the ladies all glamour, hats and dresses of every hue, the men in their lightweight suits and panama hats. Monsieur Bousigon, a neighbour and the sexton, rang the bell and everybody made their way through the parc to the church. It looked like a painting from a time long gone, as they strolled, all finery and elegance, through the trees in the sunlight. It was a beautiful ceremony, with Brian and Roger speaking both truly and wittily; the quartet played and the church was full of flowers and candles and goodwill to all men. And 150 people all crammed into a space designed for half that number.

Outside, the temperature climbed to 103 degrees; inside – well, how half the congregation didn't expire on their little wooden seats I'll never know. I suppose that it's a sadness, but Mark and Susan's wedding day is destined to be remembered not for its charm, its gaiety, or even the beauty of the bride but the heat that had every lady fanning herself with a hymn sheet and every man's shirt stuck to his back. Water, not champagne or wine, was the drink of choice; indeed, there was enough champagne and wine left over to more than cater for the thirst of the 220 guests at Katherine's wedding the following December.

Despite the heat, only the parfait melted, and the reception was all fun and laughter and the occasional tear, just as it should be. The heat of the day blended into the warmth of the evening, the live band struck up, the dancing began, Susan and Mark sang to each other, and their perfect day drew to a close as they set off for their hotel and their honeymoon down the Pacific Highway that Mark had never forgotten from that family holiday years ago. The following day, we held a lunch in the marquee for all the guests, a buffet, and Monsieur Bousigon, who had been so instrumental, with his wife, in preparing the church, instructed everybody in the arcane art of sucking armagnac through a sugar cube. And, hallelujah!, it rained. It's the only time I've ever heard an Anglo-Irish crowd applaud the rain. More speeches, more laughter, more of whatever you're having yourself; and then it was time for the panama hats and the summer dresses to depart, leaving Helen and me with the happiest memories of one of the happiest days of our life.

My beautiful daughter, Katherine Helen Bernadette Wogan, had always dreamed of a winter wedding, and on 6 December 2003 her dream came true. She has never really been that enthused over the 'Bernadette', claiming that her mother chose it for her confirmation name without consultation, at a time when Katherine was too young to put up much of an argument. It's certainly not something you could accuse Katherine of in maturity. This is a modern young woman with a mind of her own, a forceful way with words, and a short-arm left cross of which Sir Henry Cooper would not have been ashamed. In this, she is not unlike her mother, who can also punch her weight. (Incidentally, Mark Wogan's confirmation name should not go unremarked; as his brother Alan reminded us at Mark and Susan's wedding, my eleven-year-old second son insisted on 'Mark' for his third Christian name. Mark Paul Mark Wogan – those who know and love him were not surprised.)

Mark and Susan's French country wedding took some organising, particularly as it was being done from a distance, but in retrospect it was a languid *déjeuner sur l'herbe* compared with Katherine's. Again, it was to be an ecumenical wedding, her fiancé, Henry Cripps, being Church of England and Katherine, a Catholic. This time, the nuptials were to be celebrated in the Church of England by our local vicar, the Revd Alan Dibden, with my redoubtable old chum, Father Brian D'Arcy, keeping a close eye on any loose Reformist talk or heretical tendency.

Katherine and I arrived by vintage Rolls, entering the beautiful Church of St Nicholas Taplow, aglow with candles and the warmth of family and friends. Creamy white roses were everywhere, trailing over the pews with ivy and lilies, but my daughter and I were just concentrating on making it to the altar rails without breaking down. We nearly did it, too, until we both caught sight of the groom, dear Henry, his chin quivering, his eyes full of tears. Katherine nearly fainted at the altar rails, just as her mother had done in Rathmines Church, Dublin, a lifetime before. They signed the register to a lovely choral arrangement of Elgar's 'Nimrod', and the bride and groom exited, all tears forgotten, with smiles and laughter, to 'Adeste Fideles'.

Thanks to our friends from the north, Mahoods, the marquee that covered the terrace and lawn was truly a winter wonderland. Christmas trees from Henry's parents' land, with a dusting of fake snow and twinkling with pea-lights; great pots of white-painted twigs; the theme of white roses with amaryllis carried through to every table; glass panels on both sides looking out on to trees and bushes of the garden covered with lights. And the pièce de résistance: the vaulted room of the marquee covered in black cloth with a thousand little stars shining through. In the course of my speech, with which I will not trouble you, I made passing reference to the Mahood's enormous structure, saying that, along with the Great Wall of China, it was probably the only other man-made object that could be seen from the moon. They called it 'Terry's Tent'. We went north for the food as well, and Heathcotes did us proud, right down to mini fish and chips and hamburgers in the wee small hours. However, the one thing everybody who was there seems to remember, just as they remember the heat of Mark and Susan's great day, was the *coup de théâtre*, as the curtain behind the top table was drawn back to reveal the dance floor and Jamie Cullum with an eight-piece band.

Henry and Katherine took the floor to 'More', and the hooley was off and running. They boogied to the fish and chips and far beyond; Henry and Katherine left, trailing laughter and tears, a friend caught her bouquet, and married herself, this year. Helen Wogan breathed a sigh of sadness and satisfaction – nothing would ever be quite the same again. The little Wogan family was growing bigger, and better, and now there's Freddie, our only grandchild to date . . .

On the other side of the Irish Sea, the other branch of the family was set to spread its wings as well. In 2004, my brother Brian's daughter Jane kept the Wogan wedding ball in the air by marrying a New Yorker, Richie Notar, in Portofino, in a beautiful monastery overlooking the Gulf of Genoa and the spectacular Ligurian coast. We stayed in Santa Margarita in the kind of charming little hotel that only Italy can provide, a simple room with a little balcony overlooking palm trees and the sea, where we ate warm croissants and drank good coffee, and dreamed of being young again . . .

The night before the wedding, everybody gathered in a quay-side restaurant, a get-together to bind the two families and their friends. The priest who was celebrating the marriage, a Jesuit from Rome, came too. With his guitar. Useless for me to protest that one of the reasons I left old Ireland was to get away from singing priests. The warm Italian night air was pierced by Elvis

Presley favourites, and every rock 'n' roll rabble-rouser from the long-dead past.

The trouble about singing priests is the same problem we have with the Royal Family: nobody ever tells them to shut up. Everybody applauds and sings along because it's a priest with a guitar. He's never been told that he's rubbish, and so he infests every social gathering to which he's invited, in the mistaken notion that he can not only play the guitar, but sing as well. He came to the wedding reception, of course, and I was relieved that there was no sign of the dreaded guitar. Silly me – he had it under the table all the while. He did requests in between the courses. Richie and Jane have since had a little daughter, and Richie said that on first sight, she had little piggy eyes like her grandfather, my brother Brian. She'll be lucky – Brian has the light, bright blue eyes of our father, Michael T. Little Freddie Cripps, Katherine and Henry's son, has Helen's father's magnificent head of auburn hair. So it goes on, the only immortality . . .

11

Where do we go from here?

⟳

Over the past couple of years, television shows have come and gone. *Children in Need* and the Eurovision are hardy annuals, and I count myself very fortunate to be associated with both of them. Along with my radio show, it's more than enough to keep me going; I'm not exactly looking for work. I've very few ambitions left for radio or television; looking back, it's hard to believe how much I've done, how far I've come since that first evening in the old Henry Street studios of Radio Eireann in Dublin, and the cattle market report, my first broadcast.

With the seemingly ever increasing success of *Wake Up to Wogan* on the radio, it has occurred to some BBC Television executives that possibly I may still have something to offer. Whenever I meet one or more of them socially, it's the same old song: 'We really *must* find something for you on television . . .'

I've heard it so often I could put it to music. They never follow through, of course; if anything happens, it'll be an accident. Most of what happens on television is an accident. Sometimes it's fatal, and less frequently you walk away unscathed, with a BAFTA. Bruce Forsyth's reincarnation on *Strictly Come Dancing* is entirely due to a young producer who, pretty unfamiliar with the great man's work, saw him play a blinder on *Have I Got News For You*, and, bingo!, the old boy's back in town. Who could have predicted that ballroom dancing would make a comeback? There are people on the sixth floor of Television Centre who still don't believe it. But what have we always said? Right. In this business, nobody knows anything . . .

As far as I'm concerned, BBC TV can't think outside the box, so it's *Making Your Mind Up*, selecting the UK's entry for the Eurovision, or a cheap and cheerful pull-through of the Song Contest's sillier moments. *Auntie's Bloomers*, of course, could have turned me into a fatter, smaller version of Denis Norden if I hadn't walked away. Then there's *Points of View* – always a joy to do, but shunted around the Sunday evening schedules like the stopgap they obviously think it is. If you can find it, even the duration varies – and they don't show it during the peak viewing months of autumn and winter. Obviously they're not really interested in viewers' opinions, otherwise the programme would be given the status and time it deserves. As I know from my radio show, the public love to comment on what they see on the box, but ten minutes on a Sunday evening in the summer is hardly throwing open the network for viewers' opinions.

However, the world of television no longer revolves solely around the BBC, and a couple of years ago Chris Evans, just returned from his two-year sabbatical and newly wed to the delightful Billie Piper, sold my friend Kevin Lygo, at that time Head of Everything on Channel Five, now just Five, on the idea of Gaby Roslin and me presenting a daily morning magazine show. It seemed a good idea at the time – and Chris is one of the great salesmen of our time, so I bought into it. The trouble was, Kevin Lygo bought out, just before the thing started, so we lost our most important supporter. He headed off into the sunlit uplands of Channel 4, Ant and Dec, Davina McCall and *Big Brother*. I should have seen the writing on the wall then, remembering what had happened to *Wogan's Web*, when its most important mentor, BBC Head of Daytime, moved on just before the series started.

The Terry and Gaby Show came live from County Hall, London, with marvellous views of the Thames and the Mother of Parliaments, but no clear view of what it was or who it was aimed at. Gaby ratcheted up her bubbly personality several notches, and never really lost her conviction that we were trying to appeal to the readers of *Heat*, or those viewers who had made her into a star, with Chris, on *The Big Breakfast*. Although we'd worked together amicably and successfully on *Children in Need* for ten years, we never really gelled on *Terry and Gaby*. I should have been able to carry my radio audience with me, but after a couple of weeks they stopped writing about the show; they had lost interest. It was too noisy, too frantic for them, and it wasn't me. Not that it wasn't a cheery, lively little show, but it needed much more publicity than Five was prepared to pay for, and, rather like the apathy shown by listeners on my return to radio, you can't get an audience if they don't know you're there.

Despite the fact that I was convinced that we were screaming into the wind, directing our efforts in entirely the wrong direction, it was one of the happiest shows I've ever done. I will always remember Danny Baker saying, at the little party we held when Five pulled the plug, that all the young floor managers, researchers, production assistants and runners should treasure the memory of *Terry and Gaby*, because nothing they would ever do in the future on television would ever give them so much fun again.

Lack of publicity was not a mistake UKTV Gold made with *Wogan – Now and Then*. They covered any available site with huge posters of our hero as he was and as he is. It's not the most salubrious sight at quarter to seven on a Monday morning as you're bowling down the A40 into London, to be confronted with, not one, but two large pictures of yourself, the one rosy-cheeked and fulsomely sideburned, and the other a raddled shadow of his former self. And it wasn't only on the roadways of Britain that people's sensibilities were assailed; posters were all over London's underground as well.

To see yourself as others see you is bad enough. To see yourself as they saw you twenty years ago . . . You'll see the word 'legend' freely bantered about here. I'm sure that it's meant in a complimentary way but you and I know very well that 'legend', like 'icon' and 'veteran', is merely a euphemism for 'past it', 'over the hill', and 'forgotten but not gone'. My radio listeners were on to it, like ravening wolves: 'Those posters on the Underground are a jolly good idea – they keep people away from the edge of the platform.' 'I thought ventriloquism was dead and buried – which one of you is Archie Andrews?' They speculated cruelly on the name and very nature of the programme. 'What's it called – "*Wogan, Never Again?*" "*Not Again?*" "*Here and There?*" "*Over and Out?*"'

Whatever about the programme, the posters paid off, and after the first week of the show, UKTV Gold were taking full-page ads in *Broadcast* to boast of an unprecedented (for satellite programmes) audience of 1,700,000 viewers. I was surprised, delighted and not a little flattered that major stars were prepared to rake over the coals that were twenty years cold, but they came, and happily. We interspersed the retrospective with names that I hadn't had the pleasure of interviewing before, like Jordan, Ricky Tomlinson, Simon Cowell, but it was a real pleasure to see again Rory Bremner, Nigel Havers, Christopher Lee, Eric Sykes and all the old Wogan riff-raff; and David Icke, no longer a gentle soul convinced that he was descended from the God-head, that wearing turquoise was the way to salvation, and that we were all doomed, but now a ranting demagogue convinced that we were all manipulated sheep, and, of course, all doomed ... The production team and the crew made this another show that was a pleasure: relaxed and fun.

At the time of writing, I don't know how many more *Now and Thens* are in the locker, but I suspect that whatever their success, there must be a limit to the number of stars who want to see themselves as they were, apart from the considerable number who have fallen off the perch in the intervening years. The general consensus was that *Wogan – Now and Then* was a good thing, and I'll take that, because you're never going to do better. The begrudgers we have always with us, whether it be through misanthropy, jealousy, sheer bloody-mindedness or downright nastiness; you have to learn to accept the knocks, however mean-spirited or unnecessarily vitriolic. It would be a queer career indeed if you didn't sometimes deserve them. As I've said before, the wounds could be fatally deep if you don't understand that for every one who listens and watches with pleasure, there's another who loathes the very ground you walk on, and others – the vast majority of the population – who couldn't care less, and who think, whenever they bother, that if you're not Michael Aspel, you could well be Tony Blackburn.

This is one up on that fine body of men, the security guards at BBC Television Centre. They don't know who anybody is. All they know is that it's their job to keep you out. Nowadays, their ignorance can be excused by the fact that many seem to have only lately arrived in Britain, and could hardly be expected to know who the Prime Minister is, not to mind the Director-General or some fly-by-night hobbledehoy. The result is a daily traffic jam on Wood Lane as the queue of lorries, vans and cars passes excruciatingly slowly through the one narrow entrance gate. It's a good job nothing is 'live' any more on BBC TV; there'd be a lot of missed deadlines. It's not new of course, it was ever thus. Jobsworths will be jobsworths, and who do you think *you* are, anyway? I've been called 'Logan?' a lot lately, but even when I was 'Wogan', I had to endure my share of 'Who? Why?' and 'Just a minute while I ring reception and see if they know anything about you'. I mind well the occasion when dear old Kenny Everett was kept waiting so long that he turned his car around and went home. An hour later, blind panic in the studio at the non-appearance of the star: 'The audience is in, we start in ten minutes, where is he?' 'He's at home, says he thought you didn't want him today . . .'

The best BBC executives of my generation, David Hatch, Bill Cotton Jnr, Michael Grade, Mark White, all understood that any radio or television service is only as good as the people who make the programme. Hundreds of other things are important too –

budgetary control, administrating buildings, human resources, compliance; the list grows every year in the BBC – but what really matters, or should, in any broadcasting organisation, and certainly in the world's greatest, is what happens at the sharp end; the tiny bit of the iceberg that is audible and visible to the outside world, the reason for the whole huge edifice's existence: the programmes. Without good people to make and present these programmes, the new Broadcasting House, the White City Broadcast and Media Centres, and all the security men and project managers in the world are as chaff in the wind. Everything a broadcasting organisation does must be directed towards its end product. However, in one as big as the BBC, this simple truth can be easily forgotten. We have a 'talent' department, of course, but I wouldn't know where to find it. I've certainly never met anybody from it, nor, indeed, anybody in or out of the business who knows anything about its function. Perhaps it *is* mysteriously discovering and nurturing the writers, producers, directors, actors and presenters of tomorrow, but could somebody possibly open the door an inch or two so that we might get a glimpse of the burgeoning 'talent'?

I've recounted already the early days, when the talent was expected to travel third class while the producer went first. That attitude had to change, as ITV, commercial radio and satellite broadcasting took to the airwaves, but there is still detectable in the BBC a certain mindset: 'Stars may come, and stars may go, but we'll still be here . . . Nobody is bigger than the BBC . . .' The old mantra misses the point. Stars *are* the BBC. Without popular actors, presenters and newsreaders, nobody's going to watch or listen, and you can't keep asking for a licence fee from a public that isn't interested. But old habits die hard; only lately has it occurred to somebody that you can't ask anybody to sit all day in a tiny dressing room with tacky curtains and stains all over the carpet. For twenty years of *Children in Need*, I spent ten hours in just such a room, and if I didn't like it, well, nobody else was complaining, were they? Things have improved, mainly because independent production companies are using the BBC's facilities, and won't accept the old BBC 'they should be grateful they're here' mentality. My recent experiences of working with independents show them to be worlds ahead of the BBC in people skills. Everybody is looked after, and while nobody believes that every whim should be catered for, a bouquet of flowers or a scented candle are the little touches that help the performer to a better frame of mind, and bring them back for more. It all comes down to commercial reality: independent production companies live or die by success or failure; the BBC will carry on. Which is where we came in . . .

Putting complacent attitudes aside, nobody with any regard for broadcasting standards in this country would wish it otherwise. It is the independence of the BBC, the licence fee that frees it from the yoke of commercialism, that sustains it as the greatest broadcasting organisation in the world. As Michael Grade said when running Channel 4, it's the BBC that keeps all the rest decent. The BBC is the keeper of the flame, the guardian of standards, and if ever a misguided government or deluded population decide to dispense with the licence fee, television and radio in this country will go to hell in a handcart. CBC in Canada, ABC in Australia, both built in the proud image of the BBC, are now mere shadows, like PBS in the States: barely alive on handouts and charity.

All of which does little to alleviate the impatience that can be provoked by the BBC's cheese-paring. For the past two years, at the request of the Managing Director of Radio, Jenny Abramsky, I have presented the Corporation's own award ceremony, in which the unsung heroes are properly lauded – cameramen, engineers, producers, directors, sound men, the people who actually make the programmes – while the likes of me get the applause. It's an honour and a privilege to host the evening, and I gladly do it for nothing, apart from a hotel bed, because the do has a tendency to run on a bit. What does tend to niggle, just a tad, is that the bed is *all* I get from the BBC. Breakfast I have to buy myself . . . Incidentally, the awards so proudly received by the unsung heroes are old slates from the original Broadcasting House roof. With the BBC, sometimes you don't know whether to laugh or cry . . .

12

TOGs! Can't live with 'em . . .
Can't live without 'em

~~~

I've never encouraged common sense, fair comment or reality on the old show, and as nobody ever writes in under their real name, for fear of being laughed at in the street, it's only fitting that none of the contributors to *Wake Up to Wogan* are known by their own names either. There's Deadly Alancoat, the Voice of the Balls, the Wealdstone Wonderboy. Boggy Marsh, Masked Star of Films for Discerning Gentlemen, Shed-dweller and Organist. Frank Godfrey, Traffic Totty and Mimi (Me, Me, Me, Me, Me . . .). People sometimes misguidedly refer to these underlings as my 'team'. Nothing could be further from the truth. It's everybody for themselves, and watch your back. They jostle, shriek and elbow for the microphone, so that the simple and retiring star of the show can hardly get a word in edgeways. Occasionally, I admonish them gently.

'Whose show *is* this, anyway?'

'We give up,' they chortle. 'Whose is it?'

'Mine,' I softly remind them. '*Wake Up to Wogan*.'

'Oh,' the bitter ingrates riposte, 'we thought it was, *Wake Up Wogan*, or *Wake Up with Wogan, 7 to 9, Monday to Saturday, BBC Light Programme*.'

It's my own fault. In my usual selfless way, I've encouraged them, and I've bred monsters: the Voice of the Balls, Deadly, is so named because, in his relentless pursuit of the almighty dollar, he intones the numbers on the National Lottery. He claims to live in faded decency in Harrow, but everybody knows that he lives above a hairdressing salon in Wealdstone, on the wrong side of the Hill, albeit with a splendid view of the automatic bollards that are Wealdstone's finest feature. He plays a full, if somewhat seedy, part in the town's activities.

What follows is only a fragrant nosegay of the rafts of denigratory letters aimed squarely at the vitals of the 'Voice of the Balls'. It makes not the slightest bit of difference – it's the original brass monkey:

Deadly has been at it again.

He was at a bus stop in Wealdstone yesterday when an elderly lady asked him when is the number 44 due. Quick as a flash Deadly said it last appeared two Wednesdays ago. Then something about it had made 48 appearances in the last few weeks. The lady was totally confused and hailed a taxi.

Perhaps you could have a quiet word.

Many thanks,

Paul Valter

Actually, he has no idea when any ball made its first or last appearance. He makes it all up, and who's going to know any different?

Mr Dedicoat,

As you will be aware, this weekend sees the opening of the brand new Wealdstone Ornithology Centre, the Wealdstone 'Bird-a-Rama', and we need a well-known local to perform the opening ceremony. Even though you are currently rated as an 'E'-list celebrity, you are the best we could come up with.

Please be aware that Mrs Betty Bickerdike's synchronised ferret jugglers will be performing and we would prefer not to have a repeat of their last performance involving you, the cactus and the balloon full of liquidised black pudding, which caused such mayhem in the park. Mrs Bickerdike is making her first appearance since that unfortunate incident, now that her hair has grown back.

Apparently your mate Eric Walters has offered to give us a slide show – he says he has several hundred slides of birds, gathered over the years by use of a camera with a very long lens. I never knew that there was such wildlife in and around the Harpenden Nurses' Accommodation.

Please bring your other friends: the Irishman who hasn't a clue where he is and the grumpy little yellow chap, but not the posh lady who attended the band concert in the park last week and terrified the young conductor by offering him lessons in how to use his baton. Out-of-date scotch eggs and buckets of Pinot Grigio will be available to you and your guests.

Shona Mercy,
Wealdstone Development Council

We are delighted that your North London announcer has reduced the number of references to Pinot Grigio in his ramblings. (It is well established that Dedicoat has a marked tendency to a certain variety of Italian plonk. Place a vat of it before him, with a side of ham, and apart from the slurping, gargling and munching, a blessed silence will reign.) It had been having a serious impact on our otherwise successful marketing efforts to create an aspirational image for this beverage.

I think it is fair to say that Alan Dedicoat was to Pinot Grigio as Lorraine Chase was to Campari.

By way of thanks, a mixed case of Black Tower, Blue Nun and Mateus Rosé is winging its way to the Wealdstone Wineorama where he should be able to collect it this evening, with our compliments.

Neil Woodcock

The oaf's insistent denial of his Wealdstone birthright fools nobody . . .

There was a young man from Wealdstone
So handsome and so tall
He lived above the fish shop
Right next to the marble hall
His only claim to fame was
He could whistle like a sparrow
And say 'I'm not from Wealdstone
I really come from Harrow'
Be not ashamed young Deadly
To tell whate'er is true

TOGs! Can't live with 'em . . . Can't live without 'em

> *The good folks up in Harrow*
> *Wouldn't have the likes of you!*
>
> Wilting Baz

'Wilting Baz' is also known as 'Baz of Wilts', a relentless sales-man, who also applies his marketing skills to selling the TOGs calendar and helps to raise a ton of money for *Children in Need.* He sometimes turns up in the morning with a box of biscuits. I never give any to Deadly . . .

From: Radio Licensing Officer – Wealdstone District

Dear Mr Dedicoat,

We are delighted to inform you that we have approved your application to run 'Wealdstone FM', your planned new 'cutting-edge' radio station for the Wealdstone and Northolt area.

We were impressed with your experience – the list of top people who have worked under you reads like a *Who's Who* of recent broadcasting, and we particularly liked the testimony from Phil Walters, who we know used to work with the Irish chap in your Radio 2 department. His eulogy about your broadcasting talents was particularly impressive, although we were surprised that he had signed it in purple crayon, and we were also confused by the Pinner postmark, as we thought he lived in Harpenden.

We like your ideas for the station – the idea that the presenters should inter-act with the newsreaders sounds par-ticularly interesting. We have heard Terry Wogan try the idea without much success, but we feel that freed from his petty restrictions you may well make it work.

Nora Treadwell sounds like a splendid choice for the breakfast show DJ, and we look forward to visiting her Tan and Touch-Up Emporium, and using the special vouchers that you sent us here on the licensing committee.

We have one reservation – you are not able to scramble the signal to avoid the 'riff raff from Harrow on the Hill' listening to the show. You will have to include something for everybody, even them. Try and be all-inclusive.

Good luck, and thanks for the wine.

Infamy! Infamy! . . . but you know the rest! The honest listener is not gulled by false bonhomie. He knows well the treachery and back-stabbing that is such an attractive part of everyday life at the BBC.

From: Harrow & Wealdstone Home for Fallen Women

Good Morning, Mr Wogan, (then there's the moral decay . . .)

We have recently had a sudden upsurge of young women whose lives have been sullied by the activities of a certain Algernon Beddicoat, whom we understand is known to you.

The sad story is always the same, in that they are approached by Beddicoat, who informs them that he holds an important position in the entertainment world. Furthermore having guided your career from that of a humble bank clerk, to the eminent role you now play in the BBC.

With promises of fame and fortune he lures these poor unfortunates into letting him have his way with them, then discards them. Perhaps you could use your influence to dissuade him from such behaviour in the future as our resources are now stretched to the limit. Thank you.

Thomas Bikersdike

Proprietor

One foolish day, Deadlyballs made passing mention of one of the great glories of his environs, the Northolt Swimerama. After a few weeks of this kind of thing, he wished he hadn't . . .

Dear Mr Dedicoat,

The plans you submitted for the redevelopment of the Wealdstone Swimerama have been rejected by the planning committee. Some of the proposed shops are a little suspect to say the least.

Religious Books – Psalmarama
Italian Delicatessen – Palmarama
Security Specialist – Alarmarama
Bondage Equipment – Harmarama
Meditation Suite – Calmarama
Ointment Specialist – Balmarama

We would also like to point out that the suggestion from your associate of Neicearama is out of the question. I trust you will resubmit your revised proposal. Otherwise we will have no alternative but to grant the application sent to us by Miss Godfrey to establish a number of units devoted to tradesmen to be called FRANS HAREEMARAMA.

John Brown

From: Dickie Mountshaft
Proprietor
The Wealdstone Stainerama
Belvoir Cuttings
Wealdstone

Dear Mr Dedicoat,

I refer to the garment you left with us, wrapped in plain Brown Paper, with a request that it be cleaned using our 'Bespoke Service for Discreet and Discerning Gentlemen'.

I have to advise that the garment is now ready for collection. However, I would make the following observations:

1. The stain on the 'seat' of the garment has not been totally removed despite our best efforts.
2. The codpiece has suffered a degree of shrinkage; however, I am assured by my Manageress, Mrs Betty Bickerdyke, that it should pose no problems for a gentleman of your dimensions.
3. We would recommend that if the garment is to be worn again only cotton undergarments are used as man-made fabrics may cause a static charge to develop leading to spontaneous combustion.

Thank you for your custom and *I do hope that my West End Agent, Andy Nutherthing, duly delivered the provinder for your personal consumption.*
D. Mountshaft

All pretty distasteful, but as Paul Walters always says: 'I only print 'em'. And as I always say: 'I only read 'em . . .'

Dear Mr Dedicoat,

Here at the Wealdstone Development Corporation, we appreciate your continued efforts to find a suitable venture for the Northolt Swimarama site, as it gives us all a good laugh when you send us another suggestion.

We are not dismissing out of hand your idea for a 'super-pub' on the site, as we understand that such establishments are catching on nowadays and there could well be a local demand. However, some of your plans may prove somewhat fruitless.

We do not think that you will stop binge-drinking by setting a minimum age of 40. As you yourself well know from experience, you older types can put it away better than most. You will just have to have a good team of cleaners.

We also think you may be confusing two different sets of legislation and directives. You appear to have applied for a 24-hour smoking licence, whilst banning drinking throughout the premises as you will be serving food. You may get an interesting set of customers this way, but we do not think you will have much chance of making any money.

Finally we are also unhappy about your co-licensee, Ms Nora Treadwell. We have already had several problems with Ms Treadwell and her 'Tan and Touch-uparama' in the High Street. She is continually trying to claim her seedy premises serve a long-felt need for the gentlemen of the area, and the fact that you are her most regular client does not sit well with your application. However, if you can arrange a discount for council staff, we may be able to consider this more favour-ably. See what you can do.

The Wealdstone Weather-Boy claims to hail from Hollywood, but it's the one in Birmingham, not LA. He has a full England cap for eating, but is fastidious in his gourmandising; at dinners in our mutual golf club, Mid-Herts, he will allow no plate to return to the kitchen until it is licked clean. By him. I have feasted on balti with the ne'er-do-well in his native purlieus, the Midlands, where he walked out of the restaurant on the grounds that the balti was served on a table with plates, forks, spoons and napkins. The Voice insists that the true balti connoisseur sits on the pavement, while the dish is hurled at him from the door of the restaurant. As you have read, Deadly has been refused ham on a British Midland flight, and has never forgotten the slight. Frankly, I feel that he showed more front than was wholesome to demand meat while travelling steerage.

If only the whole rotten business would stop with Dedicote, but there's more – and it gets worse. Best avert your eyes . . .

Boggy Marsh is a failed television cameraman and Radio 4 announcer with something of a reputation as a Lothario, based on a tissue of lies and an overwrought imagination. However, there's one born every minute, or two, if you count Tudor and Anita Bush, producers of Exotic Films Ltd. They've made him the star of their doubtful celluloid romps:

Dear Terry,

Good morning. We were disappointed last weekend that we couldn't film our latest production for the discerning gentleman, it was going to be a remake of the classic Hitchcock thriller *The Birds* only none of the birds in our film would have been crows, because John had informed us he had a prior engagement playing your quaint English game, cricket. Well that got me thinking and we have scrapped the idea of doing *The Birds* in favour of a new production based on cricket entitled *Legs Eleven*. This will star our hero as a classic all-rounder and a succession of beauties taking to the field with him, all of them game, to say the least. John tells us he's the finest long leg in the business, although some of the girls seemed to think he'd be better at short leg! We've brought in a demon bowler from the Swedish ladies' cricket team and she'll deliver a couple of bouncers that'll have him reeling. Mind you her googly is pretty stunning too. Our hero will, of course, bowl a maiden over, well quite a few maidens actually as he delivers a series of spinners before taking up his bat and practising a few strokes at the bowler's end. Seems there could be a few innings in this one.

Best wishes,

Anita Bush

Lead Actress

Exotic Films Ltd

Frankly, it sounded like a celluloid winner to me. I can't imagine what some people got so upset about. Boggy was all eagerness to play his part. Up for it, you might say . . .

Hollywood's a far cry indeed from the pretty town of Uckfield, which Boggy calls home. Actually, his home is not strictly his home, as he spends most of his conscious hours in his shed, with his collection of magazines and buckets of his home-made wine. In moments of quiet recollection, he resembles nobody so much as Vincent Price in the role of Dr Phibes, the insane organist. I wonder if you are familiar with the old Victorian crowd-pleaser, 'Seated one day at the organ, I was weary and ill at ease, and my fingers wandered idly, over the noisy keys'? It ends with, 'I struck one chord of music, like the sound of a great amen . . .' And that's the way Boggy plays the organ. For keeps. It's not just his organ-playing, Bogs brings out the worst in people – witness those appalling Bushes – but also, it must be said, the best. Mick Sturbs, an ungainly fellow with a strange way with words, writes regularly with homespun tales of Janet and Boggy (let's call him John, for that is his real name). The Janet and John stories have become a watchword among my listeners, for their simplicity, homespun charm, and truly disgusting double-entendres.

Janet and John go to the horticultural show

Today, Janet and John are going to the horticultural show. Horticultural is a big word, isn't it?

Do you know what it means? Horticulture is all about growing things. John knows how to grow things.

Clever John.

Janet goes to talk to Mrs Harrison from the college. John sees Mrs Norris.

'Hello, Mrs Norris,' says John. 'What a nice display,' says John. 'I can't grow fruit as I have a lot of trouble keeping the birds off my plums.'

John's friend Reg knows a song about that.

John says, 'Are those conference pears?'

'Yes,' says Mrs Norris. 'My Charlie grows these. You can feel that they're a bit firm for eating just now, but they would be nice cooked. Would you like some?'

Kind Mrs Norris.

'Thank you,' says John, 'I'll have them tonight.'

Do you like pears? John does.

Then John sees Mrs Waller.

'Hello, Mr Marsh,' says Mrs Waller. 'Are you not exhibiting? Your rocket was the talk of the village last year!'

'No,' says John. See John blush. Paint John's face red.

Mrs Waller says, 'I have something for you to try, Mr Marsh, it's okra with thyme. Call in on the way home and I'll let you have the recipe, or if you fancy a snack now, I think I have some lettuce here.'

John says, 'Thank you, Mrs Waller, but I don't want to spoil my dinner.'

Sensible John.

John sees Janet coming back. Janet has bought some new shears.

'Have you been a good boy?' says Janet.

'Yes, of course,' says John. 'I saw Mrs Norris. I told her I was looking for a nice firm pear, so she let me try her Charlie's. Then I saw Mrs Waller. She told me I could have wild thyme if I popped in later, or if I couldn't wait, she'd lettuce behind the stall.'

See Janet get out the shears.

Can you hit twenty miles an hour in two seconds? John can.

Poor John.

Little old ladies constantly approach me to tell me how much they enjoy 'Janet and John'. I can't believe that they get all the double meanings. Don't tell me Britain's grannies are going to the dogs – we're all doomed.

Janet and John go to the garden centre

Today, Janet and John are going to the garden centre. Janet wants to buy a climber to cover up one of John's sheds.

(Janet says that John's sheds are an eyesore.)

See Janet looking at all the flowers. Do you like flowers? Janet does.

John is looking at the garden ornaments.

John is laughing at how funny the big concrete gnomes look with their round bellies and white beards.

John is watching the workmen make the gnomes. See the men tip concrete into the moulds.

See the workmen point at John and laugh. Poor John.

John sees Mrs Perkins from the Co-op.

'Hello, Mrs Perkins,' says John.

'Hello, Mr Marsh,' says Mrs Perkins.

What fun!

Mrs Perkins says, 'I am looking for a nice *Thymus serpyllum* for my window-box, and I wanted to find something to perk up the privet in my front garden. It is very dull in the winter, and I can't seem to find anything here that suits dry soil. I was wondering if I could have a cutting from your *Clematis vitalba*?'

'Of course,' says John. 'I will see if I can find you one.'

Kind John.

Do you know what clematis is? John does. John has lots of helpful books in his shed.

John says, 'Janet is looking for a climber.'

Mrs Perkins says, 'You ought to try *ipomoea purpurea*. My Doug has a nice reliable one at the back of the woodshed. Get Janet to pop round to see if she wants a cutting.'

'Thank you,' says John.

John walks around looking at the flowers until he sees Janet.

'Hello, John,' says Janet. 'Who was that lady I saw you talking to?'

See the warning signs.

John says, 'That was Mrs Perkins from the Co-op. She was after a wild thyme, and asked if she could have a bit of my Old Man's Beard in her front hedge. She said that in exchange, Mr Perkins has a purple Morning Glory that you could look at behind the woodshed.'

See Janet push John into one of the big tubs of concrete. Do you think John looks like a garden ornament? Janet does. See Janet waiting for the concrete to set.

Poor John.

The 'Janet and John' epics are the work of a TOG, a brilliantly witty man who has given me permission to include them in this poor effort. I'm sure that he'd prefer to be known by his *nom de grâce*, Mick Sturbs. It was Mick who set up the TOGs website, it's Mick who provides us with our weekly horoscopes, under the pseudonym of Xavier Mousepractise. If he ever gives up, I'm banjaxed . . .

Janet and John go to the seaside

Today, Janet and John are going to the seaside. John is very excited. John likes the seaside.

Janet is making bloater-paste sandwiches. John does not like bloater-paste.

Do you know what dry-heaves are? John does.

Soon it is time for Janet and John to catch the bus at the

end of the lane. Janet gives John a barley-sugar twist to suck. Janet has to wipe John's beard with a wet hankie. See John wriggle.

When they arrive at the seaside, Janet gives John his bucket and spade, his sandwiches, and some money to spend on the pier.

Janet says, 'I am going to the Bingo now. I will see you by the candy-floss stall in an hour. If you've been a good boy, you can have some candy-floss.'

Do you like candy-floss? John does.

John skips down to the pier. John likes the pier. See John throw his sandwiches to the seagulls.

John goes to the shellfish stall and buys some winkles. John likes shellfish.

John sees Mrs Bickerdyke. 'Hello, Mrs Bickerdyke,' says John.

'Eh-up Fluffywhiskers,' says Mrs Bickerdyke. Mrs Bickerdyke is from Yorkshire – see Jeremy Clarkson.

'What are you doing here?' says John.

Mrs Bickerdyke says, 'I came down for the American ice-cream tasting, they are trying out some new flavours. Are those winkles any good? I bet they aren't as good as they are down in Devon. They do them hot from the pan with cider vinegar down there. I'll be having some of those next week when I go on holiday. Now I can't stand here listening to you all day, I'm going to pop me flip-flops on and take t'whippet for a walk on the beach.'

Do you know how to get a word in edgeways? John doesn't.

John walks down to the beach and makes a big sandcastle.

Soon it is time to go back and meet Janet.

See John cross the road and stand by the candy-floss stall. Janet sees John.

'Hello, John,' says Janet. 'What have you been doing?'

'Well,' says John, 'I walked down to the pier to look at the stalls and I saw Mrs Bickerdyke. Mrs Bickerdyke had just spent all afternoon tasting Ben and Jerry's. Next week she is going to Devon to get some hot winkles in cider. Then she got her flip-flops out and said it was time to let her whippet out on the beach . . . Can I have some candy-floss now?'

See Janet push John's head into the candy-floss machine and switch it on.

See John go pink and fluffy.

Poor John.

'Winkles in cider' . . . truly, a gem in the diadem. Sturbs, we bow before you . . .

John learns how to be a journalist

John is not a journalist. John reads the news. Journalists make it up.

John is on a conversion course.

Do you know what a conversion course is?

A conversion course is something you do when you want to be taken seriously. John is not taken seriously. People point and laugh. Poor John.

For his homework, John has to have dinner and some wine in a restaurant, and then write all about it.

If he writes a nice story, he will get six gold stars. Lucky John.

John's friend Alan knows all about food and wine. Paint Alan's nose red.

Alan suggests a nice restaurant near Waterloo Bridge.

John looks worried.

'What's the matter, John?' says Alan.

John says, 'I have to take someone with me, but I don't know who to ask.'

See John blub.

'There, there,' says Alan. 'I will ask Amanda on reception. I've heard that she will do anything for a nice meal.'

Kind Alan.

John and Amanda go to the restaurant. Do you think Oxo is a funny name for a restaurant?

John is very excited. John likes his food. Amanda is a bit nervous as the restaurant is on the 8th floor and she is afraid of heights. While they wait to be served John gets Amanda some wine and she soon feels better.

Soon the waiter arrives with the food. John gobbles down his dinner. See Amanda picking bits of food out of her hair.

Soon it is time to go. Amanda does not have enough money to pay for both meals so John makes up the difference. Do you know what a hairy old skinflint is? Amanda does.

When John gets home, Janet asks what he did at work today.

'Today I was behaving like a journalist. I gave our receptionist a treat. Alan said he wanted Amanda Ryder on the desk in reception because she would do anyone a favour. We went to a very nice place to eat. But Amanda needed a few drinks because she'd never been taken up the Oxo Tower before and was a bit nervous. Afterwards she said that she would suggest it to her boyfriend.

Can you hit a moving target with a four-slice toaster? Janet can. See Janet chase John.

Run, John, run.

Let's leave it at the Oxo Tower, shall we? Here is another Musketeer – one who attracts an entirely different audience – mostly naked under a dirty raincoat.

Frank Godfrey, or Fran, as she prefers to be known, plays Tinkerbell to my Peter Pan and Pauly Walters' Smee. An elfin creature with a pleasing lilt to her voice and a tinkling laugh that would test the patience of a saint, she disturbs the early-morning placidity of otherwise sensible grown men who regularly demean themselves for her favours. She's a baggage and a tease, perpetuating the fairy tale that she is but an innocent convent girl, while in reality she spits like a sailor and swears like a trooper. And still they fawn upon her:

Ode to a Tasty Chick
by W. McGonagall
(Voted most promising poet, Brit Awards 1988)

Of those who toil at the BBC
There's only one who'll do for me.
Although I've only heard her voice,
I think she must look rather noice.
She reads the news with such aplomb,
I'd really like to take her homb.
Oh Fran! Oh Fran! Will you be mine?
The thought of you drives me insine.

Mustn't Grumble

And though I'm just a humble oik,
I'd even let you ride my boik.
But Fran if you resist my charms,
I'll run away and eat some warms.

It's a foul and contemptible calumny, but Fran brings it on herself. An excessive eagerness to please creates an impression of an 'easy woman'. Nothing could be further from the truth – unless of course, you're male. And have a pulse . . .

Dear Terry,
So no one is too old for Fran?

Come on you wizened suitors
With wrinkles like a prune
And backs bent like a hoop as
You try to make her swoon,
For Franny's made it very clear
To get her bosom heaving
With lust or love, she will not sneer
At anyone who's breathing.
So come with your decrepit charms
Though with a frame or trolley,
She'll welcome you with open arms
And especially those with lolly.

Or maybe I do her a disservice, and she's just got a fetish for high-waist trousers and enlarged prostate problems.

TOGs! Can't live with 'em . . . Can't live without 'em

Byeeee (hope this keeps till tomorrow)
Katie Mallett

Grown men build their fantasies around Fran Godfrey. I'm sure it does them good – the woman's a broadcasting enema!

A Friday Ode to Fran . . . (Hic!)

Dear Sir Terry, Fran and The Team,
An ode to Fran!!

There was a time not long ago
When Fran was young and bright,
She'd set off every evening
down the pub to spend the night.
'I'll 'ave a foaming pint, my dear,' the punters often call.
'Comin' right up, I've got one 'ere, the froth is nice and tall!'
'My goodness, that's my Guinness . . . cor blimey what a caper,
With so much foam I'll 'ave to ask for chopped nuts and a wafer!'
And while our Fran was serving in a blouse of rough delight,
The chaps all stood there leering, saying, 'What you doing tonight?'
'Oh no, Sir . . .' said the young maid . . . 'I'm a good girl and must go home to my Mum!'
'Well, 'fore you leave then come round 'ere and let us pinch yer bum!'

Now Fran was sorely tempted but knew that it was wrong,
Besides she'd told the Sister that she gone to sing a song.
Her mission was to make those men see the error of their ways;
It did seem rather strange that she'd been there for forty days.
'Young Frances, please come to my room and tell me what goes on,
I thought by now you'd have a convert keen to join our throng.·
But ev'ry night you come back here with glassy eyes and money,
And will you stop from saying to the porter, "Hello Honey"!'
Yours as ever ...

Info for Fran

Morning Tel,

Welcome backome. I have news for Fran should she ever consider cosmetic surgery:

A doctor at the University of Cosmetic Surgery has developed a breast implant with electronic music incorporated into the implant.

When asked why the doctor developed this, he replied, 'All these years women complain about men staring at their breasts and not listening to them.'

Fran will be the first to tell you that men always look her straight in the eye.

DAFTA in May

> *Not everyone can have a BAFTA —*
> *some are winners, some are duds —*
> *but here's a babe who'd win a DAFTA . . .*
> *Fran! and both her Darling Buds . . .*
>
> Byron Bonniebanks

Don't mention the BAFTA around me . . . There's Noel 'Tidybeard' Edmonds, a scant ten minutes back on the box, and he picks up a nomination. How long have I been haunting the thing? Never mind troubling the judge – I don't even trouble the starter . . .

Fran's lavish penthouse, within shrieking distance of the BBC, has been the scene of many an unsavoury tale: honest artisans imprisoned for weeks in the cupboard under her stairs, lured there on the pretext of some urgent plumbing, grouting or rendering; electricians' apprentices, sturdy lads as they enter Fran's portals, shattered husks as they emerge days later.

It's hard to credit, but each post brings the plaintive cry from newborn listeners, 'In God's holy name, what are you on about? What's a TOG?' Or, 'TOGs sound good to me – how do I join?' Or, 'I'm only sixteen, can I be a TOG?' (always answered by the traditional mantra, 'Clear off, you young limb!'). *Oldie* magazine, that splendid source of consolation for those well stricken in years, but still fondly deluding themselves that there is 'snap in their celery', asked me to define the glorious state of Togdom. I could scarce say than nay:

273

What is . . . a TOG?

For once, Chambers, Webster's and Oxford dictionaries are of one mind.

> TOGs: Terry's Old Geezers/Gals; listeners to *Wake Up to Wogan*, 7.30 a.m. to 9.30 a.m., Monday to Friday, BBC Radio 2. Thought to be in direct line of descent from the TWITS (Terry Wogan Is Tops Society), a movement which enjoyed 'a far, fierce hour and sweet' and burned out just as quickly. Rather like Wogan himself . . .

Like the aforementioned once-proud broadcaster, TOGs are well stricken in years, while remaining about twenty-five years of age on the inside. They have a fierce resentment of anybody younger than themselves: 'They don't know they're born!', and are loath indeed to allow them into their purlieus. 'Clear off, you young limb!', is the rallying cry.

TOGs usually come in flat caps, Volvos and the centre lane of the motorway at 60 m.p.h. ('I'm within my rights; 50 m.p.h. on the inside, 70 on the outside and 60 in the middle . . .'). They have a secret sign, known only to those who see it flashed, rather like some Bat Signal, on the radio every morning.

There is an even more secret Grand Master, or TOG-MEISTER, sign always exchanged under cover of darkness, or the snug of a seedy pub near Broadcasting House, which is known only to Wogan himself, the ailing producer, Pauly Walters, and the Duke of Kent.

TOGs may also be recognised by their use of such arcane

phrases as, 'Is it *me?*' or, 'I never saw a bar of chocolate until I was fourteen,' or, 'What am I doing, standing here in front of an open fridge with a torch in my hand?'

Many thousands of TOGs car stickers have been sent to eager applicants, who, once they receive them, get cold feet and hide them in the back of an upstairs drawer. Those brave enough to flaunt the sticker in the back windows of their Reliant Robin or Morris Mini-Traveller pay a terrible price, not only in loss of face among nearest, dearest and the rest of the population, but in the trade-in value: the thing is impossible to remove.

The TOGs sweater, which, like the car sticker, is rarer than hen's teeth, bears the legend: 'Do I come here often?' – a tried and trusted TOG chat-up line. There was a strong groundswell of opinion to have 'I stop for no particular reason' on the back, but it soon petered out.

Currently a movement is gathering strength to have the logos changed to 'It's never *your* fault' on the front and 'Mustn't grumble' on the back. It will come to nothing. They'll forget about it if you don't pay any attention. This condition is known to TOGs as a *'senior moment'*, a euphemism culled from America, to indicate a temporary loss of all marbles in anyone over fifty . . .

As is the current practice within the BBC itself, TOGs feel a deep-seated need to form themselves into groups, clusters or tribes. Witness this letter from a well set-up woman from Norfolk:

We decided to start our own local branch of TOGs and the very first meeting took place last week. The session started

275

with a game, to break the ice, of 'I-Spy'. This proved to be a mistake because most of the members had forgotten to bring their glasses. Undeterred, we decided to be more daring – the men then threw their false teeth into the middle of the carpet and the ladies had to pick a denture and pair off with its owner! They then adjourned to other rooms to discuss their operations. We ended with a raffle, first prize of which was a knitted pension-book cover . . .

But I see that you are all eagerness: 'How do I become a TOG?' Be of good cheer. You're in. Welcome to the club . . .

Lately, a television ad gave poor old sods a glimmer of hope: Shakespeare, as ever, got there first, but this current television ad identifies the 'Seven Stages of Ageing', espousing a miracle cream that will arrest the march of time. It has given at least one old geezer heart. After one application:

1. He may walk around a shoe shop without exclaiming, 'Ooh, they look comfy' at every pair of slippers.
2. He will stop saying 'It's bitterly cold' every time the wind changes.
3. Will not go 'Aahhh' after a first sip from a cup of tea . . .
4. . . . Nor 'Aahhh' every time he sits down.
5. He will desist from muttering 'Never did me any harm' when there's a debate on the smacking of children.
6. When anyone mentions the price of a Mars bar, he will refrain from crying out in anguish: 'That's *nine* shillings! I remember when they were threepence.'

7. And finally . . . On hearing something from today's pop charts, will not moan 'They all sound the same to me', mainly because not only is he beginning to look like his father, he's beginning to sound like him . . .

The rash of reality continues unabated on television. The keen observer will notice that what started as fly-on-the-wall voyeurism of ordinary people in *Big Brother* has been taken over by 'celebrities' who flaunt themselves before us in a variety of guises: in the jungle, in the ballroom, on the ice, on the farm, on the island – the more bizarre, the merrier. These excesses bring a daily response from my over-alert listeners. A couple of the less lunatic:

To: Terry Wogan
From: Len Horridge

Yo!! Clooney Boy!!

Hey, my creative juices have been flowing and I've just come up with a brilliantly fresh and novel idea for BBC1's evening schedules.

The programme is tentatively called **Celebrity Couples Strictly Horse Jumping and Singing on Ice in a Jungle**. Sounds like a winner already, eh?

The premise is this: celebrity couples (i.e. people you've never heard of) sing their favourite songs whilst riding on a horse and jumping over smaller celebrities who are strapped to the floor in seventies-style comedy outfits.

The winners will be the couple who stay on the horse the

longest, who sing the longest and who have hit and injured the most celebrity jumps in comedy outfits.

Oh, and don't worry about the *ice* bit. The horses are actually pantomime horses with minor radio celebrities at either end, and no animals will be injured during the making of this extravaganza.

A ratings winner, I feel.

How do you fancy co-hosting with me in a red dress?

Len Horridge

To: Terry Wogan
From: Nodding John

I have it! The key to wealth. I knew if I waited long enough I'd have an idea that would make me millions: **Newsreaders on Ice**.

Every night ten newsreaders (Deadly could take part?) start off each reading news stories whilst dancing around on ice. Every five minutes we vote someone off. You could host and on the panel could be Bruno Raviolli *et al.*

The last newsreader left gets to read the 'And finally' item.

Is it a winner or what?

If not, **Big Brother Darts** – viewers get to watch darts players twenty-four hours a day locked in a house – Sid Waddell commentates.

I am on a roll now . . .

Name:

Nodding John

To: Terry Wogan
From: Bill Shakespear

Great idea for a new reality show:

Fat Celebrity Camp on Ice Looking 10 Years Younger Because of What They Eat and How They Dress. We the public will love this as it combines six shows in one and will allow the BBC time to make much more innovative programmes such as **What's Happening at the Bottom of My Garden?**, or **Does My Ceiling Need Another Coat of Paint?**

Name:

Bill Shakespear

If you can keep your shed when all about you
    Is rising damp and condensation,
If you can read the travel as if it's true,
    Reporting three car shunts with no hesitation,
If you can play the great Widor Toccata
    Yet never make it to the end,
And people say your wife's a martyr
    'Cause your recitals drive her round the bend;

If your perfect diction never falters
    And you've a mighty organ at your fingertips,
If you can meet with Wogan and Pauly Walters
    And get those two impostors to sort their pips,
If you can fill the unforgiving minute
    When the headlines don't go quite to plan,

279

Then take my heart – for you'll surely win it
   And – which is more – I bet *you* don't need Viagra to prove
   you are a man!

Having perused the 'Are you a TOG' section of the website the memsahib and myself decided to put together a list of pointers to help decide if one is a Christmas TOG.

1. The fruitcake aunt/embarrassing uncle that every family suffers at Christmas stares back at you out of the bathroom mirror.
2. You remark (to a younger relative) on the decrepit appearance of an ageing celebrity before remembering that they were four years below you at school.
3. You wrap this year's presents in wrapping paper that you salvaged from last year's presents.
4. You go to a Christmas party and find more people that you want to slap than cuddle.
5. The knitted sweater you receive for Christmas that looks as if it was modelled on a deformed gibbon turns out to be deceptively form-fitting.
6. You see a scantily clad member of the opposite sex and your first three thoughts are:
   - They look cold!
   - They need feeding up!
   - Their mother needs a good slapping for allowing them out dressed like that.
7. You remember mince pies/drinks being bigger.
8. You insist on everyone gathering around the TV for the Queen's speech and no one can hear it over your snores.

9. Whilst being fitted for the trousers of a Santa suit your tailor asks if 'Sir' hangs 'to the left or the right?', and you answer, 'Just make them baggier at the knees!'

The annual firework display on *Wake Up to Wogan* is the highpoint of the year for many a discerning listener, and certainly the only radio firework display anywhere in the world. Furthermore, through the miracle of the internet, it is experienced all over the known world. Letters from Canada, the American west coast, China, and New Zealand bear witness to the unmatched colour, sparkle and excitement of this, the world's greatest firework display: a constant riot of every colour in the spectrum that goes on for two whole hours. A treat for adults or kiddies alike, and particularly for animal lovers. For there are *no* bangs, explosions or any upsetting loud noises to disturb the little ones, or their pets.

Dear Terry,

Fireworks on the Radio

Could you please move over a little bit because I can't see the fireworks! Or am I going blind? If there are enough sausages, do you think I could have one, please.

There will always be the whingers, of course . . .

Terry,

Who lit that last rocket?????

Although it looked beautiful, the damn stick came down in my garden and skewered the cat.

Please, please be more careful.

281

Mustn't Grumble

How heart-warming, the unsolicited testimonial . . .

To: Terry Wogan
From: Elizabeth

What a wonderful firework display this morning – colours, and such a variety! In fact my egg got cold because I was enjoying them so much – this year I got the distance from the wireless exactly right and could enjoy the colours to the full.

And because they were silent, my cat enjoyed them too – in fact she was jumping up to try and catch the sparks and colours as they flew about. Luckily we were in the kitchen so there was no chance of the carpet catching fire.

The only problem was I didn't get my sparkler and we all know you can't enjoy a firework display without a sparkler! As you couldn't get it to me on time, I would be happy to get a TOGs sweatshirt instead (extra large size)?

Elizabeth

(Love the show – best antidote to 'road rage' I know!!)

No matter how hard you try . . .

Very clever!

You've set off every smoke detector in the house and we don't have a TV licence should the detector vans come round.

Anyway, I'm not really keen on bright colours so perhaps next year you could send up a nicely camouflaged 'Sky Blue' rocket for people like me.

Ta muchly!

Katherine Weal

We even lay on the culinary delights that are part and parcel of every display – snorkers; hotdogs, roast potatoes – virtually.

Greetings, snorkermeister.

What a wonderful display!

I am finishing off the last of the pumpkin soup for breakfast whilst delighting in the sensory extravaganza. Unfortunately t'other half is in the bath and has missed the first half-hour of the masterpiece. Any chance of some edited highlights?

Can I have a hot dog, please, with onions and mustard, but no bread because I have developed a wheat allergy.

Thank you.

Des Parrot-Measures

Feed my lambs, feed my sheep. What more can I give? How far can I go? Watch this space . . .

Epilogue

So, that's the height of it. Whether it's the end of the beginning or the beginning of the end, I hope it's too soon to say. And I'm certainly not going to say that this is as far as I go. That wise man Eamonn Andrews always said to me that the three vital factors in getting the elbow were: 1. The public get tired of you; 2. You get tired of doing it; and 3. Your employer gets tired of you. Of these, he said, by far the most important was the third factor.

So far nobody in authority has suggested I fling myself off Beachy Head. Equally, my audiences for radio and television seem to be growing rather than diminishing, and I'll never get tired of talking to myself and my listener. Why else would a man of my declining years get out of bed at 5.30 on a dark and dreary January morning? I've always said that it's important, unlike Canute, to get off the beach before the tide comes in. I've seen too many once great broadcasters cling to the wreckage long after the ship has gone down. They don't know it, and nobody will tell them, but the edge has gone – no more than a half-beat, the blink of an eye . . .

There's a time to live and a time to die, but in my business, the most important of all is the time to say goodbye. I hope that

I can recognise it when it comes around, and greet it as a friend. And if I don't, keep your opinions to yourself; I'll go when I'm ready.

Index

Powell, Jonathan, 154
Presley, Elvis, 240
Price, Vincent, 261
priests, singing, 240
pronunciation, 18–19
Purslow, Ian, 231

Queen, 27
Quigley, Father Gerard, 201

Radcliffe, Mark, 86
radio, 158–68, 174, 197–200,
   208–10, 213; presenters, 35, 53,
   166, 206, 209; interviews, 72;
   outside broadcasts, 72;
   breakfast-time, 132–4; and
   popularity, 135, 137–8, 152,
   158–68, 216; local, 142, 208–9;
   national, 165; playlists, 165,
   198, 209; American, 198–9,
   209; commercial, 198–200,
   209, 247; pirate, 199; hospital,
   209; and hostile print media, 217
Radio 1, 33, 35, 133; 'Stop Wogan'
   campaign, 194–5
Radio 2, 33, 35, 38, 40, 45, 188;
   outside broadcasts, 72, 74, 79;
   auctions, 80, 84, 146–7; visits
   Aberdeen, 86; audience, 134–5;
   Music Marathon, 150; Wogan
   leaves, 151–3; Wogan returns,
   154–6; newspaper advertising,
   155–6; Lecture, 157–68; music,
   165; lack of prizes, 198; and Sony
   Awards, 207
Radio 3, 49, 165
Radio 4, 52, 260

Radio Eireann, 53, 20, 134, 170,
   197, 223, 241
Radio Luxembourg, 199
Radio Times, 34, 145, 200
RAI, 106
Ramsey, Alf, 54, 201
Rather, Dan, 55
Rathmines and Rathgar Musical
   Society, 98
Reading, Margot, Marchioness of,
   205–6
Reagan, Nancy, 19
Reagan, Ronald, 19–20
Redemptorist preachers, 14
Redgrave, Vanessa, 59
Redway, Mike, 42
Reid, Mickser, 98
Reith, Lord, 72, 166, 187
Rice, Tim, 26, 108
Richard, Cliff, 119
Richard and Judy, 152
Riga, 108, 116
Ring of Kerry Golf Club, 230
Rippon, Angela, Roberts, Julia, 2
Robinson, Anne, 32
Rogers, Kenny, 44, 77
Rome, 105–6
Rooney, Wayne, 203
Rosko, Emperor, 35, 199
Roslin, Gaby, 67, 151, 243
Ross, Jonathan, 66, 120–1, 139,
   205
Rossa, O'Donovan, 10
Round the Horne, 81
Royal Bank of Ireland, 146
Royal Variety Performance, 143
Royle, Canon Roger, 235–6

297

Index

Wogan, Rose, 22, 26, 94–5, 97, 192; family and early life, 180–1, 183–4, 186–7

Wogan, Terry: learns to swim, 17; education, 19; and languages, 19, 223; teenage years, 20–3; name, 22; courtship, 23–5, 170–1; childhood, 25–6, 94–7, 174–5; leaves shows, 32; radio show, 34–48; leaves Ireland and joins BBC, 39, 139, 188, 199–200, 209; chat shows, 54–60; salary, 54–5; experiences in America, 59–65; luck in broadcasting, 67, 171; and BBC politics, 67–9; first-class travel, 76, 82–3; and obsessive fans, 79–80; offered as auction prize, 80; visits Canada, 80–3; love of flying, 83; visits Norway, 84–5; fear of climbing, 85; gaffe in Aberdeen, 86–9; love of food, 87; joins Doonbeg advisory board, 92; has first drink, 97; love of Eurovision Song Contest, 102, 123, 132; popularity, 132–40, 168–9; awards and ceremonies, 139, 168, 204–13; pride in *Children in Need*, 140–2; impressions of, 145; dancing, 145–6; shows axed, 151–4; show returns, 154–6, 243; addresses BBC, 157–68; memories, 169–70; attitude to work, 170; family life, 170–1; suffers embarrassment, 173–4; family history, 179–91; awarded OBE, 187–8, 191;

knighted, 191–2, 195–6; and unauthorised biography, 193–4; and 'Stop Wogan' campaign, 194–5; awarded honorary doctorate, 203; becomes grandfather, 203; diary entries, 216–20; life in Spain, 221–6; buys boat, 225–6; holidays, 226–31; and horses, 228–9; life in France, 231–4; family weddings, 234–40; television projects, 241–5

Wogan, 32, 55, 59, 62, 64, 71, 132, 147; axed, 153–4, 169

Wogan in Hollywood, 60

Wogan – Now and Then, 244–5

Wogan's Guide to the BBC, 168

Wogan's Ireland, 68

Wogan's Web, 68, 243

Wolverhampton, 36

women, 16–17; in Nashville, 77

Wood, Gordon, 17, 95, 177

Wood, Keith, 95, 177

World War Two, 43, 102, 182, 196

Wright, Chely, 77

Yeats, W. B., 174

Yentob, Alan, 66

Yosemite National Park, 228–9

You Must Be Joking, 168

Young, Alisha, 32

Young, Jimmy, 28–9, 31–5, 40, 139, 164, 199

Zaragoza, 225